AN ARCHAEOLOGY
OF HUMAN
DECAPITATION BURIALS

AN ARCHAEOLOGY OF HUMAN DECAPITATION BURIALS

Katie Tucker

First published in Great Britain in 2015 by
PEN & SWORD ARCHAEOLOGY
an imprint of
Pen and Sword Books Ltd
47 Church Street
Barnsley
South Yorkshire S70 2AS

ISBN 978 1 47382 551 2

Printed and bound in India
by Replika Press Pvt. Ltd.

Typeset in Times New Roman by
CHIC GRAPHICS

Pen & Sword Books Ltd incorporates the imprints of
Pen & Sword Archaeology, Atlas, Aviation, Battleground, Discovery,
Family History, History, Maritime, Military, Naval, Politics, Railways,
Select, Social History, Transport, True Crime, Claymore Press,
Frontline Books, Leo Cooper, Praetorian Press, Remember When,
Seaforth Publishing and Wharncliffe.

For a complete list of Pen and Sword titles please contact
Pen and Sword Books Limited
47 Church Street, Barnsley, South Yorkshire, S70 2AS, England
E-mail: enquiries@pen-and-sword.co.uk
Website: www.pen-and-sword.co.uk

Contents

Introduction

My first encounter with the unusual type of burial that is the subject of this book came around ten years ago, when I was living in York and working as the human remains specialist for a large commercial archaeology unit. Excavations in advance of development in the south of the city had uncovered a number of graves, part of one of the large cemeteries that encircled the Roman town, and a number of the burials were slightly out of the ordinary. Instead of the skeletons being laid out on their back, some were on their side or their front; in some cases there were two bodies in the same grave, lying head to foot on top of one another; and most peculiarly, in a large number of the graves, the head was not where it should be, but was found placed next to the feet, on top of the chest, under the pelvis or between the legs.

I was tasked with examining the remains, determining their age and sex, taking measurements from the bones, documenting the traces of disease, and most importantly, in this case, trying to understand what had happened to them. But before I had even really started my work, the excavation had made it into the local news and one of the head archaeologists at the company was talking about these 'headless Romans' as being subjects of a bizarre burial ritual, their heads being removed after death to prevent their ghosts from returning to haunt the living. I was intrigued; how was it possible to say this with confidence when I had not even properly analysed the remains? How could we assume it had been done after death? Why would people want to do this to a body before burial?

The further I progressed in my analysis the less convinced I became that this was the only explanation, and rather than finding easy answers, more questions seemed to present themselves. The nature of the trauma, with the majority of individuals demonstrating blows to the back of the neck, did not seem to easily conform to the "post-mortem burial ritual" interpretation. They also seemed to be very different to other previously reported decapitation burials, in terms of numbers of individuals, their demographic make-up, and the nature of the trauma. But this was commercial archaeology; the funding ran out and I could not continue my research, so I handed in my report and moved on to other projects. However, the fascination never really left me and, presented with the opportunity of a PhD scholarship five years later, I knew exactly what project I wanted to take on. The disparity between the evidence from the burials in York and other decapitation burials, and between the osteological evidence and the archaeological interpretations, deserved to be investigated in detail, as it was evident that the practice was poorly understood and there were a lot of assumptions about it that did not seem to be based on the evidence. The results of that subsequent three years of research are contained in this book, and I hope it answers at least some of the questions that I posed to myself ten years ago.

Chapter 1

The Study of Decapitation Burials

The burials that are the subject of this book are referred to as 'decapitation (or decapitated) burials'. For the purposes of my research, I have used the term to refer to burials where the head has been removed from its correct position and placed elsewhere in the grave (at the feet, or under the pelvis, for example); where it is missing entirely; or where it appears to be in the correct position, but there is evidence on the cervical vertebrae, cranial base, mandible or shoulder girdle, in the form of cut marks, that the head has been removed (see plates 1-3 for examples). For non-articulated skeletal remains, it is the modification and manipulation of the whole fleshed head or 'skull' (comprising both the cranium and mandible in osteological terminology) that is of interest, and so isolated crania and cranial fragments are not generally included. However, in a lot of more general archaeological literature, the word 'skull' is used freely to describe either the whole head, isolated crania, partial cranial vaults or cranial fragments, and this has presented problems when deciding what examples to include. I have made the decision to only include cases where extra information, such as a photograph or drawing, suggests that it is a whole head that has been found, or where there is evidence for trauma (injuries) to the bone that indicate decapitation has taken place (see appendix 3 for details of the examples analysed by the author).

Early Research

The presence of decapitation burials in archaeologically excavated cemeteries was first recognised in the late nineteenth century, with examples being published by Pitt Rivers, from the Romano-British sites of Wor Barrow and Woodyates, Dorset, and the Iron Age to Romano-British settlement at Woodcutts, also in Dorset[1]. Cut marks were not noted on the decapitations from the Romano-British sites, or from the female buried in a hypocaust at Woodcutts, who was reported as probably having the head removed before burial; but the cranium of a child which was found 'thrown head downwards' into a pit at the Iron Age-to-Roman site of Woodcutts was recorded as displaying a sword cut to the back of the head[2].

Another example from Dorset was recorded at Todber in 1893 by Mansell-Pleydell, who noted that it was an adult male, found in a lead coffin, with the 'severed' head and first three cervical vertebrae placed by the tibiae[3]. Cut marks were also noted as having been made to the sixth cervical vertebra[4] of a burial from Manton Down, Wiltshire, reported in 1892, which had been buried with the head between the feet and an ampulla (a small globular flask or bottle) where the head should have been. Two decapitated burials from the Romano-British cemetery at Long Sutton, Somerset, were reported in 1894 by Morland, who recorded that the head had been found by the pelvis in one of them and between the legs in the other, but did not note the presence of any cut marks. A single decapitation with the head between the knees and the remains of hobnailed boots at the feet from Lambourn, Berkshire, was reported by Palmer in 1871, and another two examples were noted by Royce in 1882 at Temple Guiting, Gloucestershire. Another Romano-British burial from Helmingham, Suffolk, was recorded by Cardew in 1865 as having the neck broken and the head cut off but then replaced in correct anatomical position[5].

Early medieval headless burials were reported at Stapenhill, Staffordshire, by Heron in 1889 and at Linton Heath, Cambridgeshire, by Neville in 1854, the latter case having an urn placed where the head should have been. Possible examples were also reported by Foster in 1883 at Hooper's Field, Barrington, Cambridgeshire, where at least two burials had their heads displaced; by Akerman in 1860 at Brighthampton, Oxfordshire, where one burial was described as having the head on the pelvis[6]; and by Thomas in 1883 in the cemetery at Sleaford, Lincolnshire, where an adult male burial was noted as having the 'skull' of a child at the feet, and another burial as having the 'skull' by the hip and a shield boss where the head should have been. This example has been subsequently reported by Wilson, in 1992, and Reynolds, in 2009, as being a definite decapitation burial, although the original description is unclear as to whether the head had been removed and placed at the hip, or whether the body was doubled over with the shoulders and head at the level of the hips[7].

Possible examples of decapitation burials from the prehistoric period were described by Cunnington in 1884 at the Neolithic site of Bowl's

Barrow, Wiltshire, where three crania were found resting on their mandible and cranial base, suggesting they had been 'detached from the body ... when originally interred.' A cervical vertebra was also found that had been 'cut in two by some sharp instrument,' although a recent re-examination of the bone has determined that the cut was made with a metal rather than lithic (flint) blade and it therefore most probably originates from an Iron Age, Romano-British or Saxon secondary burial at the site[8].

A headless Neolithic burial was reported by Rolleston in 1876 at Swell, Gloucestershire, with the suggestion that it had probably been interred without the head, as there was little room for it by the wall against which the contracted burial lay. Smith and Brickley also re-analysed the remains from this monument and discovered a clavicle with peri-mortem cuts, which were probably related to the removal of the sternocleido-mastoid muscle (*M. sternocleidomastoideus*; one of the muscles of the neck) during the process of decapitation[9].

Headless burials and isolated skulls were also reported in the publications produced by Bateman in 1861, Greenwell in 1877 and Mortimer in 1905 on their excavations in Neolithic and Bronze Age mortuary structures, although they never specifically described these as examples of decapitation[10]. A probable Iron Age example was reported in 1886 from Worlebury Camp, Somerset, by Dymond and Tomkins, who described an individual with the head cleanly severed through C1, found in a pit with the remains of seventeen other individuals, one of whom demonstrated seven separate cuts to the cranium[11].

Examples of decapitation, both definite and possible, particularly from the Romano-British and early medieval periods, continued to be reported throughout the earlier part of the twentieth century, with publications on Iron Age hill-fort burials by Hencken, Wheeler and Kenyon[12]; Romano-British cemetery excavations by Fox and Lethbridge, Moir and Maynard, Rudsdale, Lethbridge and Calkin[13]; and early medieval 'execution cemeteries' (for a definition, see p.15) by Lethbridge and Palmer, Lowther, Dunning and Wheeler, Stone, Liddell and Hill, amongst many others[14].

A number of publications by early physical anthropologists – such as Miriam Tildesley, C.N. Goodman, Geoffrey Morant and Ian Cornwall – are distinguished by their detailed analysis of the skeletal remains, a practice which largely makes its debut in archaeological publications around this time, although the monographs published by Pitt-Rivers (see endnote 1) do contain tables of measurements taken from the cranium, mandible and long bones, and very detailed engravings or photographs of the crania and mandibulae. These analyses were concerned with determining the age and sex of individuals and also contained comprehensive details on the evidence for decapitation and other peri-mortem trauma, with particularly good examples being the analyses of remains from Sutton Walls, Meon Hill and Maiden Castle[15].

The detail contained in these publications on the skeletal remains from sites with possible or definite decapitations was not really matched until the 1990s, as the analysis of human remains for archaeological reports seemed to fall out of favour from the 1950s onwards, with the exception of publications by authors such as Calvin Wells, Keith Manchester and Don Brothwell[16].

Previous Syntheses of Decapitation

The first published synthesis of the practice of decapitation in British archaeological samples was by Clarke in 1979 and was produced as a comparison with the seven decapitated burials excavated from the Romano-British cemetery at Lankhills, Winchester[17]. It therefore only included examples ascribed to the Romano-British and early medieval periods. Interestingly, decapitation burials where 'the head was altogether missing, or where it lay only a short distance from the shoulders' were not included as they were assumed to represent entirely different practices[18]. Clarke listed twenty-nine sites from the Romano-British period, with a total of seventy-six individual decapitations. The largest numbers recorded from individual sites were fifteen out of the ninety-four burials at Cassington, Oxfordshire, and all twenty-four of the burials from Rushton Mount, Northamptonshire (although this site is probably not Romano-British in date – see p.21). However, the majority of sites contained only a single example of the practice.

Six sites from the early medieval period were listed, with a total of eight affected individuals, and only one site was listed as containing more than a single example, namely Chadlington, Oxfordshire, with three adult male decapitations.

Of the seventeen Romano-British examples where an age or sex was recorded, fifteen were adult, with eight being female and three male, with two non-adults, whilst all of the early medieval examples were adult, with all three of those that had their sex noted being male. The head was recorded as being located in a variety of positions in both periods, including in the lap, between the knees, by the lower legs or ankles, or at the feet. Clarke concluded that decapitation was a predominately late Roman rural practice, restricted to the southern and central-southern counties of England, with noticeable absences from Kent and the North.

The next major synthesis of the subject was published by Harman *et al.* in 1981, which listed forty-nine sites from the Romano-British period with over one hundred and forty-four individual decapitations, and fourteen sites from the early medieval period, with twenty-nine separate affected burials[19]. Examples were included if they demonstrated displacement of the head or had been recorded as decapitations by the original excavator, with osteological evidence in the form of cut marks on cervical vertebrae being recorded for thirty-five individuals from the two periods.

Harman *et al.* stated that decapitations were mainly found in the later Romano-British period, distributed roughly between the Severn to the west and the Wash to the east, with smaller numbers of sites to the north-east and south-west and a concentration in rural areas, although examples from urban areas and small towns were also recorded. Those from the early medieval period were recorded as having a similar distribution to those found in the Romano-British period and an association with earthworks was noted. In discussing the nature of the decapitations, no distinction was made between the two periods, with both males and females described as being affected and with a disproportionately small number of non-adults.

If the lists of decapitations contained within Harmen, *et al.* are analysed to obtain the demographic information about affected individuals, thirty-one adult males, twenty-nine adult females and seven non-adults were affected in the Romano-British period, whilst in the early medieval period, twenty-two of the affected individuals were adult males, one was an adult female and one was a non-adult. Heads were noted as being most commonly placed by the lower part of the body, although other locations were recorded, such as by the pelvis or in correct anatomical position. Cut marks were stated as having been made most commonly to the upper part of the neck, although the exact vertebrae affected did vary. They also stated that cuts were most commonly made to the front of the neck, with blows directed from both the left and right side.

This survey was followed ten years later by Robert Philpott's work, which included a gazetteer of over seventy sites where decapitation burials from the Romano-British period were found and included examples where the head was in correct anatomical location, or missing altogether, as well as where it was found in a displaced position[20].

Philpott stated that the head was most commonly severed, with a degree of care and precision, from the front between the third and fourth cervical vertebrae with a sharp instrument on a body that was either drugged or dead, and then placed in the grave, 'almost invariably adjacent to or on the lower part of the body'[21]. He also recorded a distribution mostly south-east of the Severn–Wash line, with rare examples in the East Midlands and West Yorkshire and a near total absence in the south-eastern counties of Kent, Surrey and East and West Sussex, which he ascribed to the predominance of cremation in these areas. This burial practice would preclude the identification of head displacement and obscure the presence of cut marks to the vertebrae, although a number of analyses of Romano-British cremations – including those at Braughing, Hertfordshire, and Brougham, Cumbria – have occasionally recorded a total absence of skull fragments in such deposits, which may indicate the deliberate removal of the head, whilst possible cut marks on the cervical vertebra from a cremation have also been observed[22]. Philpott also concluded that the dating evidence supported Clarke's assertion that the rite was a mostly rural one that spread to urban sites during the fourth century. The demographic profile of those affected by decapitation suggested that, with the exception of infants and children, they reflected the 'normal life expectancy' for the period, with more females subjected to the practice than males – thirty-six adult male and fifty-one adult female decapitations being recorded in the main text[23]. However, when the demographic data is extracted from the included tables, fifty of those affected are found to be adult males and fifty-three are adult females, with eight non-adults also affected, suggesting that Philpott misread his own data and indicating there is not actually that much difference between the numbers of adult male and female decapitations when the complete sample is taken into account. The presence or absence of a body container and deliberate grave inclusions were also found to mirror the wider patterns in Romano-British cemeteries as a whole.

The next author to provide a gazetteer of sites where decapitation was present was O'Brien in 1999[24]. This study focused more on examples from the post-Roman and early medieval periods, with Philpott's distribution map being used to illustrate those from the Romano-British period, although O'Brien did introduce a small number of new sites. The gazetteer included brief information about each site, with decapitations being recorded only as present, absent or possible and with no numbers or demographic information provided. There was also no detailed discussion of the practice as a whole, although some sites were described in more detail in the body of the text. The gazetteer also made no distinction between Romano-British and later sites, making it difficult to draw any conclusions about the distribution, demographics and appearance of the practice in the post-Roman and early medieval periods.

Another recent survey of decapitation burials was that included in the book produced by Charlotte Roberts and Margaret Cox in 2003[25]. This publication was an attempt to collate the evidence for pathological changes and trauma evident in skeletal remains from a large number of published and unpublished reports on the Upper Palaeolithic to the post-medieval period in Britain. For the Romano-British period onwards, Roberts and Cox included only sites from which more than 50 individuals had been excavated, giving a total of 52 sites from the Romano-British period with 5,716 individuals and 72 sites from the early medieval period with 7,122 individuals. They noted nine sites from the Romano-British period where decapitation was confirmed by the presence of cut marks to the cervical vertebrae, cranial base or mandible, with a total of fifty-eight affected individuals and nearly twice as many males as females, although the majority of these had already appeared in Philpott's study; according to Roberts and Cox, the practice 'appears for the first time in this period' and 'was a cause of death [sic][26].' They also recorded four sites from the early medieval period, with a total of fifteen decapitations and with females representing nearly half of this figure. They also stated that the practice was a 'continuing tradition' from the Romano-British period and suggested that this may have been the result of 'contact and aggression' between native populations and newcomers[27].

The most recent synthesis of the practice was by Andrew Reynolds in 2009, which concentrated on examples from the early medieval period and included individuals from attritional cemeteries where the head was displaced or absent[28]. From the earlier part of the period, Reynolds noted fifty-four individuals from thirty-two sites where the practice was found, with a distribution over much of the eastern part of England, from the southern counties as far north as Yorkshire. Males were much more commonly affected than females, with twenty-seven adult males, six adult females, nineteen adults of unknown sex and two non-adults present in the sample. However, the antiquarian nature of many of the excavations did not allow any conclusions as to the presence or nature of any cut marks.

For the later part of the period, Reynolds provided a detailed list of twenty-seven 'execution cemeteries', defined as cemeteries usually containing 'prone burials, multiple interments, decapitation, evidence of restraint, shallow and cramped burial and mutilation', and commonly including intercutting graves, varied burial orientation and an absence of finds apart from low-status dress fittings[29]. They are usually located on 'principal administrative boundaries [or] associated with earthworks such as barrows or linear earthworks'[30]. Fourteen of these sites had individuals with evidence of decapitation, with a total of ninety-nine possible examples, at least eighty-five of which could be 'confidently said' to be decapitated, and their distribution is similar to the sites from the earlier part of the period[31]. Adult males were again much more commonly affected than non-adults or adult females, who only accounted for nine of the decapitations; and the cuts to the neck were described as 'multiple or excessively violent'[32].

Other authors have also commented on the practice, although without including as many examples as are contained in the works cited above. For the Romano-British period, Reece stated that the vast majority of cut marks were recorded as having been made to the front of the neck with a 'very high degree of skill' and little bone damage[33]. A common conclusion amongst authors is that the cuts must have been made on a corpse, as a live body would have produced large amounts of blood when the arteries in the neck were severed, obscuring the view and making precise cuts impossible. Another suggestion is that a living person would have struggled, again making precision very difficult to obtain[34]. However, other writers, commentating on sacrificial practices, have made the point that the shedding of blood was an integral part of the ritual process of sacrifice[35], and no account has been taken of the possibility that the blood could have been released through initial cutting of the soft tissues of the neck, leaving limited or no traces on the skeleton, and allowing the head to be removed once the blood flow had ceased.

For the early medieval period, the 'execution cemetery' (as defined by Andrew Reynolds) is most commonly discussed, with a preponderance of younger adult males found buried in shallow graves with heads often absent and hands sometimes tied. Cut marks are often described as 'heavy' and 'clumsy'[36] and are reported as being most commonly directed at the back of the neck, with the clavicles, scapulae and cranium also often being affected[37].

For prehistoric periods, there have been no detailed surveys of the practice, although possible or probable examples are contained within gazetteers and/or commented on by a number of different authors[38], whilst compilations of nineteenth-century barrow and tomb excavations by Bateman, Greenwell and Mortimer also include some possible examples[39]. The most common findings were of isolated crania and/or crania and mandibulae in settlement sites, burial areas and defensive ditches. These include crania and mandibulae from the Iron Age Glastonbury Lake Village with evidence for peri-mortem sharp-force trauma (although none of them show definite evidence for peri-mortem decapitation)[40], and the isolated cranium and mandible with attached cervical vertebrae from the Neolithic causewayed enclosure at Yeoveney Lodge, Staines, which was reported to show evidence for blunt-force trauma to the frontal and cuts to the mastoid processes and vertebrae[41]. Headless skeletons were also recorded, especially from the Bronze Age, such as the adult male within a tree-trunk coffin found in the Bronze Age 'King Barrow' (Arne 19) in Dorset[42]. Bateman acknowledged that they were not uncommon in his excavations of barrows in Staffordshire and Derbyshire[43].

Small numbers of burials with the head displaced from its correct anatomical position were also recorded for the Bronze and Iron Ages – for example, the crouched burial of an adult with the cranium placed at the pelvis from a barrow at Hanging Grimston, North Yorkshire[44] – despite Taylor's assertion that specifically decapitated bodies did not seem to appear in formal graves in the British Iron Age[45]. In the majority of examples, very little mention is made of the possibility that cut marks could be present. Armit and Ginn stated that no direct evidence has yet been found in Atlantic Scotland[46], although Smith and Brickley did find cut marks to clavicles from the Early Neolithic sites of Swell and West Tump[47], and cut marks were originally recorded on the crania and mandibulae from Glastonbury Lake Village and Yeoveney Lodge, Staines (as mentioned above, this page), suggesting the possibility that some heads were removed from corpses whilst soft tissue was still present.

Interpretations of the Practice
For the Neolithic, Schulting and Wysocki have suggested that examples of isolated skulls should be seen either in the context of ancestor worship or of trophy-taking and that the two practices are not necessarily mutually exclusive, since the idea that the head is the core of personhood and of spiritual power could easily lead to both practices[48]. If the head of an

ancestor can be used in ritual practice to bring protection to the group, then the head of a member of a rival group could be used to remove that protection from the rival group and transfer it to that of the trophy-taker. They suggested that the placement of trophy heads in causewayed enclosure ditches may have occurred alongside the deposition of ancestral remains, both activities serving to enhance a sense of group solidarity.

For the Bronze Age, Bateman, Greenwell and Mortimer passed very little comment on isolated skulls or burials with the head displaced or absent, other than an acknowledgement that the majority of the remains appeared to have been originally buried as they were later found, suggesting that they were aware that some form of manipulation and modification of the body had occurred before burial. There has been very little written subsequently that specifically discusses possible examples from this period, with the exception of Grinsell, who, unusually, suggested a motive for these burials – namely, that the heads may have been removed to prevent the ghosts of the dead from disturbing the living[49].

For the Iron Age, much more has been written on the phenomenon of isolated skulls, with the practice often being ascribed to a Celtic 'Cult of the Head', which saw the human head as the seat of the soul and the essence of the individual. The heads could be those of enemies, collected as 'trophies', or of revered ancestors, used in rituals to ensure fertility, protection and good fortune for a community[50]. This cult is assumed to have been very widespread throughout the Celtic world, a 'fact known and proven'[51], by the symbol of the severed head which 'sum[med] up the whole of pagan Celtic religion and … as representative of it as the sign of the cross in Christian contexts'[52]. Other commentaries, notably by historians rather than archaeologists, have suggested that this presumed Cult of the Head was by no means as universal or widespread as previously thought[53], and several authors, both archaeologists and historians, have suggested that many of the human skulls found were more likely to have been a result of battle-related head-hunting in a 'secular' context[54], although it has also been suggested that Iron Age warfare was essentially a 'ritualised' activity[55].

For the Romano-British period, isolated head burials have occasionally been interpreted as offerings to the gods to ensure fertility[56], or as ritual items connected to skull cults[57]. However, the majority of interpretations have focused on articulated skeletons with displaced heads. This has occasionally been described as a continuation of earlier practices, usually of the Iron Age head cult[58], or, in one case, from the early Bronze Age[59]. It has also been characterised as a 'barbarous and pathetic'[60] pagan practice[61] that may have been carried out in response to the breakdown of centralised control in the later Romano-British period[62], whilst Dorothy Watts, writing in 1991, saw an absence of the practice as a strong indicator that a cemetery was Christian[63]. Some scholars have suggested that it was a Germanic practice[64], although Andrew Reynolds argued that it was much more a Roman form of execution, along with crucifixion, whilst hanging was more common in Germanic areas[65].

Jock McDonald, writing about decapitations from Lankhills, Winchester, all of which were associated with unusual and rich military burials or with cenotaphs, used this evidence to suggest that the decapitations were in some sense sacrificial, used as vicarious substitutes to allow the souls of people who had been denied proper burial rites to enter the afterlife at the expense of those sacrificed[66]. He believed that the individuals had been killed as part of a sacrificial ritual in which post-mortem decapitation was then carried out. Other authors have argued that there are a number of problems with this interpretation. Firstly, human sacrifice was regarded as a weird and alien rite by Roman authors, such as Livy and Plutarch[67], and had been banned in the Roman Empire in 97 BC[68]. Robert Philpott has argued that this meant it was unlikely that human sacrifice at such a large and Romanised centre as Winchester would have escaped the notice of the authorities or been allowed to continue[69]. However, other authors have suggested that the authorities may have had limited influence over death rituals[70] and that human sacrifice may have been applied by native Britons in exceptional circumstances, with the choice of victim possibly determined by their having already been condemned to death under Roman law[71]. It has also been demonstrated that a number of the bog bodies found in Britain who are assumed to have been sacrificial victims, including the decapitated Lindow III and Worsley Man, actually date to the Romano-British period rather than the Iron Age[72]. If the decapitated individuals have been presumed to have given up all possibility of their souls entering the afterlife, it has also been asked why some of these burials were provided with hobnail boots and coins in the mouth, both of which were assumed to aid passage to the otherworld[73].

It has also been suggested that decapitation of a corpse may have been an acceptable way to make a sacrifice under an administration that did not allow live human sacrifices[74]. Foundation sacrifices to ensure the immortality of a building have also been given as an interpretation of decapitated infant burials at Springhead Temple IV, Kent, and Ware, Hertfordshire[75].

Decapitation has also been interpreted as being performed to aid passage to the afterlife in cases where individuals were deemed to have died prematurely or in an unusual manner[76], although very little supporting evidence from Roman belief systems has been given as to how and why decapitation would help (interestingly, however, there is a quote from Lucretius, stating that 'the head too when cut off from the warm and living trunk retains on the ground the expression of life and open eyes, until it has delivered up all the remnants of soul', which may be one of the ancient sources from which this interpretation was derived)[77].

Contradictorily, some commentators have suggested that decapitation may have been performed in order to prevent the dead from reaching the afterlife[78], or to prevent the dead from returning to haunt the living, in cases where the individual was a difficult character during life[79]. This interpretation is the same one given for burials where the body has been weighted down with stones[80]. In one case, where an individual from the Eastern Cemetery of Roman London was found to have been buried with a key, it has been suggested that this was to ensure the spirit remained 'locked' within the tomb[81]; however, it has also been suggested that the key was a symbol to ensure that the deceased could enter the gates of the afterlife! These interpretations apply particularly to older females, who were regarded in these interpretations as possibly having been 'witches'[82]. Seemingly connected with the previous interpretation is one that sees decapitation as a means of inflicting an indignity on a corpse because the individual was deemed to have committed some crime or broken some taboo during their life, or because they were considered to be outcasts – a form of *poena post mortem* (literally translated as 'punishment after death')[83]. This was usually carried out by mutilating and destroying the statuary and portraiture of a deceased and defamed individual (*damnatio memoriae*)[84], although there are recorded cases of the decapitation of the corpses of hated and feared rulers in Rome, whose heads were then put on display – the rest of the body being disposed of, usually into the sewers or Tiber[85]. There is even one example, that of Nero's successor Galba, where the head was later reunited with the body and interred[86].

Earlier writers were often willing to interpret decapitation burials as the result of executions[87], sometimes specifically Christian martyrs[88] or for unchastity[89], although in more modern commentaries, judicial execution is often only given as an explanation for burials where the head is absent, presumably as it was thought to have been displayed after the execution, as was the norm in later periods[90], rather than being buried in the grave with the rest of the body[91]. This form of decapitation burial is rare in this period and the acceptance that only this type may be a result of execution seems to mask a reluctance to see it as a possible explanation for any other type of decapitation burial; Dorothy Watts has specifically stated that when discussing Romano-British decapitation burials, she was not talking about executions[92]. Robert Philpott and Harman *et al.* have argued that the careful treatment, provision of coffins and grave goods, and location in normal cemeteries of the majority of decapitation burials mitigates against any of them being victims of execution[93]. They do admit that the bodies of those executed by decapitation could have been retrieved by their families for normal burial but argue that if this was the explanation, the proportion of criminals in the general population was surprisingly high.

One final explanation which argues for decapitation as the mechanism of death suggests a small number of individuals were decapitated as a result of armed conflict or massacre[94].

In the early medieval period, occasional findings of isolated head burials have been interpreted as either trophy heads[95], venerated heads of important community ancestors[96], or as representing individuals who died far away from home with only their heads being brought back for burial[97]. However, the most common explanation for decapitation burials in the early medieval period is that they were executions[98]. Although Andrew Reynolds[99] has stated that hanging was a much more Germanic form of execution than decapitation (and indeed there were a few burials from 'execution cemeteries' where the mechanism of death has been interpreted to have been by hanging[100]), decapitation as a form of execution is also seen in early medieval burials from elsewhere in Northern Europe[101], and the influence of the Danelaw on areas outside their control, as well as the possible continuation of Roman forms of execution, cannot necessarily be discounted in the 'Germanic' areas of Britain in this period.

Some burials have also been interpreted as battle victims[102], whilst ritual human sacrifice has occasionally been suggested as an interpretation[103], such as for a young headless female from the cemetery site of Cleatham, Lincolnshire, who was found buried with a bird. Her cranium and mandible were found two metres away from her body next to an urned cremation burial, the interpretation being that the young female was killed to accompany the individual contained in the urn[104].

Whilst the majority of interpretations given for decapitations in this period assumed that it was the mechanism of death, a few commentators have given very similar reasons to those used to explain such burials in the Romano-British period – that it prevented ghosts from walking and disturbing the living, for example[105]. At the site of Rushton Mount, Northamptonshire, where the remains of twenty-four decapitated individuals were found, with the heads either placed by the legs, buried separately or absent, Dorothy Watts saw the heads as having been retained by the families as some form of cult item until the mandibulae became detached, during which time they would benefit from the power and protective qualities of the head. The families had then buried the skulls seemingly indiscriminately, either because there was confusion over where individuals had been buried or because the remains were being buried covertly at night[106]. However, when all the characteristics of the cemetery are examined, it appears to conform to all of those expected for an 'execution' cemetery and should probably be seen in this light, rather than as the expression of a very local continuation of head-veneration cults.

For the medieval and early post-medieval periods, very little has been written about decapitations, with the few that are well known being interpreted as battle victims[107] or executions[108].

Therefore, it can be seen from the above discussion that, as well as the phenomenon of isolated skull burials and other forms of possible evidence for decapitation, there are two very distinct types of decapitation burial discussed by previous authors, which are summarised below:

Type 1
• Usually Romano-British in date.
• Found in community cemeteries.
• Carefully laid out in the grave, sometimes with a coffin and other grave inclusions.
• Head displaced, usually found by the lower limbs or feet.
• More females than males or non-adults affected (although a detailed analysis of the lists of examples contained within a number of the previous syntheses do not seem to support this assertion).
• Cut marks are to the front of the neck and described as precise and incised.
• Usually interpreted as the result of a post-mortem burial ritual.

Type 2
• Usually early medieval in date.
• Found in community cemeteries or in distinct 'execution cemeteries'.
• Often carelessly positioned in the grave, usually with no coffin or other grave inclusions.
• Head often absent or buried some distance from the rest of the body.
• Substantially more males than females or non-adults affected.
• Cut marks are to the back of the neck and sometimes affect the cranium and shoulders, and are described as heavy and clumsy.
• Decapitation interpreted as the mechanism of death, usually as the result of judicial execution.

It is this apparently simple and clear-cut dichotomy between the types of decapitation found in the two periods and which previous research by the author has already shown to be over-simplistic, that the following chapters aim to question and address.

Chapter 2

Evidence for Decapitation in British Prehistory

The Neolithic

A total of twenty-eight sites were identified where decapitation may have occurred, with forty-four individuals being represented. Just over sixty per cent of such individuals where a biological sex was stated were identified as adult males, whilst just over thirty per cent of all individuals were identified as non-adult.

Decapitated heads

The most common type of decapitation-related deposits were isolated crania and mandibulae, sometimes with associated cervical vertebrae. These were identified during the antiquarian excavations of Greenwell in the long barrows at Rudston and Market Weighton, East Riding of Yorkshire, and by Cunnington at Bole's Barrow, Wiltshire[109], where the neck vertebra of one individual had been 'cut in two by some sharp instrument'[110], although, as stated earlier, the cut bore the characteristics of having been made by a metal blade, suggesting it was from a secondary burial, probably of Romano-British or early medieval date. Isolated crania and mandibulae were also identified at Chute, Wiltshire, and were described as having been laid in a circle on flat stones with bundles of long bones placed inside the circle[111].

More recently, a small number of associated crania and mandibulae were excavated from the ditches at the causewayed enclosure of Hambledon Hill, Dorset. Three of these crania and mandibulae were also associated with one to three cervical vertebrae, although no osteological evidence for decapitation was recorded[112]. A similar deposit was excavated from the ditch of the causewayed enclosure at Yeoveney Lodge Farm, Staines, Surrey, which was reported as displaying evidence for four blunt-force injuries to the frontal, transverse cuts to the mastoid processes and cuts to C1-C4[113]. A recent reanalysis by Schulting and Wysocki of the cranium and mandible found that they were very fragmentary and had been heavily reconstructed, making it impossible to identify any evidence for peri-mortem trauma[114]. However, they were unable to locate the cervical vertebrae originally reported as being present. As part of the present research, the cranium and mandible were re-examined and, as Schulting and Wysocki had found, it was not possible to verify the presence of any trauma to the cranium as all the broken edges were covered with plaster. However, this time, the remains of the cervical vertebrae were located and closely examined for the presence of the cuts noted in the original report. Fragments of the left arches of C1 and C2, and the left arches and bodies of C3 and C4 were identified, but there was no evidence for peri-mortem cuts or fractures to any of the elements.

Other forms of decapitation
A number of the remaining Neolithic examples of possible decapitation are represented by bodies found without their heads, such as the individual recorded by Bateman at Pickering, North Yorkshire, buried with a flint blade by their right hand,[115] and the previously mentioned (p.10) individual from Swell, Gloucestershire, found by Rolleston. Five multiple deposits of cremated human bone excavated at Trostrey Castle, Monmouthshire, containing a minimum number of fifteen individuals, were interpreted as being the result of the cremation of headless corpses. The excavators found only samples of bone from each individual rather than complete cremated individuals, but no trace of dentine or enamel was present, which was taken to indicate that the bodies had been decapitated prior to cremation[116]. However, enamel is very rarely found in cremations, even where the whole body is represented, as it shatters and disintegrates in the very high temperatures produced during the process[117], and it is not mentioned whether cranial elements (which are easily distinguished from other bones in cremated deposits because of their distinctive shape) were also absent.

Three headless burials, of an adult female, an adult male and a non-adult of *c.*10-11 years, were excavated from Whitegrounds Barrow, North Yorkshire, but, in this case, the crania of all three individuals and the mandibulae of the adult male and non-adult were found in a cache near to the prone burial of the adult female[118]. The brief report on the skeletal remains made no mention of any evidence for peri-mortem trauma to the crania, mandibulae or cervical vertebrae of any of the individuals[119]. The final example that should be mentioned is the contracted burial of an adult female found during the excavations of the chambered tomb at Ascott-under-Wychwood, Oxfordshire. The original report stated that the first cervical vertebra did not articulate with the rest of the spine, which was complete, suggesting that the cranium, mandible and C1 were from a different individual[120]. The presence of both the mandible and C1 would suggest either that the head was removed from its original post-cranial remains relatively early in the decomposition process, as the mandible detaches from the cranium prior to the upper cervical spine, or there was a deliberate attempt to re-articulate the mandible with the cranium for its final deposition. However, this non-articulating vertebra was not mentioned in the recent reanalysis of the material from the site and no peri-mortem cuts were recorded[121].

Evidence for peri-mortem trauma
Although a large number of these possible examples of decapitation from the Neolithic were reported in the nineteenth and earlier twentieth centuries and have never been subjected to detailed osteological analysis, none of the examples from more recent excavations that have been subject to such analyses have revealed any evidence for peri-mortem cuts or other traumata. This would suggest that the manipulation of crania and complete heads was occurring once decomposition was sufficiently advanced to preclude the necessity of cutting through soft tissue. This conclusion would also be supported by the observations, such as those made for the deposits at Rudston by Greenwell, that a number of the mandibulae were not found articulated with their crania or that mandibulae were articulated with crania to which they did not belong[122]. However, recent reanalysis of commingled human remains from long barrows at Swell and West Tump, Gloucestershire, have identified two clavicles with a number of incised peri-mortem cut marks to the superior surface, made with a flint blade, which would seem to be consistent with the removal of *M. sternocleidomastoideus* at its point of origin[123]. As the cranium separates from the post-cranial remains early in the sequence of post-mortem decomposition, the presence of cut marks indicates that some heads were being removed from post-cranial remains before decomposition was very far advanced. There does not seem to be any evidence for crania with cut marks to the insertion point of *M. sternocleidomastoideus* at the mastoid or to the area of the nuchal crest, where *M. semispinalis capitis* and *M. rectus capitis* (large muscles at the back of the neck) insert, or any cuts to the posterior arches of cervical

vertebrae where these muscles originate. This suggests that decomposition may have at least begun when these heads were removed, otherwise more cuts to the cranio-cervical skeleton would be expected. Such peri-mortem cuts have indeed been found on Neolithic human remains from outside Britain – for example, on cervical vertebrae at Tell Qaramel, Syria; a mandible at Köşk Höyük, Turkey; and both cervical vertebrae and mastoid processes at one of the predynastic cemeteries (HK43) of Hierakonpolis, Egypt[124]. Therefore, further research with the specific aim of identifying peri-mortem cut marks to crania, mandibulae and cervical vertebrae of commingled remains as well as isolated head deposits and articulated skeletons may reveal more evidence for peri-mortem head removal in the Neolithic period in Britain.

The Bronze Age

Forty-seven sites were identified from the Bronze Age (nearly twice as many as the Neolithic), with sixty-four individuals being represented. The percentage of adult males (just over seventy per cent of adults for whom a sex was determined) was slightly higher than in the Neolithic, and, as a consequence, the percentage of adult females (just under thirty per cent) decreased. The total percentage of non-adults also slightly decreased, although none of the differences were statistically significant.

Decapitated heads

Isolated head deposits were still the largest group represented, with half of all examples being from this category, and although this percentage represented a decrease from that found in the Neolithic, it was not statistically significant. A number of these head deposits were found in early excavations and, although a number of them were reported to have been found with attached cervical vertebrae (such as one of the three isolated crania and mandibulae found by Greenwell in a barrow at Helperthorpe, North Yorkshire, or the cranium and mandible found on Pilling Moss, Lancashire, in 1824, that also had part of C1, surviving hair and associated jet beads, all found wrapped in a coarse woollen cloth)[125], the absence of any detailed analysis of the skeletal remains made it impossible to determine whether they were the result of peri-mortem decapitation. Very poor preservation of bone also made it impossible to determine for the seven deposits of isolated heads excavated from a number of pits at Barns Farm, Dalgety, Fife, in which complete and directly associated maxillary and mandibular dentitions were the only surviving skeletal remains[126]. It is also now impossible to determine whether an adult male cranium and mandible, found with five attached cervical vertebrae, from a palaeochannel at Abbey Meads, Chertsey, Surrey, represented a deliberate decapitation or was simply the result of later truncation by quarrying of a complete burial, as the remains were stolen during the relocation of the Surrey Council Archaeological Unit stores in the 1990s[127].

Osteological analysis was carried out in the 1930s on a cranium and mandible with C1 and part of C2 attached that was excavated from a chalk-cut cist under a round barrow and directly associated with a large roughly chipped block of flint, at Easton Down, Wiltshire. The inferior border of the mandible and C2 were stated to be poorly preserved and no cut marks were observed on any of the elements[128]. Interestingly, the remains are now claimed to be in both the Natural History Museum and the Salisbury and South Wiltshire Museum, although those in the Natural History Museum appear to match the descriptions provided by Tildesley, who carried out the original analysis, which would correspond with this having taken place at the Royal College of Surgeons with the collections subsequently passing to the Natural History Museum. Unfortunately, the two vertebrae are now missing, making the original osteological observations impossible to verify.

There is only one example of an isolated head deposit from this period where osteological analysis did reveal evidence for peri-mortem decapitation and which was re-examined for the purposes of this research. This was a cranium, mandible, C1 and C2 found in a palaeochannel at the Watermead Country Park, Birstall, Leicestershire, along with a second cranium and a small number of post-cranial remains. The second cranium and post-cranial remains were radiocarbon dated to the Neolithic, whilst the articulated cranium, mandible and cervical vertebrae were dated to 990-830 cal BC, which places them within the later Bronze Age[129]. The cranium and mandible belong to a younger adult male with a possible healed depressed fracture to the anterior left of the frontal. There was no evidence for any peri-mortem injuries to the cranium or mandible, but there were four incised cuts to the posterior arches of C1 (plate 4) and at least nine separate incised cuts to the body and arches of C2 (figure 1). The majority of the cuts to C2 were made from the anterior and affect the posterior and inferior of the body as well as the anterior of the inferior articular facets. It has been suggested that these cuts indicate that the individual had their throat cut[130], but the placement of the cuts is more

27

consistent with soft tissue initially being removed from the anterior and posterior of the neck and then, once the vertebrae were visible, the blade being used to cut through the intervertebral connective tissues from the anterior until the cervical column was severed at the level of C2-C3.

Other forms of decapitation

The majority of the remaining examples of possible decapitation from the Bronze Age were represented by headless skeletons and burials where the head was present but displaced. The percentage of burials where the head was displaced showed a very slight, non-statistically significant increase from the Neolithic, but the increase in headless burials was statistically significant. Again, a number of these were excavated during the nineteenth and earlier twentieth centuries and were never subjected to any osteological analysis. These include the previously mentioned (p.16) adult male found wrapped in deer skins and buried with a shale cup in a log coffin beneath a barrow (Arne 19) in Dorset; the partial burial of an adolescent with a beaker from Fargo Plantation, Wiltshire, with the cranium, mandible and C1-C2 absent; and the contracted burial of an adult from Hanging Grimston, North Yorkshire, where the cranium was placed at the pelvis[131]. Even where burials have been excavated more recently, very few have ever

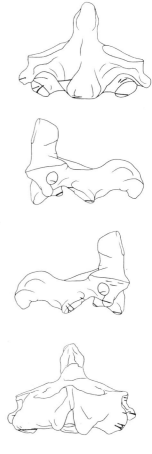

Figure 1: Incised cuts to the C2 of the individual from Watermead Country Park, Birstall, Leicestershire.

had any osteological analysis performed or, at least, published, with examples including the contracted burial of a non-adult of *c.*4 years whose cranium and mandible were described as having 'disintegrated' despite the rest of the elements being well preserved; and the headless non-adult who had been cremated *in situ* in a pit within a ring cairn at Aber Camddwr, Cardiganshire[132]. This makes it impossible to determine whether any of the cases do in fact demonstrate evidence for peri-mortem decapitation, or whether – like an adolescent male from Horsbrugh Castle Farm, Peeblesshire, whose skeleton was slightly disarticulated, with the cranium, mandible and both pectoral girdles missing[133] – the absence of the head is more likely to be the result of post-burial truncation or disturbance.

One such burial, from Babraham Road, Wandlebury, Cambridgeshire, of a partially articulated adult male, with sixty per cent of the skeletal elements absent, who had been interred in a semi-decomposed state in a large circular pit, did display evidence for an incised cut into the right petrous temporal, suggesting that an attempt had been made to remove the cranium from the post-cranial remains before final deposition[134]. This does suggest that some of the headless burials, or those with displaced heads, may actually reveal evidence that decapitation had been carried out before decomposition had become far enough advanced to allow the cranium to be removed without the need for cutting of soft tissue.

Composite skeletons

The final burial that should be mentioned, and that seems to represent a different phenomenon, is that of an adult male found beneath the floor of a building at the settlement of Cladh Hallan, South Uist. The burial was first thought to be complete and articulated, but was found on analysis to be composed of the post-cranial skeleton of one individual, the cranium and cervical vertebrae of a second and the mandible of a third, with the cranium showing signs of abrasion[135]. This, along with the absence of any evidence for cut marks, would suggest that these elements had been removed from corpses in advanced, but different, stages of decomposition. The abrasion of the cranium may suggest that the body from which it was taken had been allowed to decay above ground, with the post-mortem loss of the maxillary anterior dentition supporting this interpretation. One of the most interesting aspects of this burial is the discrepancy between the radiocarbon dates for the cranium (1500-1260 cal BC), mandible (1500-1210 cal BC) and post-cranial elements (a date of 1620-1410 cal BC from the tibia), and the date when the floor was constructed over the burial pits (1100-930 cal BC). This suggests that the composite skeletal remains were curated for at least one or two centuries before their final deposition, and there is also the suggestion that the individuals who provided the post-cranial and cranial/mandibular remains did not die during exactly the same period. It seems possible that the cranio-cervical skeleton of the main individual was removed some time after death and the remains were curated in a headless state for a number of years before replacement elements were united with the post-cranial skeleton to be further curated. Centuries later the remains were buried as a composite skeleton, possibly because it was seen as necessary or desirable that a body should appear to be whole when finally interred. Recently, a DNA analysis of an adult female burial from the same site, previously assumed to have been a single individual, has also found that it was composed of the remains of at least three different people, and it has been suggested that these composite skeletons represented a physical act designed to amalgamate different ancestries into a single lineage[136].

It is possible that this may provide an interpretation for the Neolithic burial at Ascott-under-Wychwood with the cranium that did not appear to belong to the post-cranial remains, although radiocarbon dating of cranial and post-cranial elements, coupled with a reanalysis of the remains to confirm whether the cranium does or does not belong to the rest of the skeleton, would be necessary in order to prove this theory.

The Iron Age
The number of possible or definite cases of decapitation increases again in the Iron Age, with sixty-two sites and one hundred and thirteen individuals being represented. There is also an increase in the percentage of adult males represented with a decrease in the percentage of adult females and non-adults, although the ratio of adult males to females is not statistically significantly different from the earlier periods. Deposits of isolated crania and mandibulae were again the most commonly identified group, although this represented a slight, non-statistically significant decrease from the Bronze Age. Individuals where the head was present but displaced were the second most commonly represented group, followed by headless burials, which represents a change from the Bronze Age, although it is not statistically significant. There was also a new group of burials identified from this period where the head was in correct position and osteological analysis identified definite evidence for decapitation, although this is probably largely due to the greater frequency of such analysis, which was carried out on thirty-four examples of possible or definite Iron Age decapitations (including ten analysed as part of this research).

Osteological data from the Iron Age sample
This sample of individuals where detailed osteological data was recorded allows some points to be made regarding their health status compared to non-decapitated individuals from the same period, as well as to the nature of the evidence for peri-mortem trauma amongst the group.

Of the thirty-four individuals (or parts of individuals retrieved from commingled contexts), all those that could be assigned a sex were found to be male (eleven individuals), with a few non-adult individuals also being represented. Although this does reflect the small number of adult females represented in the larger sample, it has also resulted from an unforeseen bias in the sex of skeletal remains which were available for analysis, with the articulated cranium, mandible and cervical vertebrae of an adult female from a late Iron Age well at Odell, Bedfordshire, not being available for study due to major refurbishment of the local stores[137], whilst the analysis of an older adult female from Stane Street, Baldock, who was possibly decapitated, has not yet been fully published[138].

The stature could be calculated for nine adult male individuals, with a range of 160.79cm to 178cm and a mean of 174.5cm. This is statistically significantly higher than both the general Iron Age mean of 168cm, calculated from 113 individuals by Charlotte Roberts and Margaret Cox in 2003, and the mean of 169.2cm calculated by Rebecca Redfern for Iron Age populations in Dorset[139]. This indicates that the individuals from the Iron Age who displayed evidence for decapitation were significantly taller than the general population. This may indicate a higher level of nutritional health during childhood and adolescence, which is also supported by the lower number of individuals with evidence for *cribra orbitalia* amongst the decapitated sample, compared with the samples reported by Roberts and Cox and Redfern. *Cribra orbitalia* is a porosity of the roof of the orbits that is probably a result of iron-deficiency anaemia, whether through inadequate diet or parasitic infection, although it has also been suggested that the condition may have more complicated aetiologies[140]. The possibility that the decapitated individuals may have had a better non-adult health status is also supported by the limited presence of dental enamel hypoplasia (EH), which is lower than the number of affected individuals in Roberts and Cox's sample, although not quite statistically significantly so. Enamel hypoplasia are areas of reduced enamel deposition on the dental crowns, usually manifesting as linear depressions and pitting, and are thought to relate to periods of acute ill health and increased body temperature[141].

Whether those individuals subject to decapitation were different from the rest of the population in other aspects of their health status was also assessed. Dentition could be recorded in ten individuals and, of these, three had evidence for dental caries. The percentage of the sample as a whole is slightly higher than that given by Roberts and Cox, although not statistically significantly so. The true prevalence rate (TPR) for the number of teeth affected is very similar to that reported by Roberts and Cox, but statistically significantly lower than the percentages in Redfern's sample and two samples used by Calvin Wells and Don Brothwell[142]. Dental calculus was recorded in around thirty per cent of the total sample, which is slightly lower than the percentage reported by Roberts and Cox, although it is not statistically significant. However, the TPR is statistically significantly higher than in both of the samples utilised by Roberts and Cox and Redfern.

Both dental caries and calculus are a reflection of poor levels of dental hygiene and high levels of protein and sucrose in the diet, although modern levels of dental hygiene are still not sufficient to prevent the build-up of dental calculus[143]. The fact that the decapitated individuals demonstrate statistically significantly higher levels of dental calculus whilst also demonstrating statistically significantly lower rates of dental caries suggests that the standards of dental hygiene may have been poorer amongst that group, whilst the diet may also have been different, with lower levels of sucrose than was the norm.

Periodontal disease is an inflammatory condition that affects the periodontium and which manifests as porosity and resorption of the alveolar margin (the edge of the thickened area of bone that contains the tooth sockets)[144]. It should not be confused with the continuing eruption of the dentition, a feature which is predominately recorded in individuals with high levels of dental attrition, although a lower level of continuing eruption has been recorded in populations with limited attrition[145]. Periodontal disease is usually associated with high levels of dental calculus, the bacteria within the newly deposited dental plaque being the predominant cause of the disease, and so the decapitated sample should demonstrate higher levels of the condition compared with the wider population. However, only around twelve per cent of individuals displayed evidence for periodontal disease, which is slightly lower than the percentage in Roberts and Cox's sample, although not statistically significantly so.

Dental abscesses are associated with severe carious cavities and result from an infection penetrating into the alveolar bone from an infected tooth or tooth socket, although their appearance in dry bone can be easily confused with periapical granulomata and apical periodontal cysts, both of which are also the result of infection and inflammatory processes but which are much more benign in nature[146], and so the levels should be lower in the decapitated sample, commensurate with the lower levels of dental caries. However, the percentage in the present sample was very similar to that in the sample used by Roberts and Cox.

Osteoarthritis and degenerative joint disease manifest as osteophyte formation around joints, porosity and subchondral destruction of joint surfaces, with eburnation (polishing) of joint surfaces (due to bones rubbing against bones through cartilage loss) being specific to osteoarthritis, and are a result of the ageing process and wear and tear on joints[147]. The percentage of individuals in the present sample with osteoarthritis and/or degenerative joint disease was statistically significantly higher than within the wider population sample used by Roberts and Cox. This cannot be accounted for by the age distribution of the decapitated sample, as, of the twenty-one individuals where a more accurate assessment of age was made, only three were mature adults, with the majority being young adults. This may suggest that the decapitated individuals were subjecting their joints to more wear and tear than was the norm. This is supported by the presence of Schmorl's nodes in the vertebral bodies of four individuals, which are depressions in the superior and inferior surfaces of the vertebral body. These have a complicated aetiology but are probably the result of unusual compressive loading of the spine during adolescence and young adulthood, such as carrying heavy loads on the back or head[148]. The percentage in the decapitated sample is statistically significantly larger than that in the sample used by Roberts and Cox, although if the data presented in their accompanying table is used instead, which shows the sites where Schmorl's nodes were definitely found rather than the complete sample, the percentage is almost identical to that in the decapitated sample. Enthesopathies (see appendix 1) were also seen in four individuals, which helps to support the interpretation of unusual and increased muscular stress amongst the decapitated individuals.

The unusually tall statures of the decapitated individuals, as well as the evidence for increased levels of wear and tear to joints and other increased mechanical loading and stresses to the skeleton, may suggest that the individuals were behaving differently from the rest of the population during their adult lives. This, coupled with the fact that the majority of decapitations in this period are younger adult males, could indicate a martial status for such individuals. This may be supported by the presence of ante-mortem healed fractures in four individuals, composed of two cranial depressed fractures, one rib fracture and one fracture of a metacarpal with subsequent shortening of the element. The percentage of individuals with fractures is not statistically significantly different to that quoted by Roberts and Cox, although it is interesting that there are no fractures of the long bones or claviculae amongst the decapitated sample, which are well represented amongst the samples used by both Roberts and Cox and Redfern. The fractures that are represented amongst the decapitated sample are amongst those (hand and foot, cranium, nasal bones, ribs) that are, clinically, believed to have a high specificity for a diagnosis of assault, with metacarpals often being fractured due to longitudinal compression fractures, such as occur in boxing[149]. Fractures of the ribs, metacarpals and cranium were also identified in two twentieth-century individuals known to have been boxers[150]. There is, therefore, the possibility that the decapitated individuals may have been engaging in interpersonal violence. However, if a martial context is to be suggested, it is interesting to note that there are no examples of healed sharp-force traumata, as were found, albeit rarely, amongst the sample of Iron Age burials from Dorset analysed by Redfern.

Evidence for peri-mortem trauma amongst the sample

When the evidence is examined for peri-mortem trauma amongst the group of thirty-four decapitated individuals who had been subjected to detailed skeletal analysis, thirty-two of the individuals exhibited such evidence.

A sample of Iron Age individuals from Danebury hill fort, Hampshire, previously reported as displaying evidence for peri-mortem trauma, were also reanalysed as part of this project. Deposition 238, the partial mandible of an adult ?male (possible male), was described as having a sword cut consistent with decapitation[151], although, on reanalysis, this was clearly excavation damage – the 'cut' surface demonstrating scrapes probably made with a shovel as well as pale, roughened broken bone surfaces. Excavation damage was also the likely explanation for the 'cuts' recorded to the left gonial area of two non-adult crania and mandibulae (Deposition 245) found together with a third cranium and mandible in a pit[152], although one of the crania did display three small, very superficial nicks into the inferior margin of the mandible, as well as evidence for rodent gnawing (a series of shallow parallel grooves to the exterior and interior margins) of the nasal aperture (plate 5). This does support the suggestion that the crania and mandibulae may have been displayed for a short time before deposition, as also indicated by the disarticulation of the mandibulae[153].

Post-burial manipulation

Of the individuals who did not display any evidence for peri-mortem trauma, one was an articulated adult male from Suddern Farm, Hampshire (C20), buried prone with the upper limbs flexed beneath the torso and both lower limbs flexed at the knee[154], and who was found to be substantially complete except for elements of the feet, the cranium, mandible and first cervical vertebra. This burial can be compared with another individual from Danebury (Deposition 10) who was briefly examined for evidence of peri-mortem trauma but not subjected to a full skeletal analysis. This individual was the partially articulated skeleton of an adult female with the spinal column arranged around the lower limbs and feet and with parts of the pectoral girdle, both upper limbs and the cranium and mandible absent[155], who was also found to have the entire cervical column complete except for C1. The fact that both of these individuals were missing the cranium, mandible and C1 but displayed no evidence for peri-mortem trauma could suggest that the head was deliberately removed once decomposition had progressed far enough that no cuts to the bones needed to be made but before the first cervical vertebra had become detached from the cranial base.

Post-mortem manipulation is also possible in the case of a pit burial (1111) from Winklebury, Hampshire, described as being articulated with the lower limbs crossed and drawn up and with the cranium and mandible 'placed' at the base of the spine[156]. The skeleton was found to be that of a young middle adult male with the right pectoral girdle and upper limb, both hands and most of both feet absent. There was no evidence for any peri-mortem trauma to the cervical column, which was complete, but there were ancient dry-bone fractures of the left pedicle and right inferior arch of C5 and the body and arch of C6 with some evidence for bone peel, with the distal left ulna and some of the right ribs demonstrating similar features. This fracturing may be indicative of some form of manipulation of the skeletal remains post-burial, especially as it seems to be restricted to areas in which there has been loss or movement of elements, namely the left wrist, right pectoral girdle and cervical spine. Post-mortem manipulation may also be assumed for the previously mentioned nest of three non-adult crania and mandibulae (Deposition 245) from Danebury, and the analysis of a larger sample of Iron Age burials may reveal more cases of such manipulation, including individuals with evidence for dry-bone fractures.

Decapitated heads

Of the individuals who did display evidence for peri-mortem trauma, a quarter were represented by the cranium, mandible and attached cervical vertebrae only. Four of these individuals demonstrated chopping blows through the mandible or attached cervical vertebrae, which were from the posterior (where a direction could be determined). These included the cranium, mandible and C1-C2 of a young adult ?male from the base of a ditch at Prebendal Court hill fort, Buckinghamshire[157], who demonstrated a single chop through the arch of C2 (plate 6); and the cranium, mandible and C1 of a mature adult male from a palaeochannel at Joist Fen, Lakenheath, Suffolk, who demonstrated at least four chops to the mandible[158]. One of the other examples was the previously mentioned (p.34) cranium and mandible of a non-adult individual from Danebury (Deposition 245), with evidence for very small nicks to the inferior border of the mandible, whilst a second deposit from the same site (Pit 23) – the cranium and mandible of a seven- to ten-year-old child – demonstrated a peri-mortem fracture of the right mandibular body with extensive bone peeling on the anterior margin (plate 7). The gonial area was damaged post-mortem so it is impossible to determine whether this fracture resulted from a sharp-force injury, but the anteriorly placed bone peel indicates that the blow was directed from the posterior.

The remaining two crania, mandibulae and cervical vertebrae were interesting as they both displayed evidence for non-decapitation-related peri-mortem trauma, as well as multiple incised cuts to the anterior of the cervical vertebrae. The first of these was the cranium, mandible and C1-C4 of a young adult ?male from a ditch at Stanwick hill fort, North Yorkshire, found in association with a sword and scabbard[159]. There were five chopping blows to the left and anterior of the frontal, right parietal, right maxilla and right zygomatic, directed from both the antero-superior right and left, and associated peri-mortem fracturing of the affected elements (figure 2), as well

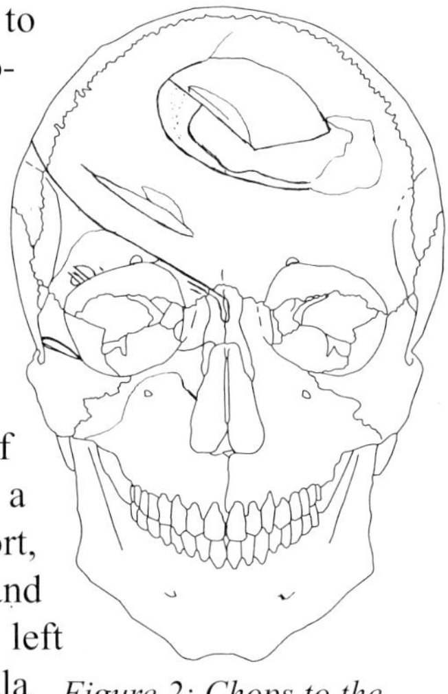

Figure 2: Chops to the cranial vault and facial skeleton of the individual from Stanwick, North Yorkshire.

as a probable contrecoup fracture of the occipital (a fracture caused by inertial stresses propagating towards the opposite end of the head from the area of impact[160]). In contrast to these peri-mortem injuries, which appear to have been produced by a heavy blade, such as a sword or an axe, there are seven fine incised cuts to the anterior of the body of C4, as well as two other deeper incised cuts that affect the inferior of the spinous process and the anterior and inferior surface of the body, and the left superior facet and superior surface of the body (plate 8). These injuries are more likely to have been produced with a knife, and their placement suggests the process involved the careful removal of soft tissue and disarticulation of the cervical column in order to remove the head. It is interesting that this was the method of decapitation chosen, rather than chopping through the neck with the same instrument that was used to inflict the cranial injuries, and may suggest that the removal of the head was not undertaken at the same time.

The second example was the cranium, mandible and C1-C2 of a young middle adult male found face down in a small pit at the settlement site in Heslington, also in North Yorkshire[161]. The individual had been hanged (there is a characteristic fracture of the arch of C2) and then decapitated, again by a careful process of soft-tissue removal and disarticulation, indicated by at least nine small incised cuts to the anterior of the body of C2 and two stab wounds to the inferior and anterior of the body[162] that are probably the result of inserting the blade between C2 and C3 to prise the elements apart (figure 3). The very similar method of decapitation in both of these examples is very different to that demonstrated by other

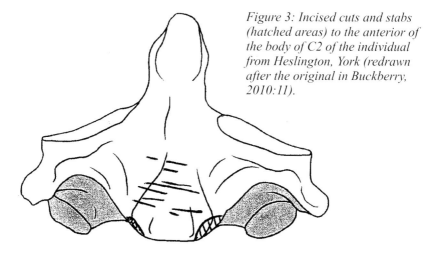

Figure 3: Incised cuts and stabs (hatched areas) to the anterior of the body of C2 of the individual from Heslington, York (redrawn after the original in Buckberry, 2010:11).

deposits of crania and mandibulae (chopping blows directed from the posterior) and the fact they are both from the same area of the country may suggest a localised form of the practice, although the number of examples is very small and the appearance of the cut marks is also very similar to those seen on the Bronze Age head deposit from Birstall, Leicestershire.

Other forms of decapitation

The other examples of peri-mortem decapitation trauma were found in skeletons where the head was displaced from its anatomically correct position, where the cranium and mandible were in correct anatomical position, where the cranium and mandible were absent, or (the most common type) where cervical vertebrae, crania or mandibulae with evidence for peri-mortem trauma were found amongst commingled or disarticulated remains. All but one of the examples that had evidence for decapitation-related trauma demonstrated evidence for chopping blows (the exception was a C2 with an incised cut to the anterior of the dens from the hill fort at South Cadbury, Somerset[163]), and the blows were directed from the posterior in all but three cases. Amongst these examples were four decapitated individuals from a mass grave of twenty-five adolescents and adult males at the hill fort of Sutton Walls, Herefordshire[164], the skeletal remains of which, although a report was produced at the time which is relatively detailed in its treatment of the peri-mortem trauma[165], can no longer be located, despite various attempts by the author and other researchers. Other cases included a C2 and C3 with five separate chops to the body and arch, all that remain of a group of three decapitated adults from the bottom of a ditch at the hill fort of Maiden Bower, Bedfordshire[166], and six cervical vertebrae (five C2s and one C1) from Sculptor's Cave, Grampian, that date to the Roman Iron Age (80-410 AD) and demonstrate evidence for chopping blows, from a single bisecting chop to eleven separate chops to a single element, all of which were delivered from the posterior with the neck flexed[167].

Individuals with extensive peri-mortem trauma

The remaining two Iron Age individuals who deserve a detailed description are both younger adult males, one found with the cranium and mandible in correct position and the other with the cranium and mandible absent. The former of these is a pit burial, from Old Down Farm, Andover, Hampshire, described as lying on their right side with both upper limbs folded under the chin in a 'sleeping' posture and with a layer of large flint nodules covering the body. The head was found in correct anatomical position but the original analysis identified fourteen separate cuts to the cranium, neck, torso and left upper limb, including two cuts to the cervical vertebrae, a cut through the left elbow and a glancing blow to the posterior of the cranium. All of the blows were identified as being made with a slashing action, apart from some of those to the ribs and thoracic vertebrae, which were identified as thrusts[168].

The re-examination of the skeleton as part of this research identified it as that of a young adult male with a stature of 173.92cm. He had suffered an ante-mortem fracture of the proximal phalanx for the fourth metacarpal with some shortening, and demonstrated large cortical defects at the insertion sites for the muscles and ligaments in the pectoral girdle that are involved in adduction, extension, medial rotation, transverse flexion and transverse adduction of the shoulder. The left humerus was also 5mm longer than the right. The presence of cortical defects suggests repeated micro-trauma to the muscle insertion sites through the particularly heavy use of the muscles, whilst the asymmetry in the length of the humeri indicates activity-related hypertrophy, probably whilst the limb was still growing, and suggests a left-sided dominance[169]. The possibility of participation in strong physical activity was also suggested by the presence of Schmorl's nodes and an avulsion fracture of the styloid process of the right third metacarpal, which was probably the result of sudden trauma to the muscle that inserts at this point and is involved in extension of the wrist.

Twenty-four separate blade injuries were identified, including two to the cervical vertebrae, one of which (which chopped into, but not totally through, C3 and the posterior of the mandible) would have partially decapitated the individual. There was also a glancing blow to the posterior of the left parietal, a number of chops to the left side and posterior of the ribcage and vertebral column, two chops to the left ilium, and a chop into the left side of the left femur, as well as stab wounds to the anterior of the sternum, left ilium, both scapulae and through the anterior and superior left of the ribcage (possibly aimed at the area of the heart). There was also a chopping injury to the distal left humerus, and proximal left radius and ulna that align if the elbow joint is held at ninety degrees flexion (plate 9 and figure 4). It is possible that this represents a defensive injury as these are commonly found on the distal segment of the upper limb[170], with a very similar injury being recorded on one individual from the War

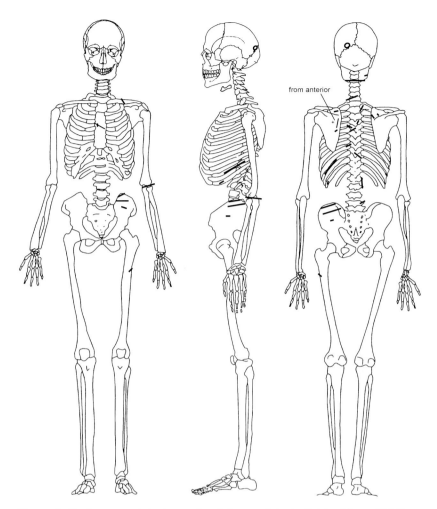

Figure 4: Peri-mortem injuries to the skeleton of the individual from Old Down Farm, Andover, Hampshire.

of the Roses mass grave at Towton, North Yorkshire[171]. It is interesting that it is the left limb that is affected, supporting the hypothesis that the individual was left-side dominant. The fact that the majority of injuries are to the left side and posterior of the skeleton could also suggest a right-handed assailant, the possibility of more than one protagonist, or the continuation of the attack once the individual was already prone on the ground.

The second individual, who bears close similarities to the Old Down Farm burial, is a young middle adult male from Sovell Down, Dorset, discovered accidently through rabbit disturbance and then subject to rescue excavation. The skeleton was in the base of a ditch lying slightly sprawled with his right lower limb tightly flexed and the cranium and mandible absent[172]. Only a small area around the skeleton was excavated, so it is impossible to determine whether they were really absent or simply unexcavated. The individual was 170.9cm in stature with Schmorl's nodes on the lower thoracic and lumbar vertebrae and large cortical defects at the attachment site for the costoclavicular ligament on both claviculae, which stabilises the pectoral girdle during movement. There were at least thirteen separate blade injuries identified, including three chops to the third and fourth cervical vertebrae (C1 and C2 were absent),

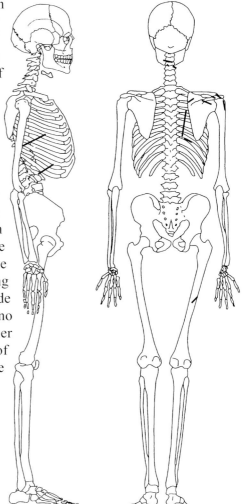

including a total decapitation between C2 and C3, chops to the posterior and lateral side of the right side of the rib-cage, at least five separate chops to the posterior and lateral of the right scapula (including ones that also affected the proximal right humerus and right clavicle), as well as a chop to the lateral side of the midshaft of the right femur (plate 10 and figure 5). Although the number of separate injuries is fewer than at Old Down Farm, the placement is very similar, although the side is reversed. The chops to the right scapula and humerus may have been intended as incapacitating injuries to a victim who was right-side dominant, although there was no evidence for asymmetry of the upper limb, or the right-side placement of the injuries may be a reflection of the position of the assailant.

Figure 5: Peri-mortem injuries to the skeleton of the individual from Sovell Down, Dorset.

41

The possible interpretation of these two burials could be that they were victims of combat, whether formal or otherwise (it would also be interesting, if they are ever located, to see whether the individuals from Sutton Walls have evidence for non-decapitation-related peri-mortem traumata, as they are assumed to have been victims of an attack on the hill fort by incoming Roman troops[173]), as the age, sex, muscular development and stature of the individuals could suggest a martial context, as already argued for the larger Iron Age sample of analysed decapitated individuals. However, the burial context is very different, with one being placed in a formal pit burial, seemingly carefully positioned and covered with flint nodules, whereas the other is sprawled in a ditch (the non-formal burial position is also seen in the Sutton Walls individuals). This could be a reflection of who carried out the burials: possibly friendly forces in the former, who may have attempted to follow traditional mortuary practices (this may also be the interpretation for the formally laid-out burials from Maiden Castle with evidence for peri-mortem trauma, including at least one individual who may have been decapitated[174]), and hostile forces in the latter, who would neither know nor care about these practices, as has been argued by Spars for more recent examples of such burial circumstances[175]. The non-formal burial of the individual from Sovell Down may also suggest a surreptitious disposal after a violent assault.

Discussion

In summary, the evidence for decapitation-related peri-mortem trauma from all individuals in the Iron Age sample indicates that the vast majority were decapitated with chopping blows directed from a postero-anterior direction. There were only two examples where this was not the case, with the head being removed by carefully incised cuts to the anterior of the cervical column, however, in both cases the individuals had evidence for other peri-mortem trauma not directly related to decapitation. There were also rare examples of individuals who had been partially or completely decapitated and who demonstrated a large number of other peri-mortem traumata, concentrated on the upper limbs and torso. The postero-anterior direction of the chops, the presence of non-decapitation-related trauma in some individuals and the fact that most affected individuals were younger adult males, as well as the indications from the osteological analysis that the decapitated sample was taller than was the norm and subject to more stress and strains on joints and higher levels of physical activity, may support the interpretation that decapitation was undertaken for head-hunting as a part of Iron Age warfare. This could also be supported by the fact that the practice is represented by both isolated crania and mandibulae and headless corpses, although head-hunting would not explain the presence of individuals who had been fully or partially decapitated but where the cranio-cervical skeleton remained with the post-cranial skeleton, which represented a significant number of the total sample. It seems likely that a number of these individuals (for example, those at Old Down Farm and Sutton Walls) were killed in some form of conflict, although it appears that the taking of heads for trophies was not as important in the Iron Age as has been previously assumed (if the individuals at Sutton Walls were indeed victims of a Roman attack, this may explain why their heads were not taken, although there are many references to such trophy-taking amongst Roman soldiers and auxiliaries – see chapter 5).

The two crania and mandibulae from Stanwick and Heslington that have evidence for careful incised cuts to the cervical vertebrae do seem to represent a different practice; if the heads were removed as trophies during conflict, it would certainly have been quicker and easier to chop them off with a heavy blade, especially in the case of the individual from Stanwick who had already been subject to a number of such heavy chopping blows to the cranial vault and facial skeleton. The precise removal of soft tissue and disarticulation of the cervical column does suggest that this was done at leisure, possibly in some form of ritual context, after the individual had been killed by other means. However, if these are examples of the 'Cult of the Head', there is no evidence for subsequent curation and display of these decapitated heads, with the example from Heslington known to have been buried almost immediately after decapitation in an anaerobic environment, which led to preservation of a large part of the brain[176]. The cranium and mandible from Stanwick were interpreted as having been displayed on the rampart of the hill fort with the sword found in association with the remains[177], although the excellent bone preservation and presence of the mandible and cervical vertebrae would suggest that display had only been very temporary if it had occurred at all.

Post-mortem manipulation of cranial remains
There is better evidence for the 'Cult of the Head' in a group of cranial remains from various sites in Britain with evidence for post-mortem

manipulation, although none of them show definite evidence for decapitation (however, decapitation can probably be assumed in a number of cases as the manipulation occurred in the peri-mortem period). These include a number of crania that have seemingly been drilled or pierced through the bone of the vault, including a non-adult frontal from Hardingstone, Northamptonshire, with an 8mm perforation through the right side of the element that appears to have been made from the endocranial side (there is a bevel on the ectocranial surface)[178]; a near-complete adult cranium from Hunsbury, again in Northamptonshire, with three 9mm perforations through the crown in the shape of an equilateral triangle; and an adult parietal, again from Hunsbury, with one, possibly two, perforations, 10mm in diameter[179]. There are also four examples from Roman Iron Age Scotland, including a partial cranium from Hillhead Broch, Caithness, with a triangular pattern of perforations[180], and an adult male frontal from Cnip, Western Isles, with a hole through it, drilled from both sides[181]. These crania could have been perforated or drilled to be suspended for display, and if so, the absence of mandibulae and attached cervical vertebrae would suggest an extended period of time before their final deposition.

Curation and display is also a probable interpretation for the calvarium of a mature adult found in the drip gulley of a roundhouse at Hurst Lane, Ely, Cambridgeshire, which had been separated from the cranial base and facial skeleton by radiating fractures as a result of two peri-mortem blunt-force injuries to the occipital and left parietal[182]. There were also a number of cut marks to the parietals that probably represented soft-tissue removal or scalping[183]. The calvarium also had an unusually polished appearance that probably indicated prolonged handling. It seems possible that this is an example of a 'skull cup', referred to in ancient sources on Celtic head-hunting practices (see chapter 5)[184]. A similar practice may be represented by a collection of cranial fragments from Billingborough, Lincolnshire, with evidence for peri-mortem removal of the cranial base and facial skeleton, and polished and abraded surfaces[185]. Fragments of the finished calvaria and 'off-cuts' of the cranial base and orbital region are both present, suggesting 'skull cups' were being both manufactured and used at this site.

Conclusion

Although these examples of modified human crania do suggest there is evidence for the 'Cult of the Head' in Iron Age Britain, they are much rarer than would be expected if the head cult was as pervasive as has been suggested, and the majority of individuals showing evidence for peri-mortem decapitation would seem to represent different practices: conflict-related head-hunting; complete or partial decapitation as a mechanism of death where the head was not subsequently removed; or ritual activity surrounding the human head where curation and display were not integral parts of the practice.

Chapter 3

Decapitation in the Romano-British Period

The sample of possible and definite decapitation burials identified from this period was the largest from any of the periods, with 532 separate individuals identified from 229 sites. For the purposes of this research, the decision was made to separate the sites associated with urban areas from those associated with 'small town'[186] and rural contexts, including villas, because many authors have recorded differences in the types and numbers of artefacts and ecofacts found on urban sites compared with rural ones[187]. The sites from small-town or rural settlements were not separated further because it is often impossible to determine to which type of settlement (especially those which have not been subject to large-scale excavation) excavated graves belong, particularly those found in small numbers in developer-led archaeological activity, which may be some distance from the associated settlement. It can also be very difficult, even where there have been larger scale excavations, to distinguish between large rural settlements and small towns[188], leading Richard Reece to suggest, using evidence from the coins (type, number and distribution), that the two types of site are actually very similar in nature[189].

The two samples of decapitated burials were then compared with data taken from twenty-nine published cemetery reports from small-town/rural contexts and sixteen from urban contexts, all of which had at least one decapitated burial amongst their number (see appendix 4 for a list of these sites). This allowed for a more accurate comparison between the decapitated and non-decapitated samples as it excluded cemetery sites where decapitation does not seem to have occurred, therefore highlighting any differences between the two samples in terms of their burial practice, as well as providing a good sample with which to compare health status and ante-mortem trauma.

Dating, Geographical Distribution and the Rural/Urban Divide
Previous syntheses of the practice of decapitation, by Clarke, Harman *et*

al. and Philpott, stated that the practice was largely restricted to the later Romano-British period[190]. The majority of the sites identified during the present research do seem to be dated to the third or fourth centuries, although, occasionally, a decapitation burial has been dated to these centuries purely on the basis of it having been decapitated, which was the case for a secondary burial from a barrow at Gayhurst Quarry, Buckinghamshire[191]. There are some burials that have been dated, either by radiocarbon dating or on stratigraphic or artefactual evidence, to somewhat earlier in the Romano-British period, such as a burial from Cuxton, Kent, presumed to be from the late first century AD[192]; a burial from Rickinghall, Suffolk, radiocarbon dated to between the first century BC and first century AD[193]; and the burials from Driffield Terrace, York, some of which were dated to between the late second and early third centuries[194]. The presence of these decapitated burials from Roman York (Eboracum) that date to the second and third centuries AD appears to contradict the assertions of both Clarke and Philpott that the practice spread from rural to urban areas in the fourth century[195]. This group of burials, composed only of adult males and non-adults and with over sixty per cent of the individuals decapitated, is very unusual compared with the majority of samples of decapitated burials from Britain, which tend to be composed of much smaller numbers of individuals, with both adult males and females represented. It has, therefore, been singled out for separate discussion (see chapter 4), although the data from the burials has also been included in the larger sample discussed below.

There are also a small number of burials that would appear, on stratigraphic and artefactual evidence, to be late Romano-British in date but which have been shown by radiocarbon dating to fall into the early post-Roman period, such as one from St Johns, Worcester, with hobnails at the feet, that was radiocarbon dated to cal AD 430-640[196]. This would suggest the possibility that a larger number of decapitated burials that initially appear to be late Roman, due to the presence of hobnails or by the fact of their being decapitated in the absence of any good stratigraphic evidence, could also actually be post-Roman, or a lot earlier than is assumed. This may have implications for the theory of continuity of the practice from the late Iron Age (although the 'typical' decapitation burial, where the head is displaced but still present within the grave, is a rare occurrence in the Iron Age – isolated heads and decapitated skeletons in non-formal burial locations, ditches, for example, being much more representative of the practice of decapitation in this period – although see p.50 for isolated head deposits in the Romano-British period), as well as the possibility of continuity into the early medieval period. There is already limited evidence for such continuity in cemeteries such as that at Wasperton, Warwickshire, where, in what appeared to be an early medieval cemetery, in use from the later fifth century to the seventh century, eighteen burials were actually found to be Romano-British, five of which were decapitated (the other five decapitation burials from the site dated to the fifth or sixth centuries), including one that was radiocarbon dated to cal AD 120-330[197].

The previous syntheses also conclude that decapitation burials have a limited geographical distribution, being largely confined to an area roughly between the Severn to the west and the Wash to the east, with a very limited number of sites to the north-east and south-west. The

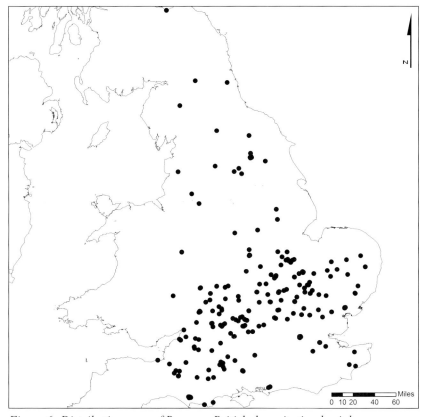

Figure 6: Distribution map of Romano-British decapitation burials.

distribution map produced for this research does seem to confirm that there is a concentration in the area south-west of the Severn–Wash line, although there are a number of sites in the Midlands and North East (figure 6). There is a strong possibility that some of this bias is a result of underlying geology leading to the poor preservation, or absence, of human bone, which would preclude the identification of decapitation burials in some areas. The preservation of inhumed bone is largely dependent on the soil pH, as acidic soil conditions lead to the destruction of the cortical bone surface or total loss of bone, although other factors, such as changes in the groundwater table or ground temperature, can also have an effect. At certain sites where there has been near or total loss of bone (such as Sutton Hoo, Suffolk), the form of the inhumed corpse can still be discernible as a so-called 'sand body'[198]. A map produced by Cranfield University that depicts the topsoil pH across the country does indicate that the areas from which there are larger numbers of decapitation burials largely coincide with those areas with a neutral or very low acidic pH, although some areas where the pH indicates there should be good levels of bone survival, such as Lincolnshire, only have very small numbers of decapitation burials. Areas with small numbers of decapitated burials, such as Kent, Surrey, and East and West Sussex, which Philpott ascribed to the predominance of cremation in these areas[199], are amongst those counties where bone preservation is likely to be poorest and so cremations, which do survive better in acidic soils, are the only type of human burial liable to be encountered in archaeological excavations.

The second factor that could bias the numbers of decapitated burials identified is the amount of archaeological excavation that has taken place, with the simple possibility that in areas where there has been more excavation, it would automatically follow that there would be more decapitated burials recorded. In order to test this theory, the number of excavated Romano-British cemeteries recorded in the Historic Environment Record (HER) for Lincolnshire (a county which, as has already been noted, has very few decapitations) was compared with the number from Cambridgeshire, a county with a very high number of decapitations. Both counties have soil conditions conducive to very good bone preservation, so this would not bias the results. The HER for Lincolnshire and North Lincolnshire contained details of 109 sites where Romano-British inhumation graves had been found, whilst that for Cambridgeshire had 169 sites[200]. The number of sites in Lincolnshire may be slightly underrepresented as a few of the entries contained details of a number of separate archaeological interventions in the same area that were given a single HER entry. The number of sites from which decapitation burials were recorded in Lincolnshire was only two, just under two per cent of the total number of sites, whilst in Cambridgeshire, there were twenty-three sites, around fourteen per cent of the total, which is statistically significantly greater. This does suggest that in areas where decapitation burials are rare or absent, it may be a real absence rather than purely a result of biases introduced by preservation conditions and the amount of archaeological excavation that has been undertaken.

The previous syntheses of Clarke and Harman *et al.*[201] stated that the practice of decapitation was largely confined to rural areas, with limited numbers of examples from urban and small-town cemeteries. However, the present research has identified such burials from Roman London, all four of the *coloniae* (Colchester, Gloucester, Lincoln and York) and five of the tribal capitals (Wroxeter, Winchester, Leicester, Dorchester and Cirencester). Decapitations are found at 60 separate sites from these urban areas with a total number of 163 decapitated burials. There are also decapitations from at least 35 sites from cemeteries that are very probably associated with small-towns with a total of 90 burials and 134 sites from rural areas with 279 separate examples of decapitation, which is 58 per cent of the total number of sites from which such burials are found and 52 per cent of the total number of individual decapitated burials. This indicates that, although there are more sites from rural areas, decapitations are anything but rare in cemeteries associated with small-town and urban areas.

Isolated Head Deposits

There are a small number of deposits of isolated crania and mandibulae from this period, with seven from urban areas and eleven from rural and small-town areas, all of which are from non-normative burial locations, such as ditches, pits, wells and bogs. Examples include the cranium, mandible, C1 and part of C2, with preserved soft tissue of a young adult male from Worsley Moss, Lancashire, radiocarbon dated to cal AD 80-220, who demonstrated a blunt-force cranial injury and decapitation-related chop-marks, and had a cord of animal sinew encircling the neck[202]; the cranium of a middle adult male with a number of decapitation-related chop-marks from a well at Rothwell Haigh, North Yorkshire[203]; and the recently analysed collection of cranial remains from the London Wall, which includes a mandible with a chop mark and a cranium with evidence for a number of injuries that could only have been inflicted if the individual had already been decapitated[204]. The osteological data on the peri-mortem trauma for examples that did show definite evidence for decapitation are included in the sample discussed later. There were also a small number of sites from which there were crania which, whilst they did not show any definite evidence for decapitation, do have evidence for peri-mortem trauma, such as the cranium of an adult male from a well at Churchill Hospital, Oxford[205], with at least three blunt-force injuries to the frontal and parietals (plate 11), and two crania from a ditch just outside the legionary fortress at Balkerne Gate, Colchester, one of which had a blunt-force injury to the frontal, whilst the other had a sharp-force injury to the occipital[206].

These examples could be taken to imply a continuation of practices from the Iron Age as regards unusual treatment of the human head, with evidence for peri-mortem trauma on the disarticulated crania suggesting that some of these heads may have been displayed or kept for a period of time. However, this is not necessarily the case, as there is a good body of evidence from Roman literary sources (see chapter 5) that the display of decapitated heads was a relatively common Roman phenomenon, especially amongst the military (three examples of these crania or crania and mandibulae with evidence for peri-mortem decapitation come from military forts). There is also limited evidence for modified crania excavated from religious sites in this period: namely, the cranium of an adolescent male, with three peri-mortem blunt-force injuries, as well as at least ninety cut marks indicative of defleshing, that appeared to have been displayed before it was finally deposited in a pit outside the temple at Folly Lane, St Albans[207]; and fragments of nine separate crania, one of which had evidence for defleshing and one that may have been trimmed for use as a skull cup, from the Baths Basilica, Wroxeter[208]. The cranial fragments also had a distinctively greasy appearance and were stated to have tested positive for vegetable oil lipids, something that was not found on the animal bone fragments from the same site. This has interesting echoes of the stories of Celtic tribes preserving the heads of their enemies in cedar oil, as mentioned by Roman writers (see chapter 5), and the possible presence of a skull cup has parallels, albeit rare, in the British Iron Age (see chapter 2). This does suggest that there may have been some continuation of practices from the Iron Age into the Romano-British period, although evidence for the 'Cult of the Head' is still relatively rare across both periods.

Burial Practice, Head Placement and Demographics
Burial practice

In order to assess whether the decapitated burials had been subject to different treatment at the time of their burial compared with the rest of the population, a number of aspects of burial practice (the presence or absence of a coffin, coins, other objects and hobnails, and whether the individual had been buried in a prone position) recorded in the sample of identified decapitation burials were compared to those seen in the wider cemetery population, separated into urban and rural/small-town samples.

It was found that, for the rural/small-town decapitated sample, there were no statistically significant differences between the burial practices observed in the decapitated group, compared with the wider cemetery population. However, the urban decapitated sample was statistically significantly less likely to have been provided with a coffin or objects and significantly more likely to have been buried in a prone position. Harman *et al.* and Philpott both note a possible connection between prone and decapitated burials[209], and, if the samples for urban and rural/small-town decapitations are combined, the number of prone burials is also statistically significantly greater than in the wider population.

When the samples were further divided into males, females and non-adults, there were no statistically significant differences in the way the different groups were treated in the rural/small-town sample, but in the urban sample, males were statistically significantly less likely than females to have been provided with a coffin, objects or hobnailed footwear. This indicates that, not only were there differences in burial practices between the urban decapitated and non-decapitated samples, but adult males were more likely to be singled out for different treatment.

Placement of the head

Previous syntheses of the practice by Harman *et al.* and Philpott have stated that the head is most commonly located in the region of the lower limbs or feet[210], and this was confirmed by the present research, with the head being found by the lower legs or feet in half of the urban examples of decapitation and in seventy-five per cent of the rural and small-town examples, a statistically significant difference. However, the head could also be located in any one of a number of different positions in the grave, as well as being found in correct anatomical position or totally absent, with the percentages of these different locations being statistically significantly greater in the urban sample, with the exception of cases where the head was absent. This suggests that there was a much greater variety in the placement of the head in decapitations from urban cemeteries, whilst those from rural and small-town areas were much more likely to have the head placed in the area of the lower limbs or feet.

Demographics

When the demographics of the samples were compared to the wider cemetery populations as a whole, statistically speaking, the number of decapitated females was significantly greater and the number of non-adults significantly smaller in rural and small-town cemeteries, whilst in urban areas, the number of decapitated males was significantly greater, and the number of females and non-adults were significantly smaller. This indicates that in rural/small-town cemeteries, adult females were more likely to have been subjected to decapitation than would be expected if the practice was carried out on a 'random' basis across the population, whilst in urban areas, it was males who were more commonly decapitated. In both samples, non-adults were less likely to be decapitated than would be expected, which is another indication that there seems to have been a selection process in choosing the individuals subjected to the practice, rather than it being carried out on a cross-section of the wider population. Harman *et al.* noted that the number of non-adults affected was disproportionally small, and whilst it has also been noted that adult females were the most commonly decapitated group[211], the present research indicates that this was only the case in rural and small-town cemeteries.

When the more detailed age and sex profile (obtained from the smaller sample of burials from which detailed osteological data had been recorded as part of the present research, as well as from skeletal analyses completed by others) was examined, it was seen that, in both samples, there were relatively small numbers of non-adults represented (as expected from the larger decapitated sample), although nearly all the non-adult age categories did have at least one example of decapitation. The numbers of young and middle adults were very similar in both samples, but there were statistically significantly fewer mature adults in the urban sample than in that from rural and small-town cemeteries.

The samples can also be compared with demographic profiles from a number of large archaeological populations, in order to determine whether there are differences in the age profile of those individuals selected for decapitation compared with the wider population. This would be a more accurate method of comparing samples, rather than relying on model life tables[212], as archaeological populations very often show distinct discrepancies to these tables, even though it can be assumed that the age structure of the archaeological population must originally have resembled one of the stable populations used to produce the models[213]. These discrepancies include a peak in mortality in archaeological populations in the middle adult years with relatively small numbers of mature adults (a result of the tendency for anthropological methods to underestimate the age of adults), as well as a shortfall in the number of non-adult individuals, particularly those from the younger age categories. This may be a result of differential burial practices for these individuals[214], and it also had been observed that the remains of non-adults are more susceptible to truncation and disturbance than those of adults, as well as being less easily recognisable to those without specific osteological knowledge[215]. However, the commonly used argument that non-adult remains are much more prone to post-burial degradation and decay than those of adults[216] has been more recently disputed by a number of writers, who have demonstrated that non-adult remains show at least the same level of bone preservation as the rest of a cemetery assemblage[217], with the bones of neonates often being more resistant to decompositional destruction as they do not possess any intestinal bacteria[218].

When the samples for urban sites were compared, the percentages in each age group for the decapitated sample were very similar to those in the non-decapitated sample, with the exception of the young child category, where the percentage of decapitated individuals was nearly double that of the wider cemetery population. However, this may simply be due to the very small sample of decapitated individuals from this age group. In the rural/small-town sample, there were no neonate or infant decapitations analysed as part of the sample. However, there was a decapitated infant of three to six months recorded amongst the decapitated individuals from the cemetery at Dunstable, Bedfordshire[219], an assemblage that was reanalysed as part of this research, although this infant was the only decapitated burial that could not be located. This does indicate that younger non-adults were represented amongst decapitations from rural and small-town areas. The other age groups were also represented amongst the decapitated samples in slightly different proportions than found in the larger cemetery populations, although this is not statistically significant for any of the age groups.

When the percentages of adult males and females in each of the age categories in the decapitated and non-decapitated urban samples were compared, it was found that, in the female samples, the percentages were very similar for each age group and were not statistically significant for any group. However, in the male samples, the percentage of decapitated middle adults was statistically significantly larger than in the wider population, whilst conversely, the percentage of mature adults was statistically significantly smaller.

Comparing the same data from the rural/small-town decapitated and non-decapitated samples, it was found that the percentages were more similar for each age group amongst both the adult male and adult female samples, with the differences between the decapitated and non-decapitated samples not being statistically significant for any of the age groups. This indicates that for both sexes and the non-adults in the rural/small-town samples, and for the non-adults and adult females in the urban samples, the decapitated group showed no apparent selection according to age compared with the wider population. However, the ages of the urban adult male decapitations did not mirror the findings in the larger population, indicating some degree of selection by age in this specific group.

Summary of data on the burial practice, head placement and demographics of the decapitated samples
• There were no differences in burial practice between the rural/small-town decapitated sample and the wider population.
• Decapitations from urban areas were less likely to have been provided with a coffin or objects than the wider population.
• Decapitations from urban areas were more likely to have been buried in the prone position than the wider population.
• There was more variety in the location of the head in the urban sample compared with the rural/small-town sample.
• There were more adult females in the rural/small-town decapitated sample than in the wider population.
• There were more adult males in the urban decapitated sample than in the wider population.
• There were fewer non-adults in both decapitated samples than in the wider population.
• There were fewer mature adults in the urban sample compared with the rural/small-town sample.

• The demographics of the rural/small-town decapitated samples and the non-adults and adult females in the urban sample mirrored those in the larger cemetery population.
• There were greater numbers of middle adult male decapitations in the urban sample than in the wider population and fewer mature adults.

Stature and Palaeopathological Analysis
Stature
Stature was calculated for all of the decapitated individuals analysed as part of this research and was obtained from as many of the individuals analysed by other researchers as possible. The mean stature was then calculated for the male and female samples, separated into the rural/small-town (170.5cm for males and 159.6cm for females) and urban (172.3cm for males and 157.9cm for females) groups. This was then compared with the average stature calculated for the equivalent non-decapitated samples (169.6cm for males and 159.1cm for females in the rural/small-town sample, and 168.8cm for males and 157.9cm for females in the urban group). It was found that the decapitated and non-decapitated samples showed no statistically significant differences in stature, with the exception of the urban male decapitations, who were statistically significantly taller than the urban male cemetery population as a whole. This may suggest that there was some form of selection as to which male individuals were subject to decapitation in urban areas, but that this was not happening with rural and small-town decapitated males, or with females in either sample. This seems to correspond to the finding that urban male decapitations seem to have been afforded different burial practices to the rest of the population.

Non-adult health status/nutritional stress
There is the possibility that urban decapitated males may have been of a greater mean stature than the rest of the population because they had a generally better health status in earlier life and better levels of nutrition. This was assessed by comparing the rate of *cribra orbitalia* and enamel hypoplasia between the males and females from the urban decapitated sample. The same was also done for the rural and small-town sample to see if there were any differences in non-adult health status between the males and females from that group. The rate of enamel hypoplasia amongst the urban male individuals was statistically significantly higher than that found amongst the females, with forty-eight per cent of males

and only fifteen per cent of females being affected. However, the rates of *cribra orbitalia* in the two groups did not show a statistically significant difference. This suggests that, if anything, the urban male decapitated sample had a lower nutritional health status than the female sample. When the rural/small-town decapitated male and female samples were compared, the rates of enamel hypoplasia were not significantly different; however, the rural/small-town male rate of *cribra orbitalia* was statistically significantly greater than in the female sample, where no affected individuals were recorded.

The percentages of pooled male and female affected individuals from the two different samples were also compared with the rates seen in the larger cemetery populations from rural/small-town and urban areas in order to determine whether there may have been differences in non-adult health status and nutritional stress between the decapitated sample and the rest of the population. The urban decapitated sample was found to have a statistically significantly higher rate of enamel hypoplasia than the population as a whole, whilst that in the rural/small-town decapitated sample was not significantly different from the rest of the population. The rates for *cribra orbitalia* were also significantly higher in the urban decapitated sample compared with the rest of the population, with no difference found in the percentages between the rural/small-town decapitated and non-decapitated samples. This suggests that the urban decapitated sample had a poorer general level of non-adult health and nutrition compared to the wider population, which would also contradict the suggestion that the mean stature of the urban decapitated males was greater because of a better level of non-adult health. This may further indicate that a taller stature may have been part of a selection process during adult life amongst those urban males who were subsequently decapitated.

Dental health

As there have already been differences noted between the urban male and female decapitated sample in terms of burial practice and health, the dental health of the two samples was also compared. It was found that there were no statistically significant differences between the adult males and females in the rural and small/town samples, whilst the urban male sample had statistically significantly lower rates of dental caries than the urban female sample, although there were no significant differences in any of the other indicators of dental health. This may be a reflection of the small number of mature adults amongst the urban adult male sample, with individuals dying before they could be affected by dental caries. However, if this is the sole explanation, the levels of periodontal disease, calculus and abscesses would also be expected to be at lower levels than in the urban female sample. This may suggest that the lower rate of dental caries is a result of the urban male decapitated individuals having access to a different diet with lower levels of sucrose.

The rates of dental disease amongst the pooled decapitated samples were also compared to the larger cemetery populations in terms of crude prevalence rates (number of affected individuals) and true prevalence rates (number of affected teeth). When the crude prevalence rates were calculated, it was found that the decapitated urban sample had a statistically significantly higher rate of dental calculus, and the rural/small-town sample a statistically significantly lower rate of calculus, than the wider population. When the true prevalence rates were examined, the urban decapitated sample was found to have higher rates of both caries and calculus than the rest of the population, whilst the rural/small-town sample had a lower rate of caries and a higher rate of calculus. This would suggest that whilst the numbers of individuals in both the decapitated and non-decapitated samples with caries was not different, those individuals with caries in the decapitated urban sample tended to have more carious teeth, whilst fewer teeth were affected amongst the individuals with caries in the rural/small-town decapitated sample. The higher true prevalence rates for calculus amongst the rural/small-town decapitated sample would also suggest that whilst the number of affected individuals was lower, they had many more teeth with deposits of calculus. This may indicate that the decapitated individuals, particularly those from urban areas, had access to a different diet than was the norm amongst the wider population.

Degenerative joint disease/activity-related changes
The rates of osteoarthritis/degenerative joint disease, Schmorl's nodes and *os acromiale* amongst the decapitated samples were compared to the wider urban and rural/small-town populations. *Os acromiale* is a failure in the fusion of the ossification centre at the acromial end of the scapula as a result of unusual and prolonged use of the rotator cuff musculature in early life[220]. Higher rates of these conditions may imply an increase in stress and strain on joints and increased mechanical loading in earlier life. It was found that the rates of osteoarthritis/degenerative joint disease amongst both decapitated samples were statistically significantly higher

than in the wider population, whilst in the urban decapitated sample, the rates of Schmorl's nodes and *os acromiale* were also significantly greater. The higher rates of osteoarthritis/degenerative joint disease in both samples cannot have been a result of there being a larger number of older adults represented, as it has already been demonstrated that the urban decapitated sample had fewer mature adults than the wider population, whilst there was no difference between the numbers of mature adults in the rural/small-town decapitated and non-decapitated samples. This would suggest that the individuals in the decapitated samples had subjected their joints to more wear and tear than would be expected, whilst the urban sample also had evidence for significantly increased rates of unusual and prolonged mechanical loading during earlier life, something that is also supported by the relatively high levels of humeral asymmetry and enthesopathies in the urban sample compared with the rural/small-town sample.

The rates of the same conditions in males and females from both decapitated samples were also compared in order to determine whether there were differences in the rates of the conditions between the sexes, but it was found that there were no significant differences between the male and female rates of any of the conditions in either decapitated sample.

Infectious disease

The rates of non-specific infection, either in the form of osteomyelitis (an infection of the medullary cavity of bones leading to diffuse compact bone, shaft expansion and cloacae for the expulsion of pus[221]) or periosteal new bone (manifesting as porous woven bone and indicating an infection of the periosteum active at the time of death, or as compact remodelled bone, thought to indicate a healed infection[222]); sinusitis (an infection of the cranial sinuses manifesting most commonly as spicules of compact bone on the floor of the sinuses[223]); and new bone on the visceral surface of the ribs (indicating the presence of a non-specific pulmonary infection, with a strong association with pulmonary tuberculosis[224]) were compared between the two decapitated samples and the wider cemetery populations.

The rates of non-specific infection in the decapitated samples were significantly higher than in the wider cemetery populations, whilst in the urban sample, the rate of new bone on the ribs was also significantly higher than in the rest of the population. It was also found that in the urban sample, females had a significantly higher rate of sinusitis, whilst in the rural/small-town sample, males had a higher rate of non-specific infection. This does not seem to be related to sex-specific differences between the conditions generally as the differences in the rates of both non-specific infection and sinusitis between the sexes in the wider rural/small-town samples were not statistically significant.

Ante-mortem trauma

Ante-mortem trauma was very common in both decapitated samples, with fifty-one per cent of the urban sample and twenty-nine per cent of the rural/small-town sample having evidence for at least one ante-mortem fracture. Both these figures are statistically significantly greater than the percentages of affected individuals in the wider urban and rural/small-town populations.

The most common sites for fractures amongst the decapitated samples were the hands, ribs, cranium, feet, fibula, tibia, vertebral arch and nasal bones, with most sites relatively equally affected in the urban and rural/small-town samples, with the exception of the tibia and fibula, which were more commonly affected in the rural/small-town sample, although not statistically significantly so. Males and females also seem to have been equally susceptible to the same type of fractures, with no statistically significant differences between the sexes for any of the fracture sites. The hands, feet, ribs, nasal bones, tibia and fibula were amongst the most common fractures in the wider cemetery populations from both urban and rural/small-town areas, with a number of these fractures (those of the hands, feet, cranial vault, ribs and nasal bones) particularly associated with interpersonal violence (see Chapter 2). This does suggest that, whilst the fracture sites amongst the decapitated samples were the same as amongst the larger populations, they sustained more fractures than was the norm, with the possibility that this was the result of higher levels of interpersonal violence amongst the decapitated samples.

This assertion is supported by the presence of three males from the urban sample with maxillary trauma associated with ante-mortem loss of anterior dentition (plate 12), and three decapitated individuals from the urban sample (all male) with healed blade injuries to the cranial vault. These include an old middle adult from Hyde Street, Winchester (Grave 3), with a healed injury just superior of the left orbit (plate 13), and a mature adult from Bath Gate, Cirencester (SK305), with a severe sharp-force injury to the right parietal with associated radiating fractures and a trephination of the frontal, both of which were healed but were suggested to have probably resulted in some form of brain injury[225].

There were also five individuals (three males from the urban sample, and one male and one female from the rural/small-town sample) with evidence for ante-mortem amputations, manifesting as slightly atrophied elements compared with the opposite side, shortening of the element with loss of the joint surface, and the presence of roughened masses of sclerotic bone at the extremity of the element. In four cases, these were of parts of the manual digits. Affected were a young middle adult male from Lankhills, Winchester (SK427), with amputation of parts of the second and fifth digits of the left hand (plate 14)[226]; an old middle adult ?female (L) with an amputation of the distal segment of a distal manual phalanx and a young middle adult male (CM) with an amputation of part of the fifth digit of the right hand, both from Dunstable, Bedfordshire; and the individual from Hyde Street, Winchester (Grave 3), with a healed blade injury, who demonstrated an amputation of part of the left thumb, as well as a traumatic flexion contracture of the proximal and medial phalanges of the left fifth digit. The other case of amputation was found in an old middle adult male from Northbrook Avenue, Winchester, who had an amputation through the distal ends of the right radius and ulna (plate 15). Ante-mortem amputation is a rare occurrence in archaeological skeletal remains and there are only a few cases recorded for the period – namely, manual digit amputation in two male individuals from the 2000-2005 excavations at Lankhills, Winchester; two males from Horcott Quarry, Gloucestershire; and one male from Kempston, Bedfordshire[227]. Finding evidence, therefore, for five such amputations amongst a relatively small sample of decapitated burials is striking.

Along with these amputations and ante-mortem blade injuries, there are a number of other individuals with evidence for traumatic injuries or other pathological alterations that would have been visible during life. These include other individuals with traumatic fusion of manual digits, including a mature adult female from Stanwick, Northamptonshire (SK6105), with the medial and distal phalanges for the right fourth digit fused in extension, and a young middle adult female from Lankhills, Winchester (SK297), with a fracture and shortening of the right fifth metacarpal and a flexion contracture of the digit. There were also three males, one from the urban sample and two from the rural/small-town sample, with evidence for torticollis[228]; a young middle adult of indeterminate sex from Dunstable, Bedfordshire (BG), with severe trauma to the right scapula and humerus that resulted in a permanent dislocation and external rotation of the humerus (plate 16); an old middle adult male from Lankhills, Winchester (SK1289), with a remodelled fracture of the diaphysis of the right humerus with subsequent early fusion of the epiphysis and substantial shortening of the element; an adolescent from the Babraham Institute, Cambridge (SK51), with a healed fracture of the left tibia with angulation and shortening[229]; a mature adult male from Jesus Lane, Cambridge (SK161), with septic arthritis[230] of both hips that resulted in restricted movement[231]; and a young middle adult male from Mundford, Norfolk (SK4), with a number of ante-mortem traumata, including fractures of the shafts of the left tibia and right ulna, a shortened left humerus, fusion of the right foot, and a fracture of the left knee which would have resulted in atrophy and an abnormal gait and posture, all of which seem to have been the result of a single incident during non-adult life (plate 17).

This concentration of unusual and relatively rare traumata and pathological conditions amongst the decapitated individuals, seemingly equally spread between the sexes and urban and rural/small-town samples (although it is possibly found more amongst adult males), may suggest that the possession of such a visible defect during life predisposed an individual to being decapitated, although by no means did all decapitated individuals have skeletal evidence for such conditions, and having such a defect did not mean that one would definitely have been decapitated.

Summary of evidence from the stature and palaeopathological analysis
• The urban male decapitations had a greater mean stature than the wider population.
• The urban decapitated sample had higher rates of enamel hypoplasia than the wider population.
• The urban decapitated sample had higher rates of *cribra orbitalia* than the wider population.
• The urban decapitated sample had higher rates of calculus, and the rural/small-town sample lower rates, than the wider population.
• Both decapitated samples had higher rates of degenerative joint disease than the wider population.
• The urban decapitated samples had higher rates of activity-related changes than the wider population.
• Both decapitated samples had higher levels of non-specific infection than the rest of the population.
• The urban decapitated females had a higher rate of sinusitis than the males.

• The rural/small-town decapitated males had a higher rate of non-specific infection than the females.
• The urban decapitated sample had a higher rate of new bone on the ribs than the wider population.
• Both decapitated samples had higher levels of ante-mortem fractures than the wider populations, although the sites of fracture were the same.
• Decapitated individuals had a high number of amputations compared with the wider population.
• There was a possible association between visible trauma or pathology and decapitation.

Peri-mortem Trauma

Of those individuals where a detailed skeletal analysis was undertaken as part of this research, or where information was available from previous analyses, 193 had evidence for peri-mortem trauma, the majority of which was directly related to the process of decapitation. Of these, 96 were from urban areas and 93 from rural and small-town cemeteries. When the data on the type of decapitating cut (whether chop, incised or a combination of both) for the two samples was compared, it was found that there were no statistically significant differences between the samples, with chopping blows being predominant in both. There were also no significant differences in the type of cut between males and females in either sample. This is in contrast to the conclusions of previous syntheses, which have stated that decapitation is usually undertaken with incised, 'careful' cuts. The present data suggests, on the other hand, that incised cuts are very much a minority, with less than five per cent of the urban sample and less than ten per cent of the rural/small-town sample demonstrating these cuts in isolation. In the vast majority of individuals, the chopping blows were very fine and clean with very little evidence for fracturing of the margins of the chop, suggesting that the instrument used was very sharp with a fine blade.

When the direction and the number of blows was analysed, it was found that the urban sample had statistically significantly more individuals with decapitating blows directed from the posterior than the rural/small-town sample, with urban males representing significantly more of this number than urban females, whilst urban females had significantly more blows directed from the anterior. The urban sample also had significantly more individuals with a single cut than the rural/small-town sample, with males making up a significant proportion of that number. The urban females had significantly more individuals with two or three cuts, whilst the rural/small-town sample had significantly more individuals with four or more cuts. There were no differences in the direction or number of cuts between males and females in the rural/small-town sample.

This is also interesting in light of previous assertions that decapitations were normally performed from the anterior, as it indicates that whilst this is predominately the case for decapitations performed in rural/small-town areas, those from urban areas, particularly of male individuals, were usually performed from the posterior with a single blow, whilst a number of blows was the norm in rural/small-town areas.

The number of individuals from each sample who had evidence for cuts to the cranium, mandible, clavicle or scapula directly related to their decapitation, as well as those with evidence for non-decapitation-related peri-mortem trauma to the cranial and post-cranial skeleton, were also recorded. It was found that there were no differences between the urban and rural/small-town samples. There were also no differences between males and females in either sample.

Decapitation types
When the detailed information on the nature of the peri-mortem trauma in the two samples was analysed, it became apparent that there were a number of different types of decapitation with different skeletal signatures: namely, 1. incised cutting of the cervical column; 2. incised cuts to the anterior of the cervical column associated with incised cuts or chops to the cranio-cervical skeleton; 3. chopping blows through the cervical column associated with additional incised cuts or chops to the vertebrae, cranium, mandible, scapula, clavicle or ribs; 4. a single chop to the cervical column with no other cuts present; and 5. chops to the cervical column associated with peri-mortem trauma to areas of the cranial or post-cranial skeleton that would indicate they are not directly related to the process of decapitation. Each type of decapitation is described and discussed below and possible interpretations are given for how the different signatures may have been produced.

1. Incised cutting
There was a very small number of individuals (four from urban areas and three from rural/small-town areas, there being no statistical difference between the two samples) who demonstrated this type of decapitation,

consisting of a number of incised cuts to the cervical column with no other cuts or other evidence for peri-mortem trauma. Examples of this type of decapitation include an adolescent from Lankhills, Winchester (SK348), who had been buried supine with the lower legs flexed at the knee, and with the cranium, mandible, C1 and C2 placed by the right knee[232]. There were a total of seven separate incised cuts to the anterior of the left and right superior articular processes of C4 and the anterior of the inferior articular processes of C3, with the cuts angled left-superior to right-inferior on the left arches, and right-superior to left-inferior on the right arches (plate 18)[233]. Another individual from the same cemetery (SK427), a young middle adult male, buried supine with the cranium and mandible by the right knee and a coin found in the mouth[234], demonstrated five incised cuts to the anterior and inferior of the neural arch of C3, all of which were angled right-superior to left-inferior[235] (figure 7); whilst a young middle adult male from Mundford, Norfolk (SK6), buried supine and extended with the lower limbs crossed at the ankle and the cranium and mandible found by the feet[236], had evidence for at least four incised cuts to the inferior surface of the body of C2 that must have been made with the neck extended (plate 19).

Figure 7: Incised cuts to the anterior of the arch and inferior facets of C3 of SK427 from Lankhills, Winchester, Hampshire.

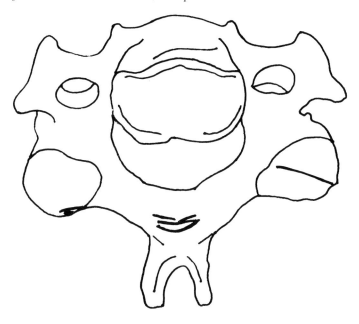

The position of these cuts and the fact that they were all made by incising the bone, along with an absence of any other peri-mortem cuts or fracturing of the cervical column, would suggest they relate to the careful severing of the intervertebral ligaments and cartilage[237] after the soft tissue of the neck had been cut through (without leaving any cut marks on the bone); the head was then removed by careful disarticulation, without fracturing any of the elements.

The absence of cuts associated with the severing of the soft tissue of the neck may suggest that these decapitations were carried out once the decomposition of the corpse was already well advanced. However, the *in situ* photographs and drawn plans of the skeletal remains show the burials to be fully articulated with no obvious evidence of disarticulation of the hands and feet, areas of the skeleton which are the earliest to lose articulation in the decomposition process, indicating that they must have been interred soon after death. This would also suggest that the process of decapitation took place in the immediate peri-mortem period, whilst the precision in the placement of the cuts would suggest that the individuals were already dead when the decapitation was carried out. It is possible that they could have been unconscious rather than dead, although the sudden release of a large quantity of blood when the carotid arteries were severed[238] would have made precise cuts difficult, and the decapitation process would have needed to have been an extended one to allow time for the blood flow to cease.

2. Incised cuts to anterior of vertebrae, usually associated with additional cuts or chops
There was a larger minority of individuals (four from urban areas and sixteen from rural/small-town areas, which was statistically significantly greater) who had evidence for incised cuts to the anterior of the cervical column, usually associated with other incised cuts or chopping blows to the vertebrae. There was one mature adult male individual, from South Parks Road, Oxford, buried supine and extended with the cranium, mandible and C1-C3 found between the distal lower limbs and parts of an accessory vessel placed where the head should have been[239], who demonstrated a single incised cut to the anterior and inferior of the body of C3 with no other associated cuts[240]. There was also an older child/adolescent (11-13 years) from Woodyates, Dorset, buried supine and extended with hobnails at the feet and the cranium and mandible placed by the right distal lower limb[241], who had evidence for a single

66

incised cut across the anterior of C3 and C4 and a stabbing injury to the anterior and inferior surface of the body of C4. Three other individuals demonstrated an incised anteriorly placed cut associated with additional incised cuts, typified by a young adult male from Barrow Hills, Radley, Oxfordshire (SK1018), buried on the left side with the distal limbs flexed and the wrists crossed, and with the cranium and mandible beneath the right knee[242], who had a single incised cut across the anterior of the body of C2, as well as at least thirteen separate cuts to the bodies and arches of C2 and C3, all of which were made from the anterior, including five cuts to the anterior of the spinous process of C2, which must have been made once the vertebrae were largely separated[243].

Five other individuals (two from urban areas and three from rural/small-town areas) had evidence for incised cuts to the anterior of the cervical column associated with additional incised cuts and chopping blows. These included an old middle adult male from 1-3 Driffield Terrace, York (SK47), buried supine and extended with the cranium and mandible placed at the head end of the grave out of anatomically correct position[244], who had evidence for five incised cuts across the anterior of the bodies of C4-C7 (plate 20). There was also evidence for two additional small incised cuts to the right side of the arch of C3 that were directed from the posterior right, and five chopping blows to C2-C5 (figure 8) and the mandible (four of which were delivered from the posterior, including

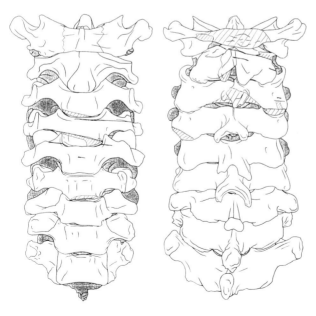

Figure 8: Incised cuts and chops to the cervical vertebrae of SK47 from 1-3 Driffield Terrace, York.

one that would have been struck when the neck was flexed), as well as a peri-mortem blunt-force injury to the right frontal and sphenoid, with endocranial bevelling and radiating fractures (plate 21). Another individual in this category was the supine and extended middle adult female from Rickinghall, Suffolk, whose cranium and mandible were absent, although they may have been originally placed at the feet, which had been truncated[245]. This individual had three or four incised cuts across the anterior of the body of C4, as well as at least eleven separate incised cuts to the posterior of the arches of C3 and C4 and a single chopping blow through the arch of C3 delivered from the posterior[246].

The final group of decapitations in this category were those with an incised anteriorly placed cut with additional chopping blows. These include a mature adult female from Cowdery's Down, Basingstoke, Hampshire (SK5), who was supine and extended with the cranium and mandible placed at the edge of the grave, level with the right knee[247]. There were two incised cuts to the anterior of the body of C4, as well as three posteriorly directed chopping blows through the arches and bodies of C4-C6, only one of which totally bisected the element (that to C4; figure 9). There was also a middle adult female from Lankhills, Winchester (SK445), tightly compressed on the right side with both hands and feet together[248], who demonstrated a single incised cut to the anterior of the body of C5 (plate 22), as well as two chopping blows to C3 and C4, both of which were directed from the anterior (figure 10)[249]. The old middle adult male from Hyde Street, Winchester (SK3), buried in a slightly contracted position with the cranium and mandible by the left knee[250], had evidence for an

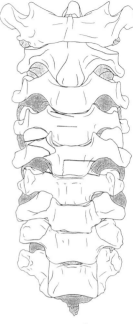

Figure 9: Incised cuts and chops to the cervical vertebrae of SK5 from Cowdery's Down, Basingstoke, Hampshire.

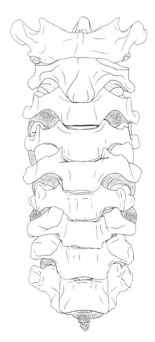

Figure 10: Incised cut and chop to the cervical vertebrae of SK445 from Lankhills, Winchester, Hampshire.

incised cut across the anterior of the body of C3 (plate 23), as well as a number of chopping blows (figure 11), including one that passed through the arch of C1, the odontoid process of C2, the left ascending ramus of the mandible (with severe associated peri-mortem fractures) and the left occipital condyle and mastoid process, delivered from an antero-posterior direction (plate 24). There were also two additional chops through the body of C2, one through the pedicles of C3, and one through the right ascending ramus and body of the mandible, as well as two stabbing injuries to the posterior of the occipital directed from the posterior right (figure 12)[251].

The most interesting individual with this type of decapitation was the old middle adult male from Winchester Street, Andover (SK4), buried slightly on his left side with the right lower limb flexed and both hands together by the left femur, and the cranium and mandible to the right of the knees[252]. There was evidence for at least two incised cuts

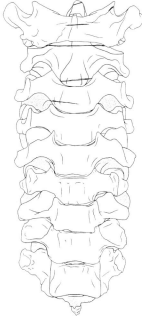

Figure 11: Incised cuts and chops to the cervical vertebrae of SK3 from Hyde Street, Winchester, Hampshire.

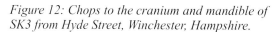

Figure 12: Chops to the cranium and mandible of SK3 from Hyde Street, Winchester, Hampshire.

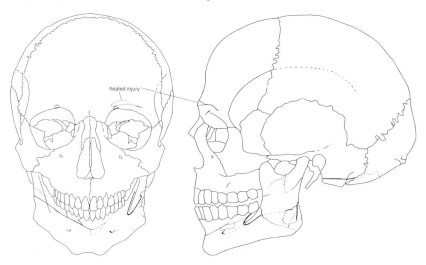

healed injury

across the anterior of the bodies of C3-C5, and at least twenty separate chopping blows affecting the inferior cervical and superior thoracic vertebrae, mandible (with associated fractures of the right ascending ramus), corpus sterni and manubrium, right clavicle, right rib 1 and glenoid fossa of the right scapula. The individual also had evidence for multiple peri-mortem fractures of the anterior and posterior dentition (figure 13, 14, 15, plate 25).

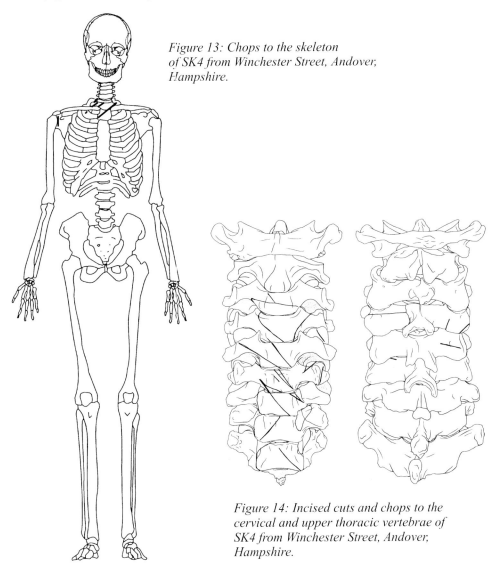

Figure 13: Chops to the skeleton of SK4 from Winchester Street, Andover, Hampshire.

Figure 14: Incised cuts and chops to the cervical and upper thoracic vertebrae of SK4 from Winchester Street, Andover, Hampshire.

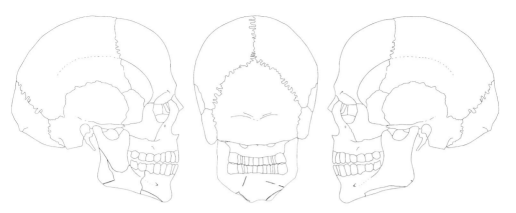

Figure 15: Chops to the mandible of SK4 from Winchester Street, Andover, Hampshire.

The placement of the incised anteriorly directed cuts in all of these individuals would suggest that they relate to a cutting of the throat. Kimmerle and Baraybar illustrated a similar cut to the anterior of C3 in an individual from a modern mass grave that they also suggested related to a cut throat[253]. Cutting of the throat has also been the interpretation of cut marks to the anterior surfaces of cervical vertebrae in a number of South American skeletal samples[254]. If these cuts are to be interpreted in this way, this may suggest that this was carried out whilst the individuals were still alive. Slitting of the throat of a corpse would seem to be an unnecessary part of the process of decapitation and, as can be seen from the relatively small numbers of individuals with such evidence for a cut throat, was not common amongst the decapitated sample. It is possible that throat cutting was undertaken in order to release the blood, considered to be an important part of any sacrificial process (see chapter 1), and is, therefore, something that would only happen to a live individual. There are also a number of bog bodies (usually considered to be sacrificial victims) with evidence for having had their throat cut[255], with sacrifice also being the favoured interpretation for the South American examples[256]. However, throat slitting is also seen in cases of murder and judicial and extra-judicial execution[257], so its presence in the Romano-British examples does not necessarily imply human sacrifice.

Once the throat of the individual had been cut, the additional cuts and chops would appear to be related to the removal of the head, sometimes by relatively carefully made incised cuts and sometimes by chopping blows. In cases where chops are identified, there is usually more than one blow administered, suggesting that there was a main decapitating blow

71

and then additional chops, undertaken in order to completely remove the head. These additional chops could sometimes be numerous, as in the individual from Winchester Street, Andover. The idea that the process of head removal was not necessarily always a quick and tidy one was suggested by Andrew Reynolds in reference to the post-mortem decapitation of Oliver Cromwell, which required eight blows even though he had died three years previously[258]. However, the original Sainthill manuscript suggests that the number of blows was required largely because the body was wrapped in six layers of cerecloth (strips of fabric impregnated in wax and used to wrap the dead) at the time of the decapitation[259].

The fact that these additional blows were administered, plus the displacement of the cranium and mandible in all of these individuals, would indicate that, rather than it just being necessary to kill the individual, the complete removal of the head was an important part of the process of decapitation. That the separation of the head from the rest of the body was not necessarily carried out once the individual was dead is suggested by a number of factors present in the individual from Winchester Street, Andover. These include a peri-mortem blade injury to the glenoid fossa of the right scapula that would not seem to be directly related to the decapitation process and may represent an attempt to cut through *M. pectoralis major*, possibly as an incapacitating injury to the right pectoral girdle of a live and unwilling victim. The fact that the decapitating blows were delivered from a number of different directions may also suggest that the individual had been moving during the process. Another possible piece of evidence is the multiple peri-mortem fractures of the dentition, which affected the right maxillary canine, left lateral incisor, canine, premolars and third molar, and the mandibular right fourth premolar, second and third molars and left third premolar. These manifested as oblique root-crown fractures or as fractures of the surface of the crown and root, removing slivers of the tooth. Fractures of the anterior dentition are usually the result of direct force, such as a blow to the face, whilst fractures to the premolars and molars are a result of forced occlusion through indirect force, such as in forceful contact between the chin and a hard surface[260]. The presence of fractures on both the anterior and posterior dentition in this individual would suggest that a direct blow to the face, or a fall onto the face, had been sustained but also that indirect force had been applied. This may have occurred as a result of post-mortem damage to the decapitated head by being dropped or thrown onto the ground or another hard surface, or the fractures of the posterior dentition could have resulted from forced occlusion due to the act of decapitation. It is possible that the blows to the mandible could have produced the posterior dental trauma, but it is difficult to determine whether this could occur in a corpse, or whether the individual would have had to be alive to produce such forced occlusion.

The clinical and archaeological literature on peri-mortem dental trauma is very sparse. One forensic case from Kosovo presented with multiple incomplete dental fractures, which were suggested to have been caused by upward blows to the mandible whilst the teeth were biting into a hard object[261]. There are also only a small number of examples reported from archaeological sites but with no comment on their possible aetiology[262], with the exception of a few individuals from the medieval Battle of Towton, who had suffered blade injuries to, and fractures of, the dentition as a result of trauma to the mandible[263], and an adult male from Opi Val Fondillo, Italy, who had sustained multiple dental fractures from a blow to the chin, probably in an accidental fall[264]. However, a peri-mortem fracture of the mandibular left second molar in Lindow Man (the famous bog body from Lindow Moss, Lancashire) was suggested to have been a result of forced occlusion from the peri-mortem blunt force injury to the frontal, as there was no post-mortem process that could have caused it[265]. Peri-mortem dental fractures were recorded in a further thirteen decapitated individuals during the present research and there is the potential that it could be one means of distinguishing decapitations that were the mechanism of death from those carried out as a post-mortem act.

Flexion of the neck during decapitation, which was recorded in one individual in this category (1-3 Driffield Terrace, York, SK47), may also be a very good method of distinguishing individuals where decapitation was the mechanism of death, as this neck position is virtually impossible to achieve in a corpse lying prone on the ground[266]. A total of nine individuals analysed as part of this research had evidence for decapitating blows delivered with the neck flexed, again supporting the assertion that a number of the decapitations were potentially performed on living individuals.

This may also be suggested by the slightly unusual burial position recorded in a few individuals, including the crossed wrists of one of the individuals (mentioned earlier, p.67) from Barrow Hills, Radley, Oxfordshire (SK1018), which may indicate that they had been tied.

Another individual, this time from Lankhills, Winchester (SK451), a relatively poorly preserved adult male with no evidence for peri-mortem trauma on the surviving upper four cervical vertebrae[267], was buried prone with both upper limbs behind the back with the distal upper limbs parallel[268], suggesting some form of restraint. There were other individuals analysed as part of this research that also had evidence for having had their wrists tied, and this may be used, particularly where it is associated with possible incapacitating injuries, cut throats or flexed necks, to suggest that decapitation may have been the mechanism of death.

3. Chopping blows associated with additional cuts or chops
Fifty-two individuals from within the decapitated sample had evidence for this type of decapitation, which was characterised by two or more chopping blows, usually associated with additional incised cuts or chops. There was no significant difference between the urban and rural/small-town samples in the numbers of this type of decapitation (twenty-five and twenty-seven individuals respectively), although there were statistically

significantly more females in the urban sample with this type of decapitation than males. Examples of this type include an older child (8-10 years) from Stanwick, Northamptonshire (SK6038), buried prone with the lower limbs flexed at the knee and the cranium and mandible by the distal left lower leg[269], who had evidence for four separate chops to the arches of C2-C4, all of which were directed from the posterior right (figure 16, plate 26), as well as peri-mortem fractures of the maxillary right second deciduous molar and mandibular permanent left first molar; and a mature adult ?female from Southfield House, Dorchester (SK66), buried supine and extended in a wooden coffin with the cranium and mandible between the ankles[270], who had two separate chops

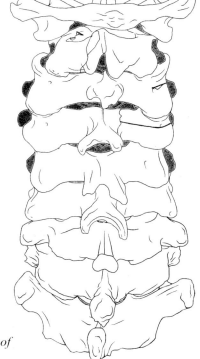

Figure 16: Chops to the cervical vertebrae of SK6038 from Stanwick, Northamptonshire.

through the arches of C4 and C5, one of which must have been made when the neck was hyperextended (figure 17), as well as peri-mortem fractures of the maxillary incisors. Other examples include a young middle adult male from 1-3 Driffield Terrace, York (SK41), who was supine and extended with the cranium and mandible on the left knee, and who demonstrated two separate posteriorly directed chopping blows, one of which affected the spinous processes of C2 and C3 and must have been made with the neck flexed (the occipital was not affected by the blow), and the other of which bisected the body and arch of C7 (figure 18, plate 27).

In examples such as these, with a (usually small) number of separate chopping blows, it is often not possible to determine whether there was a main decapitating blow and it seems possible that the head was removed using two to five separate blows delivered from the same direction. However, there are examples where this does not seem to be the case. These include a young middle adult male from Water Lane, Towcester, Northamptonshire (SK29), who was buried supine and extended with the cranium and mandible over the distal lower limbs[271], and who had evidence for five separate chops to C1 and C2 that also affected the right mastoid process and ascending ramus of the mandible, all of which were directed from the posterior. There was also a single incised cut to the posterior of the arch of C1 and a large number of incised cuts into the superior facets and odontoid process of C2, one of which overlays a chopped surface (figure 19, 20, plate 28). There were also a

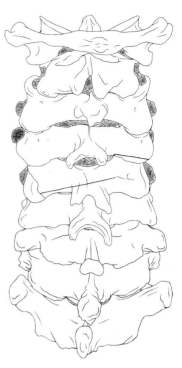

Figure 17: Chops to the cervical vertebrae of SK66 from Southfield House, Dorchester, Dorset.

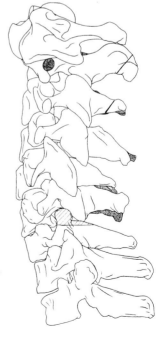

Figure 18: Chops to the cervical vertebrae of SK41 from 1-3 Driffield Terrace, York.

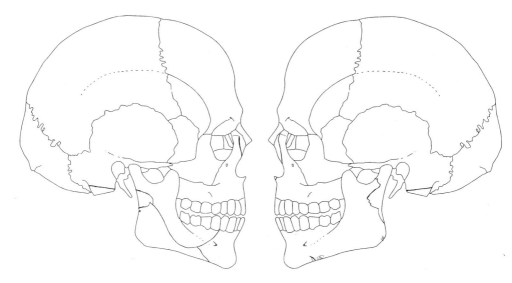

Figure 19: Chops to the mandible and mastoid processes and incised cuts to the mandible of SK29 from Water Lane, Towcester, Northamptonshire.

number of incised cuts into the gonial area and inferior border of the body of the left side of the mandible. This suggests that the initial chopping blows to the neck did not succeed in completely removing the head and additional incised cuts were required to sever the remaining connective tissue.

Other examples of this type include a mature adult female from Mundford, Norfolk (SK6), supine and extended with the cranium and mandible by the feet[272], who had evidence for a posteriorly directed chopping blow that bisected the body of C3, as well as three additional blows, also directed from the posterior: one chopped into the right ascending ramus of the mandible and fractured the gonion (plate 29), one chopped through the acromial end of the left clavicle and the third resulted in a peri-mortem fracture of the midshaft of the right clavicle. There was also a young adult of indeterminate sex from Dunstable,

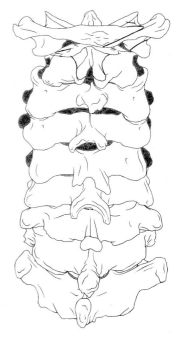

Figure 20: Chops and incised cuts to the cervical vertebrae of SK29 from Water Lane, Towcester, Northamptonshire.

Bedfordshire (AD), buried supine and extended with both hands together by the right side of the pelvis and the cranium and mandible between the femorae[273], who had a chop that bisected the arch of C3 and body of C4, directed from the anterior, as well as two chops into the inferior facets of C4, also directed from the anterior, that did not affect the arch or body of C5 (figure 21).

The evidence from these individuals for a, usually, single main chopping blow followed by additional incised cuts or chops suggests that an initial decapitating blow was delivered, and when this did not succeed

Figure 21: Chops to the cervical vertebrae of skeleton AD from Dunstable, Bedfordshire.

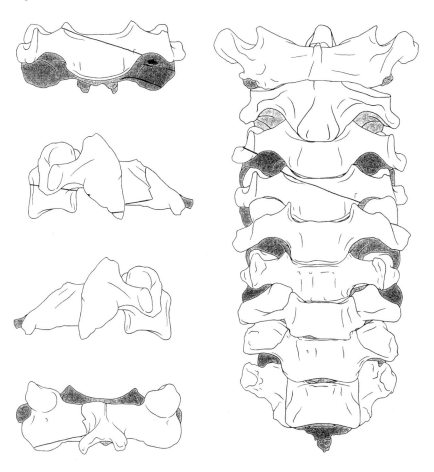

in completely removing the head, additional chops or peri-mortem fractures were made in order to remove the remaining soft tissue (to the clavicle or mandible, or to parts of the cervical vertebrae that would have been inaccessible without the column being already partially severed), or a number of incised cuts were made to sever the intervertebral ligaments and cartilage. This also suggests that, in these types of decapitation, it was a necessary part of the process that the head was completely removed. In the majority of cases, it is not possible to determine whether the decapitation was the mechanism of death, although where there is evidence that the neck was flexed (the only case in this category being SK41 from 1-3 Driffield Terrace, York – see above, p.75), or where there were peri-mortem dental fractures (as in SK6038 from Stanwick, Northamptonshire, and SK66 from Southfield House, Dorchester – see above, p.79), or a suggestion of restraint in a slightly unusual burial position (such as may be the case with skeleton AD from Dunstable, Bedfordshire, with both hands together by the pelvis, see above, p.77), there is the possibility that decapitation may have been carried out as the mechanism of death with subsequent removal of the head.

4. Single chopping blow only

There were seventy-four individuals within the decapitated sample who had evidence for this type of decapitation, making it the most widely identified type. It represented forty-eight per cent of the urban sample and thirty-four per cent of the rural/small-town sample, although these percentages were not quite statistically significantly different, and there were no significant differences between the numbers of males and females affected in either sample. Typical examples of this type of decapitation included a young middle adult male from 1-3 Driffield Terrace, York (SK2), buried supine and extended with the wrists crossed over the chest, and with the cranium and mandible rotated and on the right side of the upper torso, who had a chop through the superior facets and body of C6, directed from the posterior (figure 22; of the forty-six individuals from this site, and the associated sites of 6 Driffield Terrace and 129 The Mount, with osteological evidence for decapitation, sixty-three per cent had evidence for this type of decapitation – see chapter 4 for a detailed description and discussion of these and other decapitation burials from Roman York); and a mature adult ?female from the Old Vicarage, Fordington, Dorset (SK10), supine and extended with the cranium and mandible between the knees[274], who had a single anteriorly directed chop that bisected the body of C5 and chopped into the right pedicle (plate 30). Individuals with a single chop directed from the anterior or from the left or right were rarer than those with a posteriorly directed chop, and represented twenty-six per cent of individuals from urban areas and thirty-nine per cent of individuals from rural and small-town areas.

Posteriorly directed chopping blows are often associated with decapitation as a form of judicial punishment and it is the presence of these types of chop marks in certain early medieval burials that has led to the interpretation that these individuals were the victims of execution (see chapter 1, and chapter 8 for examples of such burials analysed as part of this research). Post-medieval and modern decapitations by the sword or axe are often performed from the posterior, such as in Japan and the Middle East, where the victims kneel with their necks extended[275], or in Europe, where a block was often used[276]. There is the potential that a few individuals who display evidence for posteriorly directed chopping blows made

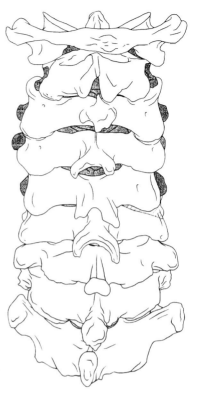

Figure 22: Chop to the sixth cervical vertebra of SK2 from 1-3 Driffield Terrace, York.

with the neck held in extension (such as an old middle adult male from 6 Driffield Terrace, York (SK21), a supine and extended burial from a triple grave, with the cranium and mandible found by the right side of the torso, and a single chop through C5 and C6) may have been decapitated with the use of such a block, although this does not necessarily mean that the decapitation was definitely the mechanism of death in such individuals, as the extended neck could also have been produced in a corpse lying prone on the ground. However, as in the previous types of decapitation, there are some individuals with supporting evidence that the decapitation was the mechanism of death, such as SK2 from 1-3 Driffield Terrace, who had their wrists crossed in the grave, possibly suggesting they had been restrained, three individuals with decapitating blows delivered with the neck flexed, and an old middle adult male from the Mount School, York (SK2), with a single chop through the arch of C2, body and arch of C3 and hyoid, who had a peri-mortem fracture of the maxillary right second molar (plate 31).

It also appears that, in certain individuals with this type of decapitation, it was not considered necessary to remove the head if it was not completely severed by the single blow. This is suggested by the position of the head in some individuals, such as SK2 from 1-3 Driffield Terrace, where the head was on the upper torso, and a second individual from the same site (SK4), a young adult male with a chop through the body and arch of C2 that also nicked into the posterior of both ascending rami of the mandible, whose head was found in correct anatomical position. This may also add weight to the possibility that decapitation was the mechanism of death in at least some of these individuals, as, if the removal of the head was one of the defining features of the act of decapitation (and it seems to be an important part of the process in the other types of decapitation), it would seem unlikely that the partial decapitation of a corpse would have sufficed. However, it would have been sufficient to kill the individual if that, rather than complete decapitation, was the aim.

5. Chopping blows with non-decapitation-related trauma
There were sixteen individuals from urban cemeteries (all of which were male, although this was not statistically significant) and ten individuals from rural and small-town areas (seven of which were male and three of which were female) with this type of decapitation, which is characterised by chopping blows (sometimes accompanied by additional chops and incised cuts) alongside peri-mortem injuries that could not be directly related to the process of decapitation. One group within this type had peri-mortem cranial injuries. This group includes a supine and extended middle adult male from Dunstable, Bedfordshire (AR), with the cranium and mandible found on the top of the grave fill[277], who had at least twenty separate chops to the cervical vertebrae, affecting C2-T1, and the left pectoral girdle, at least some of which seems to be related to the removal of soft tissue to allow complete removal of the head. The individual also demonstrated two chopping blows to the left side of the frontal and parietal with associated fracturing (figure 23, 24). There was also an adult ?male from Lankhills, Winchester (SK302), of whom only the cranium, mandible and some cervical vertebrae were excavated[278], who had a single posteriorly directed chop through C1 and the ascending rami of the mandible, delivered whilst the neck was flexed, and a chop through the

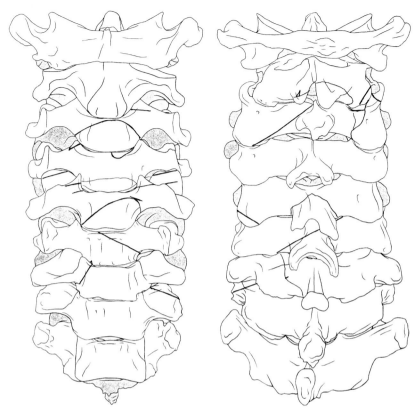

Figure 23: Chops to the cervical and upper thoracic vertebrae of skeleton AR from Dunstable, Bedfordshire.

Figure 24: Chops to the cranium and mandible of skeleton AR from Dunstable, Bedfordshire.

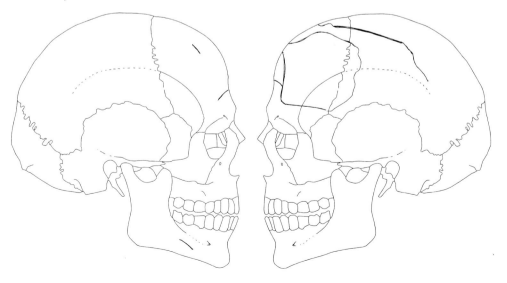

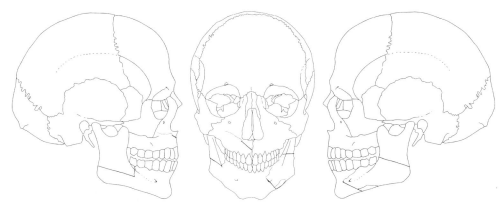

Figure 25: Chops to the cranium and mandible of SK302 from Lankhills, Winchester, Hampshire.

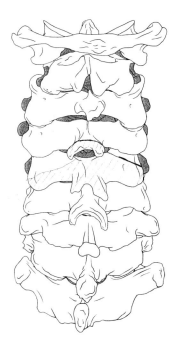

anterior of the right maxilla and left mandibular body (figure 25)[279]. There was also a small group of individuals from Driffield Terrace, York, who had evidence for peri-mortem blunt-force injuries to the cranium, as well as decapitation-related trauma, including SK47 (described above, p.73), and an old middle adult male (SK4 from 6 Driffield Terrace), who was buried supine and extended in a wooden coffin with the cranium and mandible on the knees[280], and who had two chopping blows to C4 and C5, directed from the posterior, as well as a blunt-force injury to the right parietal with endocranial bevelling (figure 26, 27, plate 58).

Figure 26: Chops to the cervical vertebrae of SK4 from 6 Driffield Terrace, York.

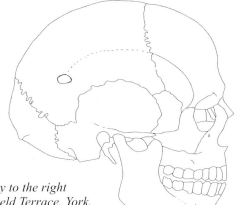

Figure 27: Penetrating injury to the right parietal of SK4 from 6 Driffield Terrace, York.

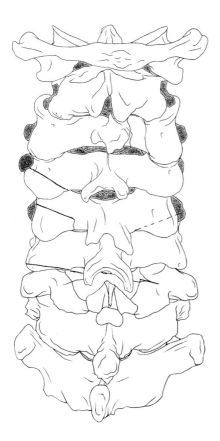

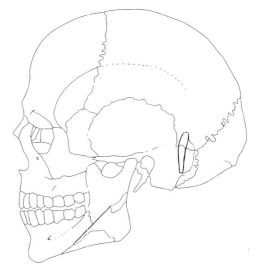

Figure 28: Chops to the cervical vertebrae of SK1118 from Little Keep, Dorchester, Dorset.

Figure 29: Chops to the cranium and mandible of SK1118 from Little Keep, Dorchester, Dorset.

The second group of burials had evidence for post-cranial peri-mortem trauma in addition to decapitation-related injuries. These include an old middle adult male from Little Keep, Dorchester (SK1118), buried supine and extended with the cranium and mandible on the right ankle[281], who had evidence for a chop to the dorsal surface of two proximal hand phalanges, as well as seven separate chops to the cervical vertebrae, right clavicle, left side of the mandible and left temporal (figure 28, 29); a supine and extended young adult male from 6 Driffield Terrace, York (SK3), with the mandible found between the femorae (the cranium had been disturbed by later activity and was recovered from a later cremation deposit)[282], who had evidence for a single chop through C4 and C5 from the posterior, as well as three chopping blows to the posterior of the proximal and midshaft of the right ulna, and a butterfly fracture of the midshaft of the same element (plate 57); and an adult male from the same site (SK9), who was supine and extended with the cranium and mandible between the femorae[283], who had four posteriorly directed chopping blows to C3-C5 (figure 30), as well as peri-mortem blunt-force injuries to the frontal and a peri-mortem fracture of the shaft of the right second metacarpal.

Other individuals in this group include an old middle adult male from 1-3 Driffield Terrace, York (SK16), who was supine and extended in a double grave with SK15 and whose cranium and mandible were found at the feet of SK15 (the cranium and mandible of SK15 had been placed at the neck end of the post-cranial remains of SK16; plate 32), and who had a single posteriorly directed chop through the arch of C6, as well as a blunt-force injury to the left parietal with an associated radiating fracture, and a stabbing blow to the anterior of the right side of the sacrum (plate 60); and a young middle adult male from the same site (SK45) who was supine and extended with the cranium and mandible underneath the right side of the pelvis, and who demonstrated a single chop through the arch and body of C5 and C6, delivered from the posterior, as well as a

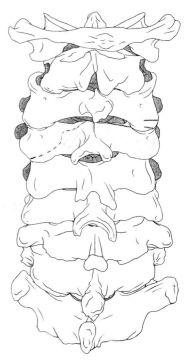

Figure 30: Chops to the cervical vertebrae of SK9 from 6 Driffield Terrace, York.

chopping blow to the distal metaphysis of the right femur that would have chopped through the major musculature of the leg, particularly *M. vastus medialis* (plate 33). There was also the young middle adult male from St Martin's Close, Winchester (SK18/19a), who had a single chopping injury delivered from the posterior that bisected C1 and the odontoid process of C2 and chopped into the posterior of both ascending rami of the mandible. There was also evidence for a number of fine incised cuts and chopping blows to the mandible and basi-occiput, including at least seven chops to the right side of the occipital and mastoid processes from a supero-posterior direction, one of which aligns with the chop through the cervical column if the neck was flexed; three small nicks to the area around the foramen magnum; and at least ten incised cuts to the right ascending ramus of the mandible (figure 31). There was also evidence for three fine chopping blows to the right side of the frontal and peri-mortem stab wounds to the posterior of L4 and L5 (plate 34), the anterior of the right ilium, the left pubis and the lateral side of a lower right rib[284].

The presence of peri-mortem post-cranial injuries on the hands and

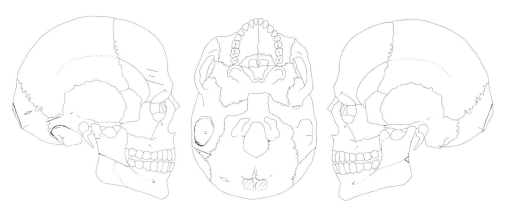

Figure 31: Chops, stabs and incised cuts to the cranium and mandible of SK18/19a from St. Martin's Close, Winchester, Hampshire.

distal upper limb of three of these individuals would suggest that they were defensive injuries, made when the upper limbs were used to shield the face and head from attack, and are, therefore, likely to indicate that decapitation was the mechanism of death in these individuals. The other injuries, focused as they are on the cranial vault, the abdomen, lower back and proximal lower limb, are probably to be interpreted as incapacitating injuries, designed to prevent the individual from escaping or, in the case of the cranial injuries, to render them unconscious. There is the possibility that the blunt-force cranial injuries could have occurred post-decapitation with the head striking a hard surface, although the presence of a 'ring fracture' of the cranial base[285] of another decapitated individual from 6 Driffield Terrace (SK12), whose cranium and mandible were found in correct anatomical position[286] (suggesting that the head was not completely removed by the single decapitating blow), makes it unlikely that the cranial injury in this case could have been caused by post-decapitation rough handling of the head (plate 35). Therefore, there is also a possibility that decapitation was the mechanism of death in individuals who demonstrated evidence for cranial and post-cranial sharp- and blunt-force non-decapitation-related injuries.

However, there is one individual, an old middle adult female from Dunstable, Bedfordshire (L), who has evidence for a different type of peri-mortem trauma. The individual was supine and extended with the cranium and mandible between the femorae, and with the distal lower limbs removed and placed on either side of the torso[287] (plate 36). Osteological evidence for decapitation was not present, as the cervical vertebrae, maxilla and mandible were not located in the archive[288], but there was evidence for peri-mortem trauma to the distal femorae and patellae, in the form of a number of incised cuts to the anterior of both patellae and chopping blows to the posterior and anterior of both femorae (plate 37). The pattern of the injuries suggests that the distal lower limbs were removed by initially chopping through the femorae from both the anterior and posterior, and then cutting through *M. quadriceps femoris* at its insertion on the patellae. This method of removal of the distal lower limbs suggests that it was undertaken post-mortem, as it seems likely that it was not a quick procedure and may represent some form of mutilation of the corpse. Interestingly, a young/young middle adult female from Tubney Woods Quarry, Oxfordshire (SK1007), originally assumed to be late Romano-British in date but recently radiocarbon dated to cal AD 535-640[289], who was found with the cranium and mandible on the knees, also had the lower limbs severed at the knee with the left distal lower limb being placed beside the torso, whilst the right lower limb was absent, although the poor skeletal preservation prevented any cut marks from being recorded[290].

Possible mutilation was also suggested in the case of an infant/young child from Stanground, Peterborough, who was found with the cranium and mandible at the knees and with the limbs severed at the joints[291]; and a mature adult female from Foxton, Cambridgeshire (SK3444), buried supine and extended with the cranium and mandible absent, and with the left humerus found lying on the lumbar vertebrae but still articulated with the radius and ulna[292]. However, cut-marks were not reported in either case and both individuals would require reanalysis in order to determine whether there is evidence for any peri-mortem trauma or whether the 'mutilation' could be the result of post-burial disturbance. However, even if these cases are accepted as evidence for corpse mutilation, the practice is still exceedingly rare amongst decapitated burials and suggests that it may have represented a practice entirely separate from that of decapitation.

Summary of evidence for peri-mortem trauma
• The majority of decapitations were carried out with chopping blows in both urban and rural/small-town samples with incised cuts in isolation being very rare.
• Decapitation was more often performed from the posterior in the urban sample than in the rural/small-town sample.
• Urban males had more decapitations performed from the posterior and urban females had more decapitations performed from the anterior.

• Urban decapitations were performed more often with a single blow than those in rural/small-town areas, which were more likely to have four or more blows.
• Urban males were more likely to have one blow than urban females, who tended to have two to three blows.
• There were five distinct types of decapitation observable in both samples: 1. incised careful disarticulation of the cranio-cervical skeleton; 2. cutting of the throat followed by incised disarticulation or chopping blows; 3. chopping main decapitating blows with associated chops or incised cuts to remove soft tissue; 4. a single decapitating chopping blow; 5. chopping blows associated with defensive or incapacitating injuries.
• There were more individuals with a Type 2 decapitation in rural/small-town areas than in the urban sample.
• There were more urban females than males with a Type 3 decapitation.
• Complete removal of the head was an important part of the process in the first three types of decapitation.
• A Type 1 decapitation was more likely to have been performed post-mortem.
• Decapitation as a mechanism of death can probably be assumed for Type 2 and Type 5 decapitations.
• Decapitation as a mechanism of death can probably be assumed for individuals with Type 3 and Type 4 decapitations in cases where there was evidence for a flexed neck, peri-mortem dental trauma or restraint of the upper limbs.
• Mutilation of the corpse, as separate from decapitation but occurring in the same individual, was very rare.

Discussion

The evidence from the large sample of Romano-British decapitations identified as part of this research suggests that previous statements made about the practice – namely that it was specifically late Roman and predominately found in rural areas but with a spread to urban areas in the fourth century – may not be strictly accurate. There are a number of such burials that have been dated to much earlier in the Romano-British period and these include some from urban cemetery areas. There are also examples of the practice in all of the coloniae and a number of tribal capitals, suggesting that it was as much an urban practice as a rural one, and that it took place during the same period in both areas. The differences between the methods of decapitation in the two samples would also suggest that the practice as it was performed in urban areas was not simply imported from rural communities, although there is the possibility that this may be due to differences in butchery techniques between the two areas (see below, p.90).

Previous statements on the geographical distribution of the phenomenon of decapitation – namely, that it was largely restricted to an area south-west of the Severn–Wash line – were confirmed by the present research and it seems that this is not simply due to biases in the preservation and excavation of human remains, although this may play some part in the near absence of decapitation burials from some areas of the country, such as Kent and Sussex. The distribution of decapitation burials does seem to be very similar to that of villas in the fourth century[293]; although there is a high concentration of villas in Lincolnshire and, as previously discussed, very few decapitation burials, even though the local geology predisposes towards good bone preservation. This does suggest that the practice of decapitation may have been linked with higher degrees of Romanisation, with some localised exceptions, which would also explain why there are relatively high numbers of decapitated burials from coloniae and other urban centres. The very limited evidence for continuity of Iron Age practices of the manipulation of the head into the Romano-British period (although this practice seems to have been rare in Britain in prehistory anyway), and the absence of the typical Romano-British decapitation burial in prehistory, would suggest that these burials, and the methods of decapitation that go with it, are very much Roman in type rather than representing a continuity of practice amongst less Romanised sections of the community, even though there are rare examples that date to very early in the Romano-British period (and see chapter 9 for comparisons between the nature of the peri-mortem trauma in the Romano-British and Iron Age decapitations). This would correspond to contemporary literary evidence (see chapter 5) that decapitation was very much a Roman practice and was performed for a variety of reasons in a number of different circumstances. However, the archaeological evidence for decapitation burials outside of Roman Britain is very limited (see chapter 6) and, although there is the potential that this may be partly due to differences in archaeological methods and research strategies, it does suggest that the phenomenon of decapitated burials with displaced cranio-cervical skeletons may be specifically Romano-British.

The practice does not, however, appear to be identical in all areas, with a number of differences between urban and rural/small-town decapitated burials. In rural and small-town cemeteries, the burial practices accorded the decapitated individuals showed no differences to those seen in the rest of the population; the decapitated individuals were just as likely to have been buried in a supine and extended position in a coffin with hobnailed footwear and other grave inclusions as non-decapitated individuals. However, in urban areas, the decapitated burials were much less likely to have been provided with a coffin or other grave inclusions, and were much more likely to have been buried in a prone position. This suggests that in terms of their burial, decapitated individuals in urban areas were singled out for 'poorer' burial rites, whilst decapitated individuals in rural and small-town areas were not distinguished in this way from the rest of the population. This may suggest that those individuals subject to decapitation in urban areas were in some way marginalised, or at least treated differently, in death, whilst this was not the case in rural and small-town areas.

The demographic profile of the rural and small-town decapitated sample largely mirrors that of the wider cemetery population, although there are much smaller numbers of non-adult decapitations and greater numbers of adult females than would be expected. This may suggest that there was some degree of selection in terms of age and sex in who was decapitated in these areas, with adult females seeming to be the focus for the practice, although the age profile of the adult decapitations mirrors that of the larger population. This may suggest that decapitation was performed on individuals who had already died from other causes (although see below, p.92), although it could just reflect a selection procedure that mirrored the general demographic profile of the population. However, in urban areas, the age and sex profile of the decapitations is very different from that recorded amongst the larger population, with small numbers of non-adults and greater numbers of adult males than would be expected, as well as there being too many middle adults and not enough mature adults amongst the decapitated burials. This indicates a greater degree of selection for age and sex amongst those singled out for decapitation in urban areas, with middle adult males seeming to be the focus. The possibility of selection is also suggested by the significantly higher average stature of the urban adult male decapitations than that recorded in the rest of the population, something not seen in the urban females, or in either sex in the rural and small-town decapitated sample, as well as the lower health status of the urban decapitations compared with the wider population.

The evidence from the palaeopathological analysis suggests that the decapitations from both samples had higher levels of degenerative joint disease and non-specific infections, and may have been eating a different diet to the rest of the population. The urban decapitations showed further differences in terms of the rates of activity-related change and chronic chest infections. There was also an abundance of evidence for ante-mortem trauma amongst both decapitated samples, with much higher rates of fractures than was the norm (most of which are associated with levels of interpersonal violence), as well as evidence for amputations and visible deformities. This also suggests that there was a degree of selection in terms of physical appearance and health status as to who was subject to decapitation, with this being more pronounced in urban areas. There is the possibility that this selection for decapitation could have been directly related to these physical differences, although this does not necessarily imply that all individuals with such differences were subject to decapitation, as evidenced by, amongst many other examples, the non-decapitated burial of a female mesomelic dwarf from Alington Avenue, Dorchester[294]. It is also possible that the physical differences and poorer health status of some individuals were related to their position or function within society and it was this that led to their decapitation (see chapter 4 for possible interpretations of the identity of decapitated individuals from Roman York).

The evidence from the decapitation-related peri-mortem trauma identified in the rural/small-town and urban decapitated samples indicate that there were also some differences between how the practice was carried out in the two areas. Chopping blows were the most common method of decapitation in both samples, with careful, incised cutting being very rare. This finding is in complete contrast to previous assertions, and may have consequences for interpretations of the practice (see chapter 1). The urban decapitated sample had more individuals with blows directed from the posterior than those in rural and small-town areas and also contained more individuals with smaller numbers of separate blows. The sample from the rural and small-town areas had a much greater number of individuals with more than four separate blows, as well as a larger number of examples of decapitation that included the cutting of the throat.

These distinctions may be related to differences in animal butchery techniques between urban and rural areas, something which has been noted in a number of analyses of animal bones from Romano-British sites[295] and which seems to be related to a need to butcher carcasses much more quickly and in more volume in urban areas than would have been necessary on rural sites. This led to a change in implement use from a knife to a cleaver in urban areas and a subsequent reduction in the number of cuts needed to dismember the carcass[296]. This may be reflected in the smaller number of blows seen in urban decapitated burials, although the predominance of knife use (to make incised cuts) in rural butchery techniques does not seem to have been mirrored in human decapitation, where chopping blows were still the most common method. The presence of both chopping blows and incised cuts in a large minority of decapitated individuals from both samples may suggest that at least two different types of implement were used to decapitate a single individual (it is relatively difficult to produce fine and carefully placed incised cuts with chopping implements such as axes and swords, as the blades are either the wrong shape or the placement of the grip is in the wrong position to allow for precise movements), although it has been suggested that the Romano-British cleaver was essentially a dual-purpose tool, designed to slice as well as chop, in contrast to modern cleavers which are specifically designed as a chopping implement[297]. This may mean that cleavers were used in the process of human decapitation and were able to produce both chopping blows and incised cuts on the same individual. This may be supported by the presence of two peri-mortem chop marks, which resulted in scoops of bone being removed from the bone surface, on the clavicle of an individual from Lankhills, Winchester (SK297), that are virtually identical to that recorded on a cattle tibia, also from Winchester, demonstrated through experimental studies to have been produced by the tip of a cleaver in stripping meat from the bone[298] (plate 38). This would also support the thesis (see above, p.92) that if complete removal of the head, which seems to have been an important part of the process in most types of decapitation, was not achieved by the main decapitating blow, the removal of soft tissue by additional chops and incised cuts was undertaken until the head could be completely separated from the post-cranial remains.

Even within the urban and rural/small-town areas themselves, there was not much evidence for consistency in how the decapitations were performed, with at least five different types of decapitation identified, examples of nearly all of which could sometimes be found in the same cemetery (such as at Lankhills, Winchester). This does suggest that, rather than differences in how decapitations were performed being simply related to differences in butchery techniques and geographic area, the different (and distinctive) types may have been different because they were carried out for specific, and distinctive, purposes.

A number of individuals displayed evidence that decapitation was likely to have been the mechanism of death, and this discovery, which was a result of the very detailed analysis of peri-mortem trauma carried out as part of this research, is a very important counterargument to the vast majority of previous researchers who have seen decapitation in the Romano-British period exclusively as a post-mortem act. There certainly are a small number of decapitations where the placement and nature of the cuts suggests that the individuals were indeed dead when decapitation was carried out; however, they are outnumbered by examples where decapitation was probably the mechanism of death and cases where it could not be determined either way. Evidence that decapitation was probably the mechanism of death came in the form of cut throats in a small number of individuals, as well as evidence for flexion of the neck, defensive and incapacitating injuries, peri-mortem dental trauma and the possibility that a few individuals may have been restrained, or in a state of cadaveric spasm (see chapter 5), at the time of interment. All of these factors have been reported in the forensic literature as indicating vitality at the time the injuries were received and so there is a very good chance that, where they are found in the Romano-British examples of decapitation, they have the same types of aetiology.

Comparisons between the types of peri-mortem trauma found in the Romano-British examples and those seen in individuals from other periods will be made in chapter 9, and a discussion of possible interpretations for all of the different types of decapitation from all periods, based on the osteological, archaeological, literary and ethnographic evidence, will be given in chapter 10.

Chapter 4

Decapitations from Roman York –
A Case Study

York (Eboracum) was founded by the Romans in AD 71 and was the site of a legionary fortress and *colonia* (the highest status of Roman city) with many public buildings, including baths and temples. It was also an imperial residence on two separate occasions: during the reign of Septimius Severus (AD 193-211) and Constantine the Great (c. AD 306-337). The settlement was surrounded by cemeteries, a number of which have been identified by tombstones and mausolea recovered during building works in the eighteenth to early twentieth centuries[299], whilst other areas have been subjected to more controlled excavation, including the Railway Station cemetery, excavated in the 1870s[300], Trentholme Drive, excavated in the 1950s[301], and various other smaller scale excavations undertaken by the York Archaeological Trust since the 1970s[302] (figure 32).

In 2004 and 2005, a series of York Archaeological Trust excavations, in the area of The Mount cemetery (1-3 and 6 Driffield Terrace and 129 The Mount), brought to light a very unusual group of eighty burials with a very high percentage of individuals showing evidence for decapitation[303]. The burials on both sites were made on a variety of different alignments and there was some intercutting of graves, indicating that the burials had taken place over a period of time. The radiocarbon dates obtained from a small number of individuals suggest that burials were taking place at 1-3 Driffield Terrace from the second century onwards[304], and at 6 Driffield Terrace in the third century extending into the fourth. Most of the burials were in single graves, although there were two double burials from 1-3 Driffield Terrace, and one double, one triple and one quadruple burial from 6 Driffield Terrace, with the evidence pointing to contemporaneous burial of individuals, rather than primary and secondary interments. Coffins were rare at 1-3 Driffield Terrace, with only four (out of fifty-four) graves showing any surviving evidence for

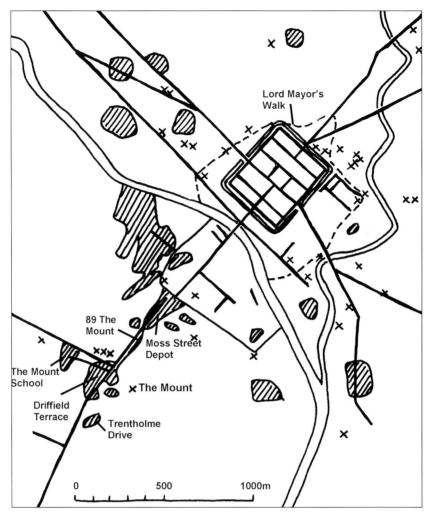

Figure 32: Map of the cemeteries of Roman York with locations of decapitated burials (the hatched areas denote named cemeteries and the "x"s denote scattered burials, redrawn from an original by the York Archaeological Trust).

them, whilst at least twelve of the graves (out of seventeen) from 6 Driffield Terrace had evidence for a coffin. Pottery vessels were found associated with two burials from 1-3 Driffield Terrace, two individuals were buried with partial chicken skeletons, and five burials had evidence for hobnailed footwear. At 6 Driffield Terrace, two burials had hobnails, whilst large numbers of horse bones, some of which had been butchered, were found within the coffins in two other graves[305].

Of the eighty individuals from the seventy-one graves, only six were under the age of eighteen at the time of death and comprised two foetuses/neonates, one young child, one older child and two adolescents, with the remaining seventy-four individuals being adult. Forty-five of these were middle adults, fourteen were young adults, and there were only two individuals who were mature adults. When this age profile was compared with that obtained from other Romano-British cemeteries within urban areas, the percentages of non-adults and mature adults were found to be significantly lower in the York sample than expected, whilst the percentages of young adults and middle adults were significantly higher, suggesting either that the population was not subject to the normal attritional processes, or that the area of the cemetery targeted by excavation was set aside for the burial of specific members of the population.

The sex ratio of the population was also very unusual, with sixty-five of the sixty-seven adults for whom a sex could be determined being male or ?male, with the remaining two being indeterminate in sex. The ratio of adult males to females in the cemetery population from Trentholme Drive was 3.6:1[306], whilst at Cirencester (also a *colonia*) it was 2.2:1[307]. This is higher than that seen in other urban cemeteries (1.7:1 in the eastern cemetery of Roman London[308] and 1.6:1 at Lankhills, Winchester[309]), and is probably a result of the numbers of retired military personnel taking up residence in *coloniae*, which were originally founded as settlements exclusively for ex-military personnel[310]. Therefore, even though cemetery populations from York should be expected to have higher numbers of adult males than females, to find a sample with no adult females at all is highly unusual. This may also indicate that the excavated area of the cemetery was specially designated for the burial of particular individuals, especially as the excavated burials from Trentholme Drive (which included at least fifty-two adult females[311]) are very likely part of the same cemetery as Driffield Terrace.

Of the eighty individuals, forty-five had osteological evidence for decapitation, with a further three demonstrating displacement of the cranio-cervical skeleton but no evidence for decapitation-related trauma due to the absence of the relevant skeletal elements (the osteological evidence for peri-mortem trauma in this group is described and discussed below, p.97ff). The presence of such a large number of decapitated individuals in one excavated sample, when decapitated burials had never been previously reported from York, was the catalyst for a re-examination of nearly all of the Romano-British skeletal remains that have been excavated from the city in order to determine whether these were really the only examples of the practice (the skeletal remains re-examined included those from the Railway Station cemetery, Sycamore Terrace, Trentholme Drive, Blossom Street, Marygate, The Avenue, County Hospital, The Mount School, plus many others[312], which came to a total of 525 individual skeletons or part skeletons). The cranium, mandible and cervical vertebrae (where present) were subjected to a quick visual examination and if evidence for peri-mortem trauma was identified, the individual was then subjected to a detailed skeletal analysis.

Individuals with evidence for peri-mortem decapitation-related trauma were identified from amongst the burials at Trentholme Drive (four adult males), The Mount School (five adult males) and Moss Street Depot (three adult males, identified and analysed by the author prior to the commencement of this research[313]). There were also two additional decapitated burials (at 89 The Mount and at Lord Mayor's Walk, both of which were adult males) identified by other authors but not available for reanalysis as part of this research[314]. All but one of these burials were from the southern cemetery area (centred on The Mount), which extended out on both sides of the road to Tadcaster (Calcaria), whilst the remaining example was from the northern cemetery area.

The percentage of decapitated individuals amongst the re-examined York sample (62 individuals out of 535) is statistically significantly higher than the percentage of such burials from Winchester (20 of 1,234 burials), and it is very interesting that they are all adult males (which is again in contrast to the decapitated individuals from Winchester, nine of which were adult males, with six adult females, one unsexed adult and four non-adults also being represented).

The mean stature of the decapitated sample from York is 172.8cm, which is very similar to that calculated for the larger urban male decapitated sample and significantly greater than the stature calculated for the urban male cemetery population as a whole. The group also had evidence for high levels of degenerative joint disease, non-specific infection, fractures closely related to low-level interpersonal violence, activity-related changes and increased robusticity, all of which were also relatively high amongst the non-decapitated individuals from Driffield Terrace. Isotope analysis of a number of the individuals from Driffield Terrace, both decapitated and non-decapitated, has indicated a very diverse range of origins, including individuals who seem to have come from the Mediterranean or North Africa, the Middle East, the Alps and eastern Scotland[315]. There were also two individuals who had isotope signatures characteristic of a mixed C3 and C4 diet (plants with different types of photosynthesis), something that has only been recorded very rarely in British skeletal remains. This indicates that they were probably eating millet, the only C4 plant cultivated in Europe, but not Britain, in antiquity, which suggests that these individuals had also originated from outside Britain[316].

When the different types of decapitation represented amongst the sample from York were analysed, the majority of individuals had a Type 4 decapitation (single chopping blow), and where a direction could be determined, all of these blows were delivered from the posterior. At least twelve of these individuals had evidence that the cranium and mandible may not have been completely removed by the single chop, as it was found in correct, or near correct, anatomical position. Twelve individuals had evidence for a Type 3 decapitation (chopping blow with additional chops or cuts), including two individuals where multiple chopping blows to the mandible may have been an attempt to mutilate the face, although they could also relate to attempts to chop through very robust neck musculature. One of these was a young middle adult male (1-3 Driffield, SK33), who was buried supine and extended with the cranium and partial mandible by the distal right lower limb. The individual had evidence for non-specific infection and healed fractures of the clavicle and rib, as well as a heavily scarred palate with large amounts of compact bone and ante-mortem fractures of the dentition, which is of unknown aetiology but could possibly be related to having had a foreign body held in the mouth (plate 39). There were four chopping blows through the cervical vertebrae that had been delivered from the posterior, including one which must have been made when the neck was flexed, as well as at least nine chops into the left and right body of the mandible, made from a variety of directions. The anterior portion of the mandible was not recovered from the grave, suggesting that this part of the face had been entirely separated from the rest of the remains prior to interment (plate 40). There were also peri-mortem fractures of the maxillary left incisors and second molar, and mandibular left first molar (figure 33, 34).

There was also evidence that three other individuals from the sample had decapitating blows delivered when the neck was flexed, which, as has been previously discussed (p.73), probably indicates that decapitation was the mechanism of death. There were also two individuals where the

97

body position would indicate they had possibly been restrained, including an old middle adult male (1-3 Driffield, SK37), who was supine and extended with the cranium and mandible by the left distal lower limb, and whose wrists were together on the right side of the torso with the right wrist in hyperflexion. Interestingly, this individual was also found with iron rings encircling both ankles that had probably been cold-forged onto the lower limbs,[317] and it is possible that these had been in place for some time before death as there were lesions on the tibiae associated with ulceration of soft tissues, as well as periosteal new bone on the tibiae and fibulae in the areas associated with the shackles (plate 41). There was evidence for a posteriorly directed rough chop through the body and arch of C2 with associated fracturing that appeared to have been produced using a different type of weapon from that used to produce the very clean and fine chop marks on the other decapitated individuals from the site, and a second

Figure 33: Chops to the cervical vertebrae of SK33 from 1-3 Driffield Terrace, York.

Figure 34: Chops to the cranium and mandible of SK33 from 1-3 Driffield Terrace, York (the horizontally hatched areas denote areas of bone absent from the grave and the diagonally hatched areas denote peri-mortem dental fractures).

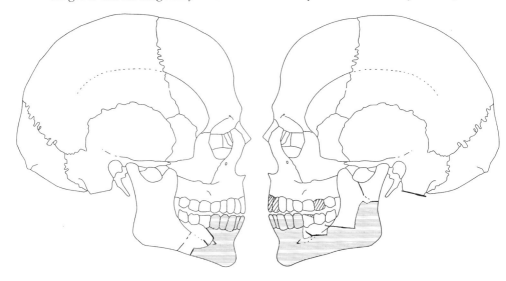

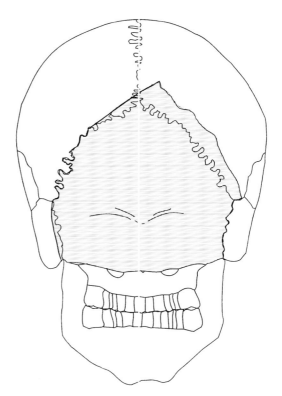

Figure 35: Chop to the posterior of the cranium of SK37 from 1-3 Driffield Terrace, York (the hatched area denotes bone absent from the grave).

chop into the posterior of the parietals and left temporal with associated fracturing and endocranial bevelling (figure 35).

There was also a young middle adult male (1-3 Driffield, SK31) who, whilst showing no evidence for restraint, had been placed in a very unusual position in the grave. He was supine and extended with the cranium and mandible in correct anatomical position, but the right upper limb was hyperflexed with the hand on the right shoulder and the left upper limb was flexed with the hand on the cervical column, the digits apparently encircling the neck (plate 42, 43). It is possible that this individual was deliberately placed in the grave in this position for some unknown reason, or there is the very slight chance that this may be a case of cadaveric spasm. This is a very rare process in which certain groups of muscles, particularly in the hands, tighten at the moment of death and cannot be released until they decompose[318]. It is an entirely different phenomenon to rigor mortis – a reversible chemical change of the muscles, which gradually stiffen from around two to three hours after death and then release again after approximately thirty-six to forty-eight hours[319]. Cadaveric spasm is usually restricted to individuals who have died a sudden and traumatic death, such as air crash victims whose fingers have been recovered gripping seatbelts, or victims of falls from a height who are found with grass and brush in their hands that they had grasped in an attempt to break their fall[320]. This individual had a single posteriorly directed chop through the body and arch of C6, which, if this is a case of cadaveric spasm, would have been the mechanism of death – the position of the hand presumably being an automatic reaction to the delivery of the blow.

All but one of the remaining individuals (who had evidence for a Type 2 decapitation: cutting of the throat with subsequent head removal, described in chapter 3) had Type 5 decapitations (chopping blows associated with incapacitating or defensive injuries). A number of these had evidence for peri-mortem blunt-force injuries to the cranial vault (described in chapter 3) and, amongst the non-decapitated individuals from Driffield Terrace, there were a further six individuals with peri-mortem cranial trauma, including an older child of six to seven years (1-3 Driffield, SK25), who had a blunt-force injury to the right parietal with endocranial bevelling and radiating fracture lines. Other decapitated individuals had evidence for probable incapacitating or defensive injuries to the post-cranial skeleton (described and discussed in chapter 3), and there was also one non-decapitated individual with this type of trauma – a young adult male (6 Driffield, SK15) with peri-mortem chops to the lateral and dorsal surfaces of the proximal phalanges for the left fourth and fifth metacarpals. Interestingly, this individual also had a small cranial vault and a comparatively large nose and face, suggesting that they may have been microcephalic (having an abnormally small head), although it cannot be assumed that this would have been accompanied by any degree of disability[321] (plate 44). In fact, of the eighty individuals from the Driffield Terrace assemblage, fifty-five had evidence for decapitation and/or an incapacitating or defensive injury (sixty-nine per cent, or ninety per cent of those individuals where the cranium, mandible and cervical vertebrae were present).

All these very unusual aspects of the Driffield Terrace population have led to an amount of speculation as to their identity, with victims of a political purge[322] and gladiatorial fighters[323] amongst the more sensational theories seized upon by journalists and television documentary makers. The first of these theories is easily discountable using the evidence that the burials took place over a period of centuries (discussed earlier, p.93), but the second interpretation was supposedly supported by the presence of a 'lion bite'[324] to the scapula and pelvis of one individual. This individual, a young middle adult male (6 Driffield, SK19), was supine and extended with the left upper limb behind the back, and was the uppermost interment in a triple burial contained within a single large wooden box[325]. The individual had evidence for a single posteriorly directed chop through the arch and body of C3 that had also chopped into the posterior of both ascending rami of the mandible, as well as a single circular perforation of the cortical bone on the posterior border of the left ilium, and two similar lesions to the lateral and anterior of the right ilium that appeared to be consistent with puncture marks from carnivore teeth[326] (plate 49). The uppermost position of this individual in the triple grave could have potentially made them accessible to scavenging animals (Roman law only required for a body to be covered with a few handfuls of soil to make it a legal burial[327]) and the size and appearance of the puncture mark would suggest a relatively small carnivore, such as a dog, rather than a lion or tiger.

The presence of large amounts of peri-mortem trauma on the Driffield Terrace assemblage has also been used to support the gladiator theory, although there is an absence of ante-mortem blade injuries, and very few post-cranial peri-mortem injuries or cranial penetrating injuries, all of which were recorded on the skeletal remains of presumed gladiators from Ephesus, Turkey[328]. Decapitation is also not recorded in any of the Ephesus individuals, although one has been reported to show evidence for a slit throat, whilst a second was recorded as having received a stabbing injury to the posterior of the neck that penetrated through the scapula and into the rib cage[329]. Decapitation is also not mentioned in any contemporary literary sources as being the means of dispatching losing gladiatorial fighters.

The demographic profile, above-average stature and evidence for activity-related changes and interpersonal violence amongst the population, as well as their varied geographical origins, may also suggest a military context for the decapitated burials from York. The Roman army did have height standards for recruits[330], which in the case of elite soldiers was at least 5ft 10in[331], and military personnel would have been used to a high degree of physical labour[332]. Anyone over the age of sixteen was considered suitable for military service[333], and if strenuous physical training was begun at this age, this may explain the high rates of *os acromiale* and humeral asymmetry amongst the population. High rates of *os acromiale* and humeral asymmetry were also recorded amongst individuals from the mass grave associated with the medieval Battle of

Towton[334], and from the skeletal remains from the Mary Rose[335], which, although they are not ideal comparative samples due to their later date, are the most extensively studied groups of known military personnel from archaeological sites. The individuals from Driffield Terrace also had very similar rates of Schmorl's nodes[336] and cortical defects[337] to those seen amongst the sample from Towton, which may also suggest similar patterns of activity amongst the two groups.

The evidence would suggest that, in at least eighteen individuals from the decapitated sample, decapitation was the mechanism of death, with there being a good possibility that this was the case for the majority of other individuals with posteriorly directed single chopping blows (see chapter 3). This may indicate that the decapitated individuals within the Driffield Terrace population, as well as the other examples of decapitated burials from Roman York (which, apart from the isolated burial of a middle adult male from Lord Mayor's Walk, supine and extended with the cranium and mandible between the femorae,[338] were all located in the southern cemetery), were victims of some form of judicial execution. This would be consistent with the evidence from the literary sources that decapitation was one of the punishments used within the military, although other Roman citizens were also subject to decapitation (see chapter 5), and it is possible that the population was composed of military and non-military individuals. The area in which these decapitated burials are concentrated (Driffield Terrace, 129 The Mount and The Mount School) is directly alongside the main approach road from the south and on a small, steep glacial moraine (the highest point in the local landscape[339]), with Trentholme Drive and Moss Street Depot, where fewer numbers of decapitations were identified, being located at the foot of this prominent landscape feature. If the individuals were decapitated on this site, as well as being buried there, this would suggest that there was a degree of 'spectacle' involved in the act, with the location of the burials designed to promote remembrance of the act amongst the local population[340]. The prominent burial location could also be a reflection of the potentially higher social standing of the decapitated individuals, which is supported by the argument from some literary sources that execution by decapitation was restricted to citizens or, after AD 211, *honestiores* (see chapter 5), and by the relatively tall stature of the individuals.

Although there have been three very different theories on the nature of the very unusual burial group from Driffield Terrace, all of them have relied on the probability that decapitation was the mechanism of death in the majority, if not all, of the individuals, something that is not contradicted by the other examples of decapitation from York identified as part of the present research. The theory that the burials were of a ritual nature with post-mortem removal of the head has not been considered since the excavation at 1-3 Driffield Terrace in 2004, when the nature of the osteological evidence for decapitation in these individuals had not yet been determined[341]. This does suggest that, in at least some cases of Romano-British decapitation, it is becoming more acceptable among scholars to describe the act as the mechanism of death rather than as some form of post-mortem burial ritual.

Chapter 5

Decapitations in Ancient European Literature, Art, Material Culture and Ethnography

Whenever decapitation is mentioned in relation to the perceived 'Cult of the Head' in Iron Age Europe, a number of Roman literary sources are quoted that refer to Celtic tribes 'cutting off the heads of the slain'[342] and then fastening them to the necks of their horses, before nailing them to their houses, or embalming the heads of their most distinguished enemies in cedar oil to display to visitors[343]. Another source refers to a tribe called the Boii cutting off the head of the defeated consul Postumius and turning it into a gilded libation vessel for use in their temple[344]. These texts are used to argue for a homogenous and widespread head cult across the whole of Northern Europe during the Late Iron Age (see chapter 10), even though the Celtic tribes referred to in the texts are localised to Northern Italy and the Mediterranean Coast. Outside of these areas, there is very little literary evidence for headhunting during the Iron Age; neither the writings of Caesar (*De Bello Gallico*) nor Tacitus (*De Vita Iulii Agricolae*) make any reference to such a practice occurring in Gaul or Britain, although Diodorus Siculus did refer to Gauls 'cutting off, according to their custom, the heads of the dead' after defeating the Roman army outside Rome in 386 BC[345], whilst Polybius mentioned Celtic auxiliaries betraying their Roman counterparts and killing them before cutting off their heads[346].

There is much more evidence in literary sources for decapitation being sanctioned by the Romans themselves, especially in military contexts, with Caesar referring to the heads of dead enemies being fixed upon swords and lances by his Gaulish troops[347], and Livy writing of enslaved conscripts being so preoccupied with decapitating the bodies of the enemy to gain their freedom that they stopped fighting[348]. Heads of the corpses of deposed leaders and rebels were often chopped off by Roman soldiers and paraded around on lances before being sent to Rome[349].

Some of these references provide interesting details on how and when heads were cut off. Lucan wrote that Pompey's head was removed before he had drawn his last breath, with his assailant 'severing the neck sinews and hacking clumsily at the bones'[350] and then impaling it on a javelin, 'though the features still worked, the lips still moved and the open eyes were still unglazed',[351] whilst Galba's head was also cut off when he was 'still half alive'[352].

Decapitation was also recorded as the method of decimation for a treacherous legion ('down on the ground, traitors – prepare to lose your heads!'[353]) and as a form of execution for Christian martyrs and other criminals, as long as they were Roman citizens[354] or, after 211 AD, when citizenship was extended to everyone in the empire[355], *honestiores* (senators, soldiers and others in the service of the emperor and members of municipal councils and their families)[356]. A single member of the imperial family, Constantius Gallus, was also subjected to execution by decapitation in the fourth century AD, whereby he had his 'hands bound up, after the fashion of a convicted thief, and he was beheaded; then his face and head was mutilated'[357]. The weapon to be used was specified as a sword[358], although Eusebius records that some martyrs were 'slain with the axe, as in Arabia'[359], and the families of the executed were permitted to recover the body for the purposes of burial[360]. Careful burial of the corpse and head of decapitated individuals is also referred to in the *Alia Acta*, a twelfth-century translation by William the Monk of St Albans of a purported late sixth-century text on the martyrdom of Saint Alban, in which his head is described as being 'devoutly placed beside his body' in a specially dug burial pit[361].

There are also depictions of Roman military personnel engaging in the decapitation of their enemies on Trajan's Column, including depictions of decapitated heads being presented to the Emperor, auxiliary troops carrying severed heads whilst in battle, and heads impaled on poles outside Roman fortifications[362]. The Great Trajanic Frieze and the Column of Marcus Aurelius also include images of decapitated heads being presented to the Emperor by auxiliary troops[363], whilst the Column of Marcus Aurelius and the Tropaeum Adamklissi depict decapitations taking place[364]. The Portonaccio sarcophagus also appears to show a severed head wearing a helmet surmounted on a trophy[365], whilst there is a Republican coin of M. Sergius Silus (in office 116-115BC) that shows a cavalryman with a sword and severed helmeted head held in his left hand[366].

Martyrdom by decapitation is apparently depicted in a relief from a column in the catacombs of Domitilla in Rome which shows Achilleus hanging on a cross whilst another figure holds a curved sword to his throat[367], and is also the subject of an interesting inscription, again from the catacombs, this time at Nepi, near Rome, discovered in 1540. Inscribed above one of the graves cut into the rock walls was the phrase '*martyrio coronatus capite truncates iacet*' (he lies beheaded and crowned with martyrdom)[368]. There is also a body of data on the intentional decapitation of imperial statuary of deposed or hated rulers (*damnatio memoriae*, see chapter 1), including two decapitated heads from bronze statues of Nero and heads from statues of Plautilla, Macrinus, Severus Alexander, Gordian and Trajan Decius, some of which were thrown into rivers or wells, as well as the attempted decapitation of a statue of Caligula with evidence for deep chisel gouges around the base of the neck[369].

In contrast to the absence of any literary evidence for decapitation in Britain, there is a small corpus of evidence from statuary and portable objects, including a stone distance slab from Bridgeness, West Lothian, depicting a cavalryman in full armour trampling four naked Britons, one of whom has been bound and decapitated[370], and a tombstone of another cavalryman from Lancaster, brandishing his sword and holding in his other hand the severed head of his opponent, whose body is slumped beneath the horse's hooves[371]. A second tombstone, of the cavalryman Aurelius Lucianus from Chester, depicts his groom displaying the severed and preserved head of an enemy[372]. A copper-alloy knife handle from South Kesteven, Lincolnshire, depicts three figures in an erotic scene, two of which are definitely male, with one of the males holding a severed human head in his arms[373]. Perhaps the most interesting example of the depiction of decapitation in Romano-British statuary is the tombstone of a soldier that was reused in the bastion of the city wall of London at Camomile Street, Bishopsgate, with the head removed and placed at the feet[374].

There is also limited evidence for decapitation in British Iron Age iconography, with Sueno's Stone, Moray (from the post-Roman Scottish Iron Age), depicting a battle scene with rows of headless corpses and a pile of human heads[375]. There are also a number of chalk figurines from Garton Slack, East Yorkshire, that have been beheaded, seemingly deliberately[376]. Similar figurines were also found at Harpham Villa and Blealands Nook, both in East Yorkshire, as well as at Maiden Castle,

Dorset[377]. There is also a coin of Cunobelinus showing a male figure holding a club or sceptre in his left hand and a severed human head in his right[378].

Iron Age sites in the South of France also have iconographic evidence for decapitation, including a pottery sherd from Clermont-Ferrand depicting a warrior on horseback with a spear in one hand and a severed head hanging from the neck of his horse[379]; a coin of Dubnorix from the Dijon area, showing a figure holding a decapitated head in their left hand[380]; pillars and lintels carved with niches to receive human crania at Roquepertuse; and a pillar from Entremont carved with decapitated heads and a seated warrior figure holding severed heads in his hands and on his lap[381].

In order to find any references to post-mortem decapitation and why it may have been carried out, it is necessary to look at medieval sources – for example, the *Life and Miracles of Saint Modwenna* by Geoffrey of Burton, who wrote about the ghosts of two recently buried peasants returning to their village of Stapenhill, Derbyshire, and causing sickness and death amongst the inhabitants. In order to stop the haunting, the graves were reopened and the heads of the corpses cut off and placed between their legs[382]. Decapitation with a spade and re-interment was the response ordered by Bishop Foliot in a case from Hereford, recorded by Walter Map, of a man who had returned from the dead and caused all those whose names he called to die within three days[383]. In Icelandic literature, the *Saga of Grettir the Strong* contains two references to bodies of revenants being decapitated and their heads being placed between their thighs to prevent their ghost from returning[384]. Saxo Grammaticus also refers to the exhumation and decapitation of an individual who caused the death of anyone who came close to their burial mound[385].

Decapitation as a means of preventing revenants from returning to haunt the living is also recorded in European ethnographic literature. In a Lithuanian tale, the body of a man who had returned as a ghost was found to be lying face down in his coffin and was decapitated by three blows, which, however, failed to prevent his ghost returning. It was only when the head was placed at the feet and the mouth filled with poppy seeds that the ghost was quietened[386]. The Romanians would, in persistent cases of vampirism, perform a very similar procedure, whereby they would cut off the head of the corpse and replace it in the coffin with the mouth filled with garlic[387], whilst the Armenians are recorded as preventing revenants by either sticking nails into the head or heart of the corpse or cutting off the head[388]. The East Prussians also advocated decapitation of the corpse with the head being replaced between the feet[389], whilst in one case, a supposed revenant, who was thought to have been responsible for a great pestilence, had their head cut off and a live dog placed in the grave with them[390]. Decapitation of the corpse to prevent the return of ghosts or vampires is also recorded in Silesia, Moravia, Hungary, Poland and Russia[391], whilst the remembrance of such a practice was recorded in Yorkshire by Atkinson in 1891, who stated that, to lay a ghost, the head was severed from the body and laid between the legs, or placed under the arm or by the side of the chest[392].

Chapter 6

Decapitation Burials from Elsewhere within the Roman Empire

Although there is a large amount of evidence in the archaeological record for decapitation in continental Europe from both earlier and later periods[393], the evidence for the Roman period is, when compared with Britain, rather slight.

In Rome itself, whilst building the Bastione di Belvedere in the nineteenth century, a skeleton was found whose head was between the legs and who had a mask or plaster cast of the head 'reproducing most vividly the features of the dead man' found where the head should have been[394]. A group of four very similar burials, dated to the third century AD, were excavated from a brick-vaulted tomb in Cumae, near Naples. In these examples, the skulls were absent but replaced in two of the burials by wax busts with glass eyes and hair on the head[395]. Elsewhere in Italy, this time dating to much earlier in the Republic (fourth century BC), three skeletons with displaced heads were excavated from tombs at Metaponto. Two of these, both adult females, had their skulls on the pelvis (Tombs 80 and 97), whilst a third adult female had the skull beyond the feet[396].

From outside Italy, there was the mature female (Burial 5) from Furfooz, Belgium, who was buried with the skull between the femorae[397], and two burials from France where an extra skull was placed into the grave with a complete, articulated skeleton. One of these (from La Brèche) had the skull placed between the femorae[398], whilst the other example (from Pouzilhac) had nails forced into the ears and the top of the cranium[399]. Eight adult male skulls, each pierced by a nail, have also recently been excavated from a third- to fourth-century church on the island of Lagonisi in Greece[400]. Van Doorselaer listed three other sites in France with decapitated burials, including d'Albert, where two sarcophagi contained decapitated burials, and Rouvroy, where one burial had the head placed between the lower limbs[401]; whilst from Germany, there was a headless individual found within a sarcophagus beneath the cathedral of

St Viktor in Xanten[402]. In Serbia, in the former area of Moesia Superior, the individual from Grave 8 at the Velika Kapija cemetery at Viminacium, dated to the third century AD, had the cranium and mandible laid on the lower limbs of the corpse[403]. It has also been reported that there were three decapitated Roman burials found in excavations beneath the cathedral of Santiago, Spain[404], although there is no reference to these burials in the source cited[405].

None of the examples described above had any osteological evidence for decapitation reported, but there are a number of cases where such analysis has been undertaken. In Modena, Italy, the partial remains of three adult males were found together on the bottom of a canal, close to a first-century cremation cemetery. The bodies were in sprawled positions, with the cranium and mandible of one individual being found between their lower legs, and with evidence for cut marks on the remains[406].

From Germany, there was an adult male (Grave 26) from Neuburg an der Donau, who was buried in a supine and extended position with the skull on the left femur, and who demonstrated chops through the left mandibular body, arch and body of C2 and arch of C3 that were directed from a postero-anterior direction[407]. From nearby, in Regensburg-Harting, the remains of thirteen individuals were recovered from two wells within a villa estate, and there was evidence they had been killed by blunt-force trauma to the cranium, with some of the individuals being subsequently decapitated and scalped[408]. Another well, this time in Jüchen, was found to contain the partial remains of a mature adult male with a chopping blow through the inferior of the arch and body of C3[409], whilst in Ellingen, a cache of three adult male skulls with attached cervical vertebrae was recovered from a small pit beneath a building. All three of the skulls had evidence for chopping blows to the cervical vertebrae, with one of them also demonstrating chops to the mandible, and, interestingly, all three also had evidence for sharp-force injuries to the left side of the cranium[410].

At Evreux, Normandy, nine individuals were recovered from a small cemetery area between the baths and theatre. All of the individuals were supine and extended in individual graves, with five of them demonstrating absence of the cervical vertebrae and skull, but with no evidence for trauma. However, the other four individuals had evidence for chopping blows to their cervical vertebrae, with one also demonstrating chops to the cranial base and mandible, although in all four cases, the head was found in correct anatomical position[411]. A mass grave from Moravia, Czech Republic, containing the remains of at least thirty-four individuals, was reported to include one young adult female with chop marks to the mandibular rami. The description of a second adolescent female from the same site, with C1-C3 and part of C4 described as being found with the displaced cranium and mandible, whilst the rest of C4 and C5-C7 were with the post-cranial remains, strongly suggests that this was also a peri-mortem decapitation[412]. A second mass grave, with the partial remains of seven adult males with evidence for traumatic sharp-force amputations of the limbs and exposure to fire was excavated from the forum of Valentia, Spain, and included one individual who had been decapitated, with the head being found between the legs[413].

From the late Roman period (fifth-sixth century AD), there is the young adult male from Canosa, Italy, buried supine in a plaster-lined tomb with the upper and lower left limb flexed and with the cranium and mandible rotated to the right with the base of the cranium resting on the bottom of the tomb. The individual displayed a single chop that severed the left mastoid and chopped through the left mandibular ramus, the left inferior facet of C1, and the odontoid process and superior surface of the arch of C2, before cutting into the left side of the maxilla. The blow was delivered from the posterior and superior left with the victim's head rotated and with his mouth open. There was also evidence that the individual had been scalped, and he displayed evidence for probable defensive injuries to the left distal upper limb, arrow injuries to the cranium, and stab wounds to both tibiae, which suggested that the individual had been killed in combat[414].

Execution was posited as the explanation for a cranium from a Roman-period mass grave in Nubia that had the left mastoid process and occipital condyle severed by a chopping blow[415], and this was also the favoured interpretation for the final examples of the practice found outside Britain, which were identified amongst skeletal remains from Israel. The first of these is a cervical vertebra with evidence for a 'sword blow' found amongst commingled remains in a ritual bath at Horvat 'Ethri, which were suggested to have been evidence for the slaughter of the inhabitants by the Romans during the Bar Kokhba Revolt[416], whilst the remainder were found amongst the remains in ossuary burials. The first of these was from Tomb D at Mont Scopus, Jerusalem, and was a mature adult male, decapitated with two chopping blows through the inferior arch of C3 and the superior arch and body of C5, both of which were delivered from the posterior[417]. A mandible and C2 from Giv'at ha-Mivtar, probably from an adult female, demonstrated a chop through both rami and the odontoid process that were probably delivered from the posterior with the neck hyperflexed[418], whilst a mandible and four cervical vertebrae from three separate crypts in the tombs of Ein Gedi demonstrated clear chop marks that penetrated through the entire element, although the blows were, in these cases, directed from an antero-posterior direction[419].

These small numbers of examples of decapitation from the Roman period outside Britain seems to indicate that the 'typical' form of decapitation burial was largely localised to Roman Britain. A large number of these examples are of isolated skull deposits, or articulated skeletons found in non-normative burial locations, and in this sense, they much more closely resemble the evidence for decapitation in earlier periods, and may suggest some degree of continuity that is largely absent in the British material. In cases where the burial resembles those in Britain, it may be evidence for the spread of the practice, but the scarcity of examples from continental Europe may suggest that it originated in Britain, rather than being introduced by immigrants from continental Europe who were reluctant to give up their local customs and practices.

Chapter 7

Decapitation in the Early Medieval Period

The evidence for decapitation in the early medieval period in Britain was secondary only to the Romano-British period in the number of sites and individuals represented, with a total number of 387 individuals from 129 sites. Decapitated or possibly decapitated individuals were identified in attritional cemeteries (91 sites with 142 individuals), execution cemeteries (19 sites with 146 individuals) and isolated burials, settlement sites and mass graves (19 sites with 99 individuals). The evidence for decapitation from each of the different types of site are discussed below with comparisons made between the decapitations in order to determine whether there are any differences between the types of individuals affected and the methods used in each category of site.

Attritional Cemeteries
This type of site is defined as a cemetery in which individuals of all ages and both sexes were buried with no evidence for selective burial based on age or sex. There were 91 such sites where possible decapitation burials were identified, with a total of 142 affected individuals. The majority of these sites have been dated to between the fifth and eighth centuries AD, with a few sites, such as Wasperton, Warwickshire, and St John's, Worcester (discussed in chapter 3), showing evidence for continuity in the use of the cemetery and the occurrence of decapitation burials from the late Romano-British period. The cranium and mandible were recorded as being displaced from correct anatomical position in just under forty-eight per cent of cases, whilst they were absent in forty per cent of examples and in correct anatomical position in just under nine per cent. The remaining few examples were deposits of isolated crania and mandibulae.

The numbers of males, females and non-adults affected by decapitation were compared with a pooled sample of early medieval cemetery populations from Wessex, which can be assumed to represent the numbers of males, females and non-adults that would be expected in the wider cemetery population[420]. This showed that there were significantly more adult males and significantly fewer adult females amongst the decapitated sample than in the wider population, whilst the numbers of non-adults in the decapitated sample was not significantly different to that in the wider sample.

The decapitated sample from which a more accurate estimation of age could be made was very small, with only seven individuals where this was the case. Of these, one was an older child, two were young adults and the remaining four were middle adults. There were no mature adults amongst the decapitated sample. When the age profile of the decapitated sample and the wider population[421] were compared, although the decapitated sample was too small to provide any meaningful statistical analysis, it was found that the age profiles in the two samples, with the exception of the 'child' category, were very different.

When the burial practices in the decapitated and wider sample[422] were compared, it could be seen that individuals within the decapitated sample were significantly more commonly buried in a prone position and significantly much less likely to have been provided with a coffin than the rest of the population. Indivuduals within the decapitated sample were also less likely to have been provided with objects than the wider population, although this is not quite statistically significant.

Examples of previously reported decapitated burials from attritional cemeteries included two individuals, one male and one female, from the eighth-century cemetery at Winnall, near Winchester. The old middle adult female (SK11) was buried on her left side with the right lower limb flexed and the left lower limb extended. The cranium and mandible were found in correct anatomical position, but the upper two cervical vertebrae were displaced in front of the face with no obvious sign of disturbance to the grave. The young middle adult male (SK23) was supine and extended with the cranium and mandible absent and, although there was some evidence for animal burrowing, this was not thought to have been responsible for the loss of the cranium and mandible, with the suggestion being made that the body had been buried headless[423]. Both of these burials were stated in the original publication to have been decapitated before interment, although caution was advised in the case of SK11, and they have been recorded as examples of the practice in the recent synthesis by Andrew Reynolds[424]. Both individuals were subjected to a detailed skeletal analysis as part of this research and it was found that three cervical vertebrae were absent from SK11, whilst SK23 was missing the cranium, mandible, first two cervical vertebrae and both clavicles, as well as displaying fragmentation of the ribs and scapulae. There was no evidence for peri-mortem trauma to either individual. It has recently been suggested that both of these graves may have been reopened in antiquity in order to move the corpse of SK11 (offering a possible explanation for the unusual body position) and to remove the head of SK23[425], although the presence of modern scrape marks on the superior surface of the arch of C3 of this individual may suggest that the cranio-cervical skeleton was truncated rather more recently.

Another case where it was stated in the original publication that decapitation had occurred was a double burial of two adult males (Grave 3) at Portway West, Andover, Hampshire, both of whom were headless[426]. These individuals were subjected to a quick visual examination as part of this research and, although the absence of the cranium and mandible were confirmed, the poor preservation of the vertebrae precluded the identification of any peri-mortem trauma.

One especially interesting site where decapitation was stated to have taken place was Red Castle, Thetford, Norfolk, where two isolated crania, mandibulae and cervical vertebrae deposits, buried in hollows lined with flint and chalk, were excavated from a cemetery where the other burials were largely complete and articulated[427]. Both crania and mandibulae were stated to display evidence of trauma to the mastoid processes, and one was also reported as displaying damage to the mandibular rami, whilst the other had damage to the occipital condyles. It was suggested that they may have been curated as decapitated heads for a time before being interred in the cemetery where they were found, based on the fact that they were much darker in colour than any of the other burials from the site. The remains were examined for this research and, whilst the damage to the cranial base, mastoid processes, mandible and cervical vertebrae was noted, this was all probably of very recent origin, as the broken bone surfaces were much paler in colour than the surrounding bone and the fracture margins were roughened and irregular. It is therefore very likely that these remains derive from disturbed and heavily truncated graves, and they certainly do not represent heads removed from the post-cranial skeleton in the peri-mortem period.

Other examples of the practice were stated to demonstrate evidence for decapitation-related peri-mortem trauma but were not available for analysis as they could not be located in the archives. These included three burials from Caistor-by-Norwich, Norfolk, reported as having had the cranium and mandible located in the area of the lower limbs, including a young adult male (SK37) who was said to demonstrate a peri-mortem fracture of the mandible[428].

Given the examples above, it is apparent that in a number of cases where individuals from attritional cemeteries in this period have been stated to demonstrate evidence for decapitation, either there is no evidence for peri-mortem trauma, the presence of trauma cannot be verified due to poor bone preservation, or the burials cannot be located in the archives because they appear to have been reburied or lost, which also makes it impossible to verify whether they had been decapitated. This was the case for twelve sites selected for analysis for this research, with only three of the individuals analysed actually demonstrating any evidence for peri-mortem trauma (this evidence is discussed below, p.124). This suggests that caution should be applied when ascribing decapitation to individuals from attritional cemeteries, unless there is definite evidence for peri-mortem trauma or the articulated cranio-cervical skeleton is obviously displaced within the grave.

Execution Cemeteries

These cemeteries have been identified as being specifically for the burial of execution victims, with evidence for shallow burial, variability in burial alignments, evidence for restraint in the position of the skeletal remains (wrists crossed behind the back), and high numbers of decapitated individuals. The cemeteries are also often located on, or adjacent to, prehistoric monuments or hundred boundaries and appear to be situated in liminal positions in the landscape (see chapter 1).

Nineteen such execution cemeteries were identified where decapitated burials were found, with a total of 146 decapitated individuals. These sites are usually dated to between the ninth and eleventh centuries AD, although one individual from Walkington Wold, East Yorkshire, has been radiocarbon dated to cal AD 655-765[429]. Heads were displaced in just under forty-eight per cent of individuals, headless burials represented twenty-three per cent of cases, seventeen per cent of deposits were of isolated heads, and heads were in the correct anatomical position in the remaining examples. Of those individuals to whom an age or sex was assigned, ninety-one per cent of individuals were adult males, seven per cent were adult females and only two per cent were non-adults.

It was rare for objects to be found with the burials, with only four cases being recorded, all of which seem to have been part of clothing or were worn or carried at the time of interment. These included an individual from Meon Hill, Hampshire (SK9), with a copper-alloy earring found adjacent to the right temporal bone, and a second individual from the same site with an iron buckle and strap end found on the pelvis and a silver coin by the right hand[430]. There was also an individual from Stockbridge Down, Hampshire (SK19), where six silver coins were found in one small area next to the torso that had probably been contained in a purse or bag[431]. There were two examples of burials being found in coffins, including an adult male from Old Dairy Cottage, Harestock, Hampshire (SK580), who, because of the presence of the coffin, was assumed to have been Romano-British in date, but was radiocarbon dated to cal AD 770-970[432]. Prone burial was relatively common, with eleven individuals being buried in this position.

In contrast to the previous category of burial, thirty-five individuals with definite evidence for peri-mortem trauma were identified (this evidence is discussed below, p.124). Eleven of these were analysed as part of the present research, whilst detailed published information by other authors was available for the remaining twenty-four individuals. These numbers could have been increased but for the impossibility of locating the skeletal remains from a probable execution cemetery at Rushton Mount, Northamptonshire, where twenty-four burials, all of which were reported as having been decapitated, were excavated during the 1960s[433]. The absence of vertebrae in the assemblage from Stockbridge Down, Hampshire, also precluded the identification of decapitation-related peri-mortem trauma in the majority of this group of individuals, although chop marks were noted on the posterior of two mandibular rami.

Isolated Burials, Deposits from Settlement Sites and Mass Graves
Decapitations from these categories of site were identified from nineteen separate locations, with ninety-nine individuals being represented. Isolated burials, which by their very nature could not be ascribed to either an attritional cemetery or execution cemetery context, were typified by the burial of a young middle adult male from Stonehenge, Wiltshire, radiocarbon dated to cal AD 600-690, who had been buried in a supine position with the cranium and mandible in correct anatomical position but twisted round in order to fit the body into the pit in which it was buried[434]; and the burial of four non-adult individuals in a boundary ditch at Fordham, Cambridgeshire, two of whom had evidence for peri-mortem trauma to the cervical vertebrae[435]. Deposits from settlement sites included

an isolated cranium from the base of a pit at Cottam, East Yorkshire, dated to cal AD 647-877, that demonstrated evidence for weathering and a perforation through the vault, both of which were used to suggest that the cranium had been displayed on a pole before it was finally interred[436]; and a pit containing the partially disarticulated remains of at least eight individuals found on the foreshore at the confluence of the Fleet and Thames in London. The individuals may have been dismembered and decapitated before burial[437], although Andrew Reynolds has stated that there was no evidence for peri-mortem trauma on any of the remains submitted for detailed analysis[438]. The majority of sites from these two categories have been dated to between the sixth and ninth centuries.

Two mass graves were identified, one of which was excavated in 2009 on the Ridgeway, Weymouth, Dorset, and dated to cal AD 910-1030. It contained forty-seven articulated decapitated heads and fifty-two post-cranial skeletons, all of which were of adolescent or adult males, with extensive evidence for decapitation-related peri-mortem trauma, as well as defensive and incapacitating injuries. The isotopic analysis of the remains indicated a varied but non-British origin for the individuals and the favoured interpretation is that they were a raiding party who were captured and executed, with some heads being retained, possibly for display. A full report on the remains has recently been published, with detailed information on the demographic profile, stature, pathologies and ante-mortem trauma of the individuals, as well as on the nature of the peri-mortem trauma associated with decapitation[439]. However, this was, unfortunately, published too late to be included in the detailed discussion of the trauma, below, or in any of the statistical analyses.

The other mass grave was discovered beneath St John's College, Oxford, and comprised the remains of between thirty-four and thirty-eight adult males who had evidence for extensive peri-mortem trauma. There were six individuals who had been at least partially decapitated, and there was evidence for charring and burning on some of the skeletal remains[440]. The remains were dated to cal AD 890-985 and isotopic analysis suggested a Scandinavian origin and diet for the individuals. It has been suggested that the burials resulted from the St Brice's Day massacre, when Danish settlers were rounded up and killed on the 13th November 1002 in response to a decree issued by Aethelred[441], although the radiocarbon date would seem to preclude this interpretation, and the recent publication on the remains suggests it was more likely to be another executed raiding party[442]. The unpublished skeletal report for this site was obtained for this research[443] and the data from it was used in the discussion of peri-mortem trauma below.

Individuals with displaced heads were the most common type of decapitation burial represented in this category with sixty-eight per cent of examples, whilst headless burials comprised eighteen per cent of the sample. The head was in correct anatomical position in ten per cent of examples, with the remaining cases being isolated head deposits. There was no evidence for a coffin in any of the burials and objects were rare, found in only four per cent of cases, whilst three per cent of the burials had been made in a prone position. Of the individuals where an age and sex was assigned, ninety-two per cent were adult males, three per cent were adult females and five per cent were non-adults. Detailed information on the peri-mortem trauma was available for eleven individuals in this category but only one was analysed as part of this research; the data on the remaining individuals was obtained from published and unpublished reports by other authors (as previously stated, the data on the individuals from the mass grave at Ridgeway Hill, Weymouth, was obtained too late to be incorporated into the detailed statistical analysis).

Comparisons between the Samples
Demographics, burial practice and position of the head
Demographics
As previously stated, the decapitated sample from the attritional cemeteries had significantly more adult males and significantly fewer adult females than the wider population. When the three decapitated samples were compared, it was found that there were significantly more adult males in the execution cemetery and isolated-burial/settlement site/mass-grave samples than in the sample from attritional cemeteries, but there was no difference between the numbers of males in the execution cemetery and isolated-burial samples. For adult females, the execution cemetery and isolated-burials sample had significantly fewer individuals than the attritional cemetery sample, but again there was no difference between the numbers in the execution and isolated burial samples. For non-adults, the execution cemetery sample, but not the isolated-burial sample, had significantly fewer individuals than the attritional cemetery sample, but there was no difference between the execution and isolated-burial samples.

More accurate estimations of age were available for seven individuals from the attritional sample, thirty-four individuals from the execution cemetery sample, and nine individuals from the isolated-burial/settlement site/mass-grave sample. The small sample sizes meant that there were no statistical differences between the samples, and so the data was pooled and compared to the data from the wider population[444].

It was found that there were statistically significantly more young adults and middle adults in the decapitated sample than in the wider population and significantly fewer mature adults.

Burial practice
The numbers were compared in each decapitated sample of individuals who had been provided with a coffin, had objects in the grave or were buried prone. There were found to be no differences between the numbers of individuals with coffins or those buried in a prone position between any of the samples. However, there were significantly fewer individuals buried with objects in the execution cemetery and isolated-burial samples compared to the attritional sample, although there was no difference between the execution cemetery and isolated-burial samples.

Placement of the head
The numbers were compared in each sample of individuals who were buried with the cranium and mandible displaced from correct anatomical position, with the cranium and mandible absent, and with the cranium and mandible in correct anatomical position, as well as those who were represented by a deposit of an isolated cranium or cranium and mandible. There were found to be no differences between any of the samples in how many individuals had the cranium and mandible in correct anatomical position, whilst the execution cemetery sample had significantly more deposits of isolated crania and mandibulae than either the attritional or isolated-burial samples. The isolated-burial sample had significantly more individuals where the head was displaced than either the execution cemetery or attritional cemetery samples, whilst headless burials were significantly less common in the execution cemetery and isolated-burial samples than in the attritional cemetery sample.

Summary of the demographics, burial practice and position of the head
• There were significantly more adult males and fewer adult females in the decapitated sample from attritional cemeteries than in the wider population.

• There were significantly more adult males and fewer adult females in the execution cemetery and isolated-burial samples than in the decapitated attritional cemetery sample.
• There were significantly fewer non-adults in the execution cemetery sample than in the decapitated attritional cemetery sample.
• There were significantly more young and middle adults in the pooled decapitated sample than in the wider cemetery population.
• There were significantly fewer burials with coffins in the decapitated sample from attritional cemeteries than in the wider population.
• There were significantly more prone burials in the decapitated sample from attritional cemeteries than in the wider population.
• There were significantly fewer burials with objects in the execution cemetery and isolated-burial samples than in the decapitated attritional cemetery sample.
• There were significantly more isolated head deposits in the execution cemetery sample.
• There were significantly more headless burials in the attritional cemetery sample.
• There were significantly more burials with displaced heads in the isolated-burial sample.

Stature, pathological conditions and peri-mortem trauma
Stature
The mean stature was calculated for each of the different decapitated samples. The males were found to range from 172.9cm to 176cm. It was only possible to calculate female stature in the execution sample, and there were only two individuals for which this could be done, with the mean stature being 172.6cm. There were no significant differences between the mean statures in any of the decapitated samples and there was also no difference between the separate and pooled mean statures for the decapitated samples (173.7cm) when compared to the mean male stature for the period (172cm[445]).

Palaeopathological analysis
A number of palaeopathological conditions were observed amongst the decapitated individuals from all three samples. The individual samples showed very few significant differences between the rates of the conditions (probably largely as a result of the very small sample sizes involved), and, as a result of this, the data was pooled and compared to

the rates in a sample of 7,122 individuals excavated from 72 sites from the early medieval period[446].

It was found that there were no statistical differences between the decapitated and wider samples in the rates of the majority of pathological conditions, including caries, periodontal disease, abscesses, enamel hypoplasia, *cribra orbitalia* and tuberculosis. However, the rates of calculus, osteoarthritis/degenerative joint disease, Schmorl's nodes, fractures and non-specific infection were all significantly greater in the decapitated sample than in the rest of the population. The higher rate of calculus may suggest that the decapitated individuals were eating a different diet to the rest of the population, although there are no equivalent rises in the rates of dental caries, periodontal disease or abscesses as may be expected if this was the case. It does, however, certainly imply that the levels of dental hygiene were poorer amongst the decapitated sample and the younger age profile of the decapitated sample may suggest a reason why this poorer dental hygiene had not yet led to correspondingly higher rates of other forms of dental disease.

The higher rates of degenerative joint disease and Schmorl's nodes imply that the decapitated sample were subjecting their joints to more wear and tear than was the norm but, again, this cannot be related to the age profile of the sample. Increased levels of physical activity also seem to be supported by the high number of individuals with evidence for enthesophytes and cortical defects, although it is not possible to compare the rates of enthesopathies in the decapitated sample with a wider population sample. That this heavy use of muscles and joints seems to have been restricted to adult life is suggested by the relatively low rates of humeral asymmetry and *os acromiale*, which, in the case of *os acromiale*, is not significantly different from that seen in the wider population. If unusual muscular loading had occurred in earlier life, these conditions could also have been expected to be higher amongst the decapitated sample.

The higher rate of fractures cannot, in contrast to the earlier periods, be ascribed to higher levels of interpersonal violence (the evidence for healed weapon trauma shows no difference between the decapitated and larger population), as there are only two individuals with rib fractures and no other examples of fractures that have a high specificity for assault. There were two individuals with compression fractures of the vertebrae, and single cases of fractures of the humerus, radius, ulna, clavicle, femur and tibia, all of which are likely to have resulted from accidental processes. This does suggest that, whatever these processes may have been, the decapitated sample had sustained more accidental fractures than the wider population, possibly because of differences in livelihood[447].

The higher rate of non-specific infection amongst the decapitated sample suggests that their health status may have been poorer, although there was no evidence for osteomyelitis or sinusitis amongst the sample and the rates of tuberculosis were not significantly different in the decapitated sample compared with the wider population. The few pathological conditions that do show significant differences between the decapitated and larger samples do suggest that the diet, health status, and activity types and levels in adult life of the decapitated sample may have been different from the norm, although other markers for diet and health status, as well as activity-related changes in non-adult life, do not show any differences.

Peri-mortem trauma
The evidence for peri-mortem trauma in the three decapitated samples was also compared, including the types of cut present, from what direction they were delivered, how many cuts were present, and whether there was evidence for decapitation-related trauma to the non-cervical skeleton, as well as cranial and post-cranial non-decapitation-related trauma. It was found that, apart from one individual who had evidence for both chopping and incised cuts, all of the individuals had evidence for chopping blows only. Blows were directed from the posterior more commonly in the execution cemetery sample, although this was not statistically significant. There were also no significant differences in the number of blows delivered, although single blows were more common in the isolated/ settlement sample and execution cemetery sample. Decapitation blows that also affected the mandible, cranium or clavicle were common amongst the sample, with no significant differences between the different groups. It was only the levels of cranial and post-cranial non-decapitation-related peri-mortem trauma in the isolated-burial/settlement site/mass-grave sample that showed significant differences to the execution cemetery sample, where no cases were recorded.

Summary of stature, pathological conditions and peri-mortem trauma
• There were no differences between the mean stature in the decapitated samples and in the wider population.
• The decapitated sample showed evidence for increased mechanical loading in adult life, a higher rate of fractures and possible evidence for

a different diet and lower health status than the rest of the population.
• All but one individual had evidence for chopping blows, delivered most commonly from the posterior in the execution cemetery sample.
• A single blow was most common with high numbers of individuals where the blows also affected the clavicle, mandible or cranium.
• The isolated-burial/settlement site/mass-grave sample had significantly more individuals with non-decapitation-related cranial and post-cranial peri-mortem trauma than the other two samples.

Types of decapitation
When the detailed information on the nature of the peri-mortem trauma recorded in the decapitated individuals was analysed closely, it became apparent that there were three different types of decapitation with different signatures. These were: 1. single chopping blows, 2. multiple chopping blows and 3. chopping blows to the cervical column associated with evidence for other cranial and post-cranial peri-mortem trauma. Each type of decapitation is described and discussed below and possible interpretations are given for how the different signatures may have been produced.

Single chopping blows
There were twenty-four individuals with evidence for this type of decapitation, comprised of one individual from the attritional cemetery sample, three from the isolated-burial/settlement site/mass-grave sample, and twenty from the execution cemetery sample. The single blow was directed from the posterior in all but three individuals, with two of these three demonstrating blows directed from the side, whilst the remaining individual demonstrated an anteriorly directed blow. Typical examples of this type of decapitation included an old middle adult male from the execution cemetery at Meon Hill, Hampshire (SK10), who was buried in a supine position but had been largely disturbed by a subsequent burial[448], and who demonstrated a chop through the superior facets and odontoid process of C2, directed from the left (plate 46); a young middle adult male from an isolated pit burial at Stonehenge, Wiltshire, who was buried supine and who had evidence for a single posteriorly directed chop through the superior of the body and arch of C4 that also chopped through the left gonion of the mandible[449]; and a young middle adult male from Bevis's Grave, Southampton, Hampshire (SK3), who was buried supine and extended with the cranium and mandible in correct anatomical

position[450], and who had evidence for a single posteriorly directed chop through the inferior of the arch of C3 and the superior of the body and arch of C4, delivered with the neck tilted to the right, that also chopped through the hyoid (figure 36, plate 47).

The cranium and mandible were found in correct anatomical position in ten individuals, suggesting that it was not considered necessary to remove the head in every case. This may suggest, as also discussed in chapter 3, that the intention of the blow was simply to kill, rather than to effect head removal. That decapitation was probably the mechanism of death in this group is also suggested by the flexed neck position of one individual, a young adult male from Meon Hill, Hampshire (SK9), with a chop through the superior of the arch and body of C6 that did not affect C5 and was directed from the posterior. This individual was buried in a supine and extended position with the wrists crossed over the abdomen[451], suggesting they had possibly been restrained. Similar upper limb and wrist positions were recorded in a further five individuals with this type of decapitation, which also contributes to the theory that decapitation is likely to have been the mechanism of death in a number, if not all, of these individuals.

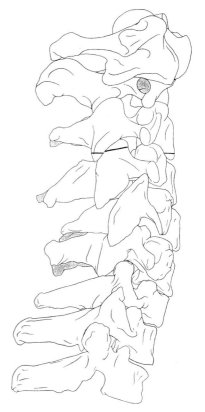

Figure 36: Chop to the cervical vertebrae of SK3 from Bevis's Grave, Hampshire.

Multiple chopping blows

There were eighteen individuals with this type of decapitation, one of whom was from the attritional cemetery sample, two from the isolated-burial/settlement site/mass-grave sample, and the remaining fifteen from the execution cemetery sample. Chops were directed from the posterior in nine individuals, with anteriorly directed chops recorded in four individuals, including both individuals from the isolated-burial/settlement site/mass-grave sample. Laterally directed chops were recorded in one individual from the execution cemetery sample, whilst chops were directed from a number of directions in four individuals, including the single individual from the attritional cemetery sample.

Six individuals had multiple chops to the cervical vertebrae but were buried with the cranium and mandible in correct anatomical position, suggesting that, even with a number of separate blows, the head was probably not completely removed by the decapitation in these individuals. These included an old middle adult male from the execution cemetery at Chesterton Lane Corner, Cambridge (SK8), with five posteriorly directed chops that affected C3 to C7[452], and both individuals from the isolated ditch burial at Fordham, Cambridgeshire: namely, an older child (HB2) who was buried supine and extended with the cranium and mandible in correct anatomical position but with the neck extended, and who had evidence for two anteriorly directed chops, one of which affected C4-C6 and one of which chopped into C1; and an older child (HB4) who was buried on the left side with the upper and lower limbs flexed, and who had two anteriorly directed chops that affected C5-C6 and T1-T2[453]. As in the examples with a single chopping blow, the fact that these multiple blows did not remove the head would suggest that the decapitation was the mechanism of death, and it was not then necessary to ensure that the head was completely separated from the post-cranial remains. This interpretation is supported by the suggestion of restraint in the body position of one individual (SK1 from Meon Hill, Hampshire) who had the lower limbs flexed, the feet together and the upper limbs behind the torso with the wrists crossed[454].

The position of the cranium and mandible in the remaining individuals indicates that the head was completely removed, and these included one individual (SK7 from Walkington Wold, East Yorkshire) where the cranium and mandible were absent and who had evidence for two anteriorly directed chops to the body of T1. There were also three individuals from the same site who were represented only by a cranium, or cranium, mandible and associated cervical vertebrae, including one (Skull 2) that had three posteriorly directed chopping blows to the occipital and parietals that must have been directed with the neck in extreme flexion[455].

Four other individuals had multiple chopping blows to the cervical vertebrae with complete removal of the head, including a young adult male from London Road, Staines, Surrey (SK454), who was buried prone and extended with the cranium and mandible between the ankles[456], and who had four separate chops to the bodies and arches of C4 and C5, all of which were directed from the posterior (figure 37, plate 48). In these individuals, it was not possible to determine whether there was a main decapitating blow with additional chops, but two individuals had evidence that the head may not have been removed by the initial blow and that additional chops were required in order to sever the remaining soft tissues, allowing the head to be completely removed. These comprised another young adult male from London Road, Staines, Surrey (SK451), buried supine and extended above another individual in a double grave, and with the cranium and mandible found in the space created by the flexed right upper limb[457], who had a chop through the superior arch of C4 directed from the posterior, as well as an anteriorly directed chop to the inferior border of the mandible (plate 49); and a young middle adult male from Meon Hill, Hampshire (SK7), with the cranium and mandible found between the femorae[458], who had three posteriorly directed chops through the arches and bodies of C3-C4 (figure 38), as well as two chops through the acromial end of the right clavicle (plate 50), one of which also chopped through the acromion of the right scapula, that were directed from the superior left. This individual was buried in a prone position with the upper limbs behind the torso and the wrists crossed, suggesting the possibility that the individual had been restrained.

The evidence of restraint, flexion of the neck and correct anatomical position of the cranium and mandible even when a number of blows had been delivered, suggests that decapitation may have been the mechanism of death in the majority of these individuals.

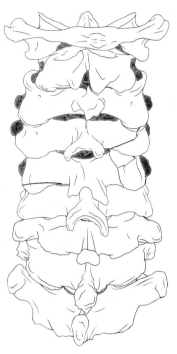

Figure 37: Chops to the cervical vertebrae of SK454 from London Road, Staines, Surrey.

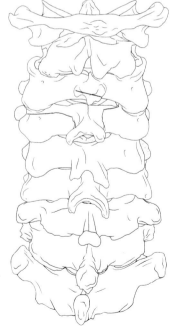

Figure 38: Chops to the cervical vertebrae of SK7 from Meon Hill, Hampshire.

Extensive peri-mortem trauma

There were seven individuals with evidence for extensive peri-mortem trauma, one of whom was from the attritional cemetery sample, with the remaining six coming from the isolated-burial/settlement site/mass-grave sample. The individual from the attritional cemetery sample was an old middle adult ?male from Great Chesterford, Essex (SK128), who was buried in a supine and extended position with the lower limbs crossed at the ankle, and with the cranium and mandible in correct anatomical position. The individual was buried with a pottery vessel at one shoulder, a glass beaker at the other, a knife at the right hip and a buckle on the pelvis[459], and had evidence for healed tuberculosis of the right hip that had completely destroyed the head of the femur. There was a single chop through the left mastoid process and two chops to the superior surface of the lateral side of the left clavicle, all of which were directed from the superior left and probably at least partially decapitated the individual, although there was no evidence of trauma to the cervical vertebrae. There were also three chops to the left side of the frontal and left parietal with associated radiating fractures, also directed from the superior left (plate 51), and a stabbing injury to the posterior and inferior margin of the right rib 12 that also nicked into the right superior facet of L1.

Five of the remaining individuals came from the mass grave found beneath St John's College, Oxford, and included a young adult male (1866) with a single chopping blow to the anterior of the arch and body of C2, two chops to the mandibular rami, five chopping blows to the frontal and left parietal, three chops to the right humerus, one to the left humerus and a penetrating injury to the anterior of the left ilium. There was also a heavily truncated adult male (1898) with a chop to the anterior and inferior of C5 that also chopped into the anterior of the left side of the mandible, as well as chopping blows to the distal left humerus and proximal radius and ulna, and puncture wounds to the cranium[460]. The peri-mortem trauma in all of these individuals, including the one from the attritional cemetery sample, could possibly represent incapacitating blows or defensive injuries, directed as they are to the cranium, abdomen, upper limbs and lower back, and, as the cranium and mandible were found in correct anatomical position in all the individuals, complete decapitation does not seem to have been an important part of the assault. The injuries to the cervical vertebrae seem almost to be incidental, with the majority of individuals found in the mass grave at St John's College, Oxford, having no evidence for injuries to the cervical vertebrae despite having extensive cranial and post-cranial peri-

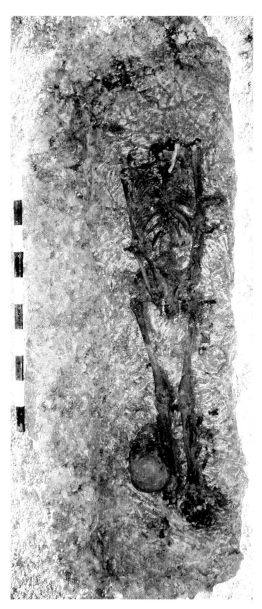

Plate 1: Decapitated burial of a mature adult male (Burial 1047) in a wooden coffin from Little Keep, Dorchester, Dorset. (image © Wessex Archaeology).

Plate 2: Decapitated burial of an old middle adult female (Burial 1069) from Little Keep, Dorchester, Dorset (image © Wessex Archaeology).

*Plate 3:
Reconstruction of
the decapitated
burial of an
adolescent/young
adult female
(SK2021) from
Great Casterton,
Rutland (drawing by
Alexander Thomas).*

Plate 4: Peri-mortem incised cuts to the first cervical vertebra of the individual from Watermead Country Park, Birstall, Leicestershire.

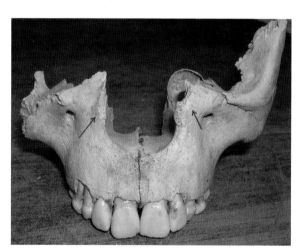

Plate 5: Rodent gnawing around the nasal aperture of Skull 1, Deposition 245 from Danebury, Hampshire.

Plate 6: Chop through the spinous process of C2 of the decapitated head (SF4002) from Prebendal Court, Aylesbury, Buckinghamshire.

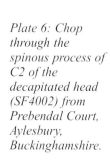

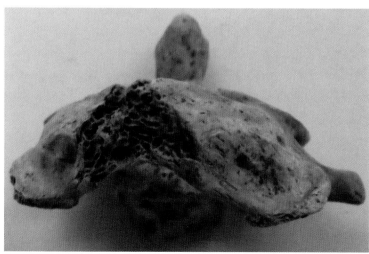

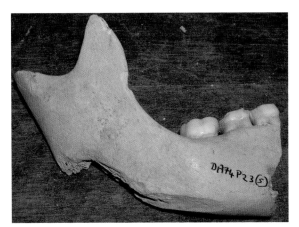

Plate 7: Peri-mortem fracture of the mandible of Skull 1, Deposition 23 from Danebury, Hampshire.

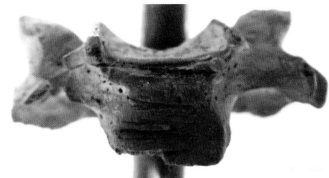

Plate 8: Incised cuts to the anterior of the body of C4 of the decapitated head from Stanwick, North Yorkshire.

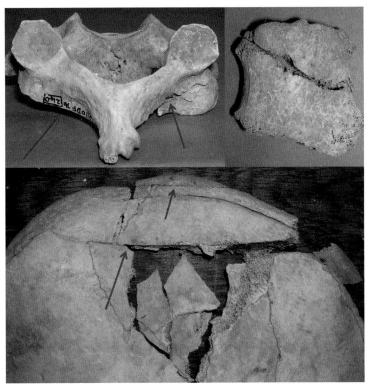

Plate 9: Peri-mortem injuries to the individual from Old Down Farm, Andover, Hampshire – clockwise from the top left: chop to the arch of C3; stab to the sternum; two chops to the left os coxa.

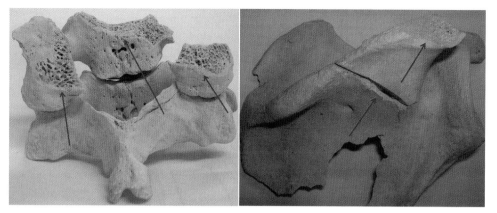

Plate 10: Peri-mortem injuries to the individual from Sovell Down, Dorset – left: chop to the cervical vertebrae; right: chops to the posterior of the right scapula.

Plate 11: Cranium from Churchill Hospital, Oxford, with multiple peri-mortem blunt-force injuries.

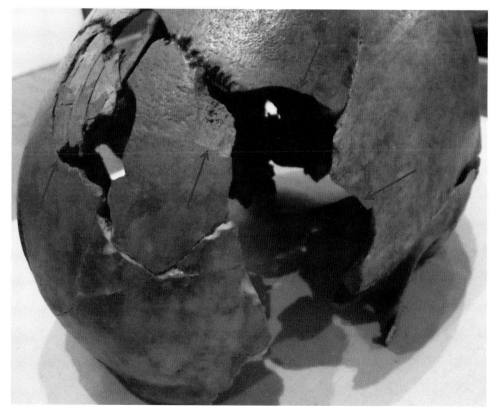

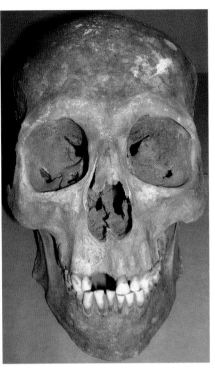

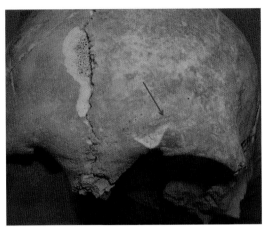

Plate 12: Ante-mortem loss of anterior dentition in SK8 from 6 Driffield Terrace, York.

Plate 13: Healed blade injury above the left orbit of SK3 from Hyde Street, Winchester, Hampshire.

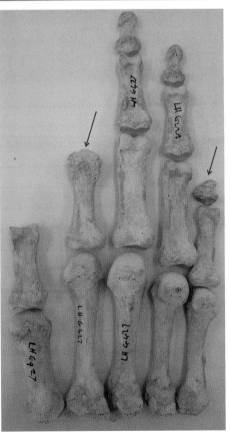

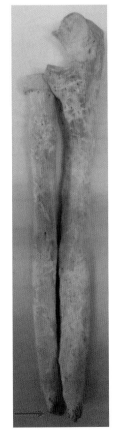

Plate 14: Ante-mortem amputation of parts of the second and fifth digits of SK427 from Lankhills, Winchester, Hampshire.

Plate 15: Ante-mortem amputation through the distal right radius and ulna of SK57 from Northbrook Avenue, Winchester, Hampshire.

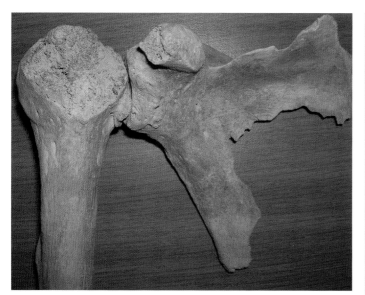

Plate 16: Ante-mortem trauma to the right humerus and scapula of skeleton BG from Dunstable, Bedfordshire.

Plate 17: Ante-mortem trauma to the left knee of SK4 from Mundford, Norfolk.

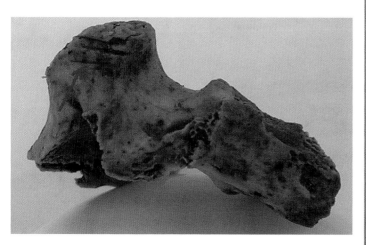

Plate 18: Incised cuts to the anterior of the articular process of C4 of SK348 from Lankhills, Winchester, Hampshire.

Plate 19: Incised cuts to the inferior and anterior of the body of C2 of SK4 from Mundford, Norfolk.

Plate 20: Incised cut to the superior surface of the body of C6 of SK47 from 1-3 Driffield Terrace, York.

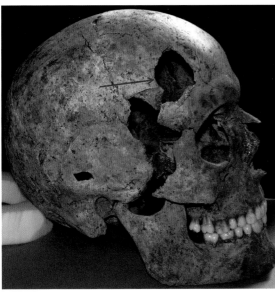

Plate 21: Blunt-force injury to the right side of the frontal of SK47 from 1-3 Driffield Terrace, York.

Plate 22: Incised cut to the anterior of the body of C5 of SK445 from Lankhills, Winchester, Hampshire.

Plate 23: Incised cut to the anterior of the body of C3 of SK3 from Hyde Street, Winchester, Hampshire.

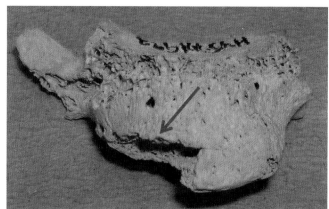

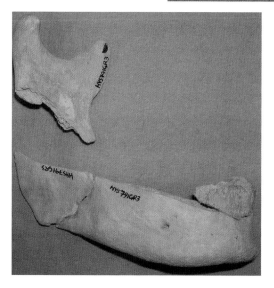

Plate 24: Chop through the mandible of SK3 from Hyde Street, Winchester, Hampshire.

Plate 25: Peri-mortem injuries to SK4 from Winchester Street, Andover, Hampshire – top: chops to the manubrium (sternum); bottom: fractures of the dentition.

Plate 26: Chops to the arch of C2 of SK6038 from Stanwick, Northamptonshire.

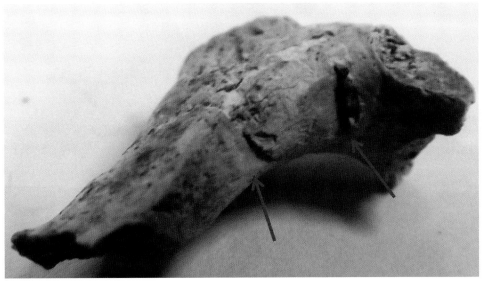

Plate 27: Chop through the arch of C7 of SK41 from 1–3 Driffield Terrace, York.

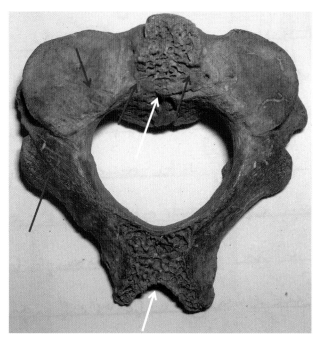

Plate 28: Chops (white arrows) and incised cuts (red arrows) to the arch, superior facets and odontoid process of C2 of SK29 from Water Lane, Towcester, Northamptonshire.

Plate 29: Chop to the right ascending ramus of the mandible, with associated peri-mortem fracturing, of SK6 from Mundford, Norfolk.

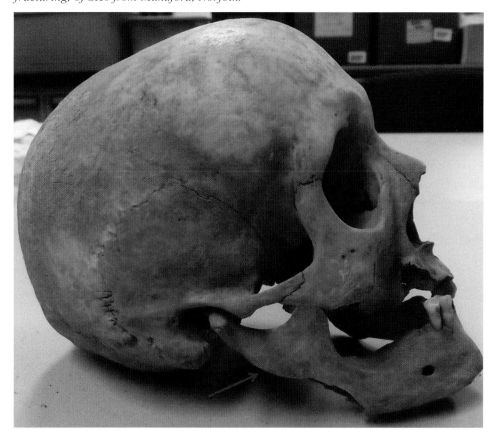

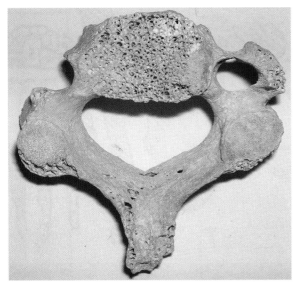

Plate 30: Chop through the inferior surface of the body and right inferior facet of C5 of SK10 from Old Vicarage, Fordington, Dorset.

Plate 31: Peri-mortem injuries to SK2 from The Mount School, York – top: chop through the arch and body of C3; bottom: chop through the inferior surface of the hyoid.

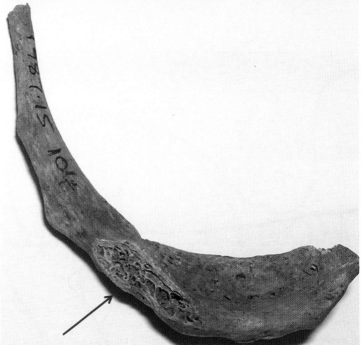

*Plate 32:
Reconstruction of the
burial of an old middle
adult male (SK16) and
a young middle adult
male (SK15) from 1–3
Driffield Terrace, York,
with the head of SK16
at the feet of SK15.
(drawing by Alexander
Thomas)*

Plate 33: Chop to the medial and distal shaft of the right femur of SK45 from 1–3 Driffield Terrace, York.

Plate 34: Stab to the posterior surface of the arch of L5 of SK18/19a from St Martin's Close, Winchester, Hampshire (the stab is partially disguised by post-mortem degradation of the bone surface).

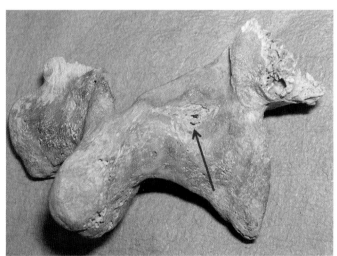

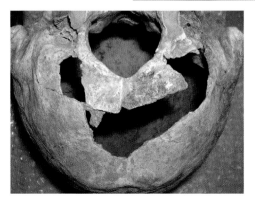

Plate 35: Ring-fracture of the cranial base of SK12 from 6 Driffield Terrace, York.

Plate 36: Reconstruction of the burial of a mature adult female (skeleton L) from Dunstable, Bedfordshire. (drawing by Alexander Thomas)

Plate 37: Peri-mortem injuries to skeleton L from Dunstable, Bedfordshire – top: incised cuts to the anterior surface of the patellae; bottom: chops through the distal shafts of the femorae.

Plate 38: Small 'scoops' of bone removed from the surface of the right clavicle of SK297 from Lankhills, Winchester, Hampshire.

Plate 39: Heavily scarred palate and ante-mortem damage of the dentition of SK33 from 1–3 Driffield Terrace, York.

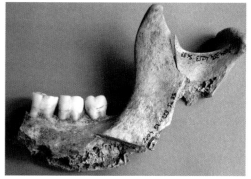

Plate 40: Multiple chops and peri-mortem fractures of the mandible of SK33 from 1–3 Driffield Terrace, York.

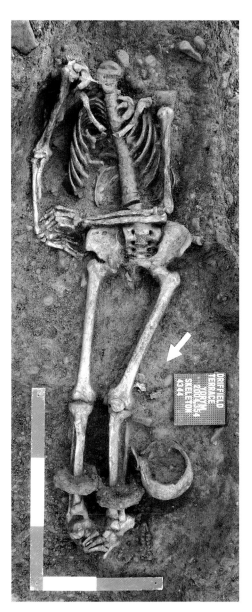

Plate 41: left: burial of an old middle adult male (SK37) from 1–3 Driffield Terrace, York, showing the unusual position of the hands and the shackles around the distal lower limbs (image © York Archaeological Trust); right: reconstruction drawing of the same burial. (drawing by Alexander Thomas)

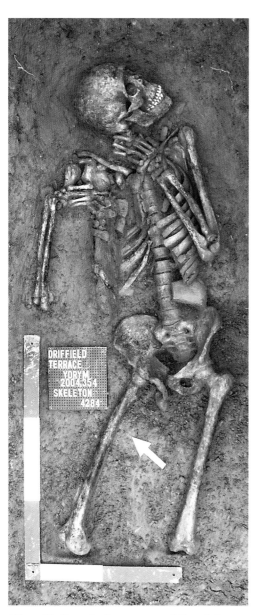

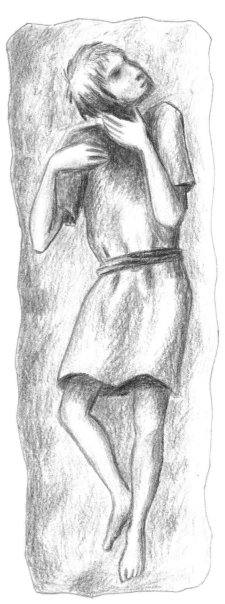

Plate 42: Burial of a young middle adult male (SK31) from 1–3 Driffield Terrace, York, showing the unusual position of the left hand. (image © York Archaeological Trust)

Plate 43: Reconstruction drawing of the burial in plate 42. (drawing by Alexander Thomas)

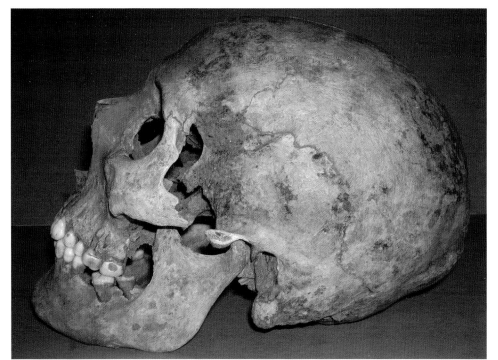

Plate 44: The cranium and mandible of SK15 from 6 Driffield Terrace, York, with possible microcephaly.

Plate 45: Carnivore tooth-mark on the posterior surface of the os coxa of SK19 from 6 Driffield Terrace, York.

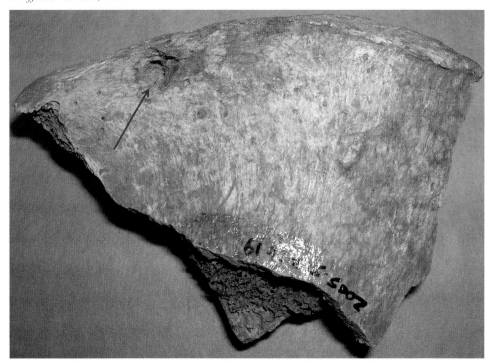

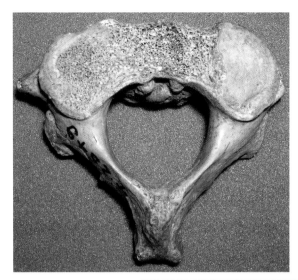

Plate 46: Chop through the odontoid process and superior facets of C2 of SK10 from Meon Hill, Hampshire.

Plate 47: Chop through the hyoid of SK3 from Bevis's Grave, Hampshire.

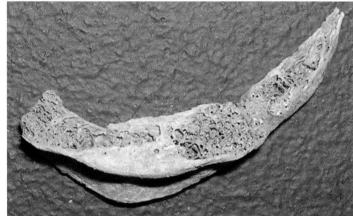

Plate 48: Chops through the arch and body of C5 of SK454 from London Road, Staines, Surrey.

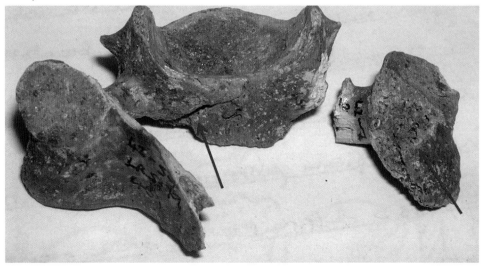

Plate 49: Chop through the inferior border of the mandible of SK451 from London Road, Staines, Surrey.

Plate 50: Chops to the right clavicle of SK7 from Meon Hill, Hampshire.

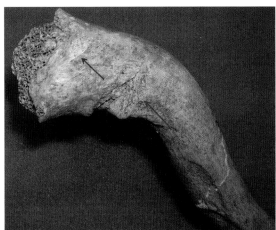

Plate 51: SK128 from Great Chesterford, Essex – left: tuberculous destruction of the head of the left femur; right: chops to the cranium.

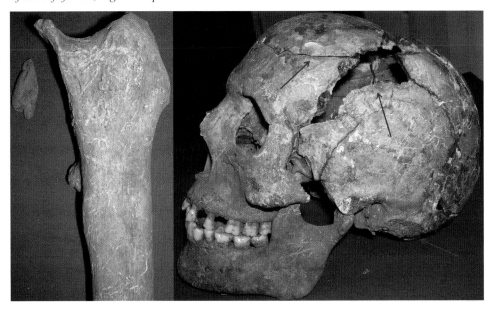

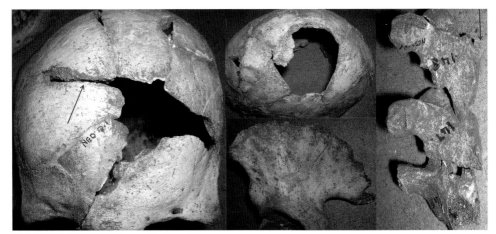

Plate 52: Peri-mortem injuries to Q1 from Maiden Castle Long Mound, Dorset – left: chop to the frontal; top middle: chop to the left parietal; bottom middle: chop to the left os coxa; right: vertical chop through the arches of the thoracic vertebrae.

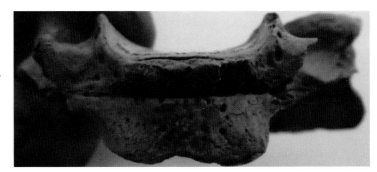

Plate 53: Chop to the anterior surface of the body of C5 of SK50 from Fishergate, York.

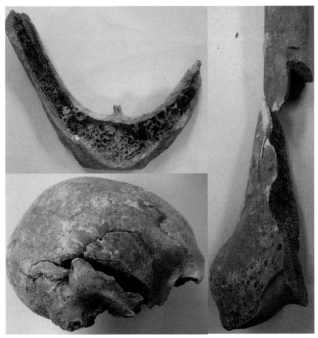

Plate 54: Peri-mortem injuries to SK171 from North Elmham, Norfolk – top left: chop through the mandible; bottom left: chop to the right parietal and temporal; right: chop to the lateral and distal shaft of the left femur, with associated peri-mortem fracturing.

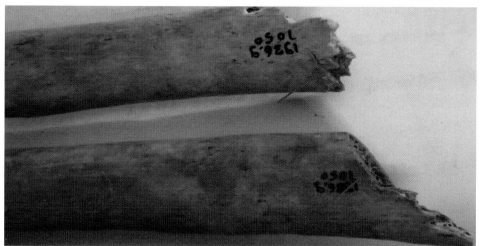

Plate 55: Stab to the lateral side of two left ribs of SK41 from Fishergate, York.

Plate 56: Peri-mortem fracture of the shaft of the right fifth metacarpal of SK65 from George Street, York.

Plate 57: Peri-mortem butterfly fracture of the midshaft of the ulna of SK3 from 6 Driffield Terrace, York.

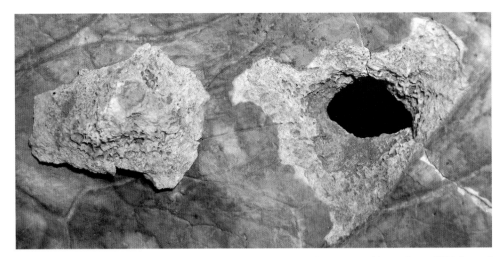

Plate 58: Peri-mortem endocranial bevel with detached fragment of bone from SK4 from 6 Driffield Terrace, York.

Plate 59: Peri-mortem chops to the humerus of Q1 from Maiden Castle Long Mound, Dorset, showing fine striations running parallel to the direction of the blow.

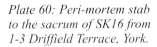

Plate 60: Peri-mortem stab to the sacrum of SK16 from 1-3 Driffield Terrace, York.

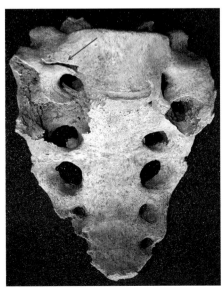

mortem trauma. The presence of this extensive peri-mortem trauma in the decapitated individuals, with the focus being on incapacitating injuries, as well as the presence of defensive injuries in at least one individual, would suggest that the partial decapitation, or the other peri-mortem injuries, were the mechanism of death.

The final individual from this category was an extremely interesting case and seems to represent an entirely different phenomenon. This was a young middle adult male (Q1) excavated from the Long Mound at Maiden Castle, Dorset, who was found partially disarticulated with some elements and joints, including the distal lower limbs, right *os coxa* and femur, distal upper limbs, hands and wrists, and feet and ankles remaining in articulation[461]. The burial was initially thought to be Neolithic in date but the identification of sharp-force peri-mortem trauma made with a metal blade resulted in radiocarbon dating being carried out in the 1960s, which produced a date of cal AD 555-715[462]. Previous analyses had been conducted with the remains embedded in the soil matrix in which they had been originally lifted and displayed but, for the present research, permission was granted by the Dorchester Museum to remove all elements from this matrix in order to conduct a detailed skeletal analysis.

There was evidence for at least fifty chopping blows, along with two stabbing injuries, peri-mortem fractures of the dentition, and peri-mortem fractures of the shafts of the ribs. There were at least eight chopping blows and a penetrating injury to the cranial vault, as well as four chops to the endocranial surface that must have resulted from blows that penetrated completely through the vault and brain, and there also seems to have been an attempt to separate the facial skeleton from the cranial vault. A chopping blow to the posterior of the mandibular rami seems to be consistent with an attempt, however successful, at decapitation, and there are numerous chopping blows to both pectoral girdles and upper limbs, with complete separation through the elements and skeletal regions in at least five places. There are also similar chopping injuries to the lower limbs and pelvis with severance at five locations. The pelvis and spinal column had also been chopped through vertically, with horizontal chopping blows through the lower lumbar vertebrae and superior surface of the ilia also present, whilst the rib cage had been opened, resulting in fractures to the posterior shafts (figure 39, 40, 41, plate 52, 59).

The severing of the limbs, decapitation, and vertical and horizontal separation of the torso into segments was also recorded in an individual from Hulton Abbey, Staffordshire, dated to cal AD 1215-1385 and interpreted as

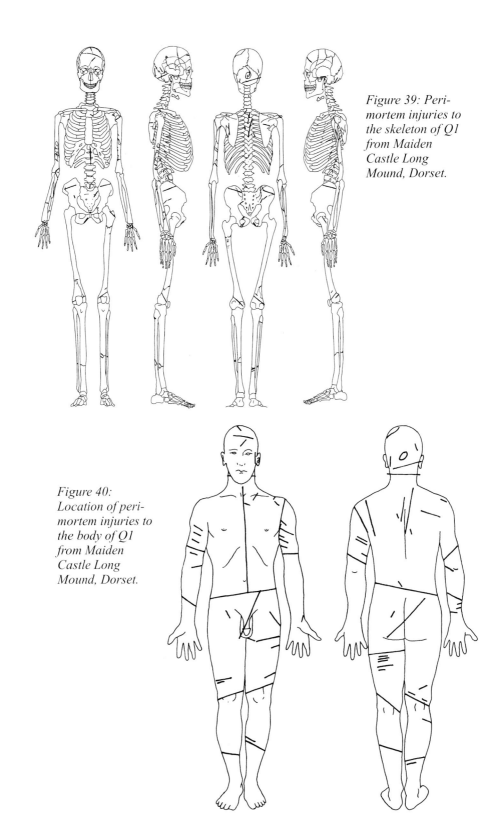

Figure 39: Peri-mortem injuries to the skeleton of Q1 from Maiden Castle Long Mound, Dorset.

Figure 40: Location of peri-mortem injuries to the body of Q1 from Maiden Castle Long Mound, Dorset.

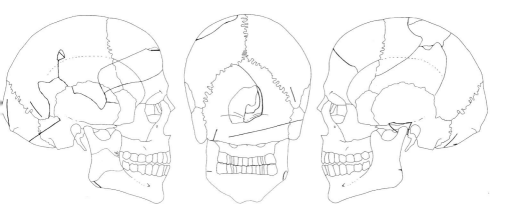

Figure 41: Peri-mortem injuries to the cranium and mandible of Q1 from Maiden Castle Long Mound, Dorset.

representing an individual who had been subject to hanging, drawing and quartering (described in detail in chapter 8)[463]; it is very possible that a similar process was responsible for the peri-mortem injuries in the individual from Maiden Castle.

Summary of the data on the types of decapitation
• There were three different categories of decapitation from this period: namely, 1. single chopping blows, 2. multiple chopping blows and 3. extensive peri-mortem trauma including decapitation.
• Examples of the first two types of decapitation were found in all three samples.
• Examples of the third type were found in the attritional cemetery sample and the isolated-burial/settlement site/mass-grave sample.
• In the first two types of decapitation, removal of the head does not seem to have been necessary in all cases, which suggests the decapitation was the mechanism of death in these individuals.
• In the first two types of decapitation, there was evidence for flexion of the neck and restraint in the position of the body in some cases, suggesting that decapitation was the mechanism of death in these individuals.
• In the third type, decapitation appears to have been largely incidental, with the majority of peri-mortem injuries appearing to be incapacitating and defensive injuries and suggesting that decapitation was the mechanism of death in these individuals.
• The peri-mortem trauma in the individual from Maiden Castle appears to have been related to quartering and decapitation of the body, indicating that this was likely to have been the mechanism of death.

Discussion

The analysis of the evidence for peri-mortem trauma amongst the decapitated burials from this period, as well as the evidence for restraint in the position of the body, has indicated that decapitation was either the probable mechanism of death in the majority of individuals, or it was an incidental part of a more extensive suite of peri-mortem injuries that were also very likely to have led to death. This supports the thesis of previous researchers (see chapter 1) that, where decapitated individuals are found in specific 'execution cemeteries', decapitation was the method of execution used. The nature of the decapitation-related trauma is also very similar to that previously reported, with posteriorly directed chopping blows, and associated injuries to the cranium, mandible, claviculae and scapulae in a large number of individuals. However, it is interesting that, although the numbers are very small, individuals showing evidence for decapitation from attritional cemeteries and isolated burials and settlements also demonstrate this type of decapitation, which may suggest that these burials also result from some form of judicial punishment.

Where radiocarbon dates are available, the attritional cemeteries in which decapitated burials are found date to between the fifth and eighth centuries, with a number of the isolated burials and deposits from settlement sites also having a similar date range, whilst the majority of execution cemeteries seem to have been in use from the ninth to the eleventh centuries, although the dates from Walkington Wold, East Yorkshire, suggest that some sites came into existence as early as the seventh century. This suggests that prior to the establishment of specific burial locations, decapitated, and therefore possibly executed, individuals were being accorded burial in attritional cemeteries or were being buried in isolation but that this ceased once these execution cemeteries had come into existence.

It is also interesting to note that a number of the isolated burials, and both of the mass graves with evidence for decapitation, are associated with boundaries or earlier man-made landscape features, with the mass grave from Oxford being on the site of a Neolithic henge monument[464], whilst the most obvious examples are the isolated burials at Stonehenge and Maiden Castle. This placement on or alongside boundaries or earlier landscape features is something that Andrew Reynolds has noted for a number of the execution cemeteries[465]. The association between monuments and sites of execution is also depicted in the early eleventh-century Harley Psalter, with one scene showing three decapitated male bodies on, or within, a mound. The same scene shows decapitations in the process of being carried out, using both an axe and a sword, and the position of the body (flexed at the pelvis but with the neck straight, also shown in other medieval depictions of decapitation, or upright with the neck extended) may explain why there are very few cases of analysed individuals where the decapitation seems to have been carried out with the neck flexed[466].

Although Andrew Reynolds[467] has suggested that decapitated burials in the earlier attritional cemeteries resulted from 'superstitious motives' and were probably undertaken in the post-mortem period, the very small number of individuals with recorded evidence for decapitation-related trauma makes this very difficult to assess, and where peri-mortem trauma has been recorded, it is of an identical nature to that seen amongst the later 'execution' burials. It is unfortunate that in the two cemeteries in which there is definite evidence of continuity in burial and decapitation from the Romano-British period into the early medieval period (Wasperton, Warwickshire, and St John's, Worcester), poor bone preservation has precluded the identification of peri-mortem trauma, making it impossible to determine whether the method of decapitation also showed evidence of continuity. However, it has already been demonstrated in chapter 3 that there is evidence in many Romano-British burials that decapitation may also have been the mechanism of death, potentially making an interpretation of post-mortem decapitation in burials from early medieval attritional cemeteries less tenable.

Within the attritional cemeteries, decapitations were more likely to have had the head absent than in the other samples and this may suggest that the cranium and mandible were being removed in order that they could be displayed in other locations. This is suggested by the isolated cranium found at the base of a pit at Cottam, East Yorkshire, with evidence for weathering and a perforation through the vault, suggesting it had been displayed above ground for a period before being buried in the pit[468], as well as the discovery of three crania and mandibulae, with associated cervical vertebrae that had evidence for sharp-force trauma, in a chalk pit at Heytesbury, Wiltshire[469]. However, in this case, the fact that they were excavated in an articulated state suggests that if they were displayed, it cannot have been for an extended period. However, isolated crania were still very rare amongst the isolated-burial/settlement site sample, suggesting that many of the heads removed from burials in the attritional cemeteries have never been located. However, there is also the possibility that they were being reburied in the same, or another, cemetery (the isolated cranium and mandible of an adult female, unfortunately never subjected to skeletal analysis, accompanied by a copper-alloy pin and pottery vessel, was excavated from a stone-lined feature within the cemetery at Bidford-on-Avon, Warwickshire[470]).

Isolated crania and headless post-cranial remains were relatively common in execution cemeteries (although the majority of burials had their cranium and mandible displaced from correct anatomical position) and there is evidence, especially from Walkington Wold, East Yorkshire, that the crania may have belonged to the post-cranial skeletons that were also found, but had, in the majority of cases, been displayed for an extended period of time, allowing the mandibulae and cervical vertebrae to detach from the cranium[471]. This is very interesting in the light of the discovery of an execution cemetery at Harestock, near Winchester, Hampshire – the derivation of the name 'Harestock' being the Saxon *heafod stocc*, which has been suggested to refer to stakes set up on boundaries of ploughlands[472] or to groups of pollarded trees[473], but has more generally been accepted to refer specifically to places where the heads of criminals were displayed on posts or stakes[474]. However, there were no isolated heads found amongst the excavated burials at this particular site.

In all three decapitated samples, there were more males present than females and non-adults, and there was a total absence of mature adults. The lower numbers of adult females and non-adults would also support the theory that decapitation was the mechanism of death, although females and non-adults were not totally excluded from the practice (the tenth-century Laws of Aethelstan state that anyone over the age of twelve would be put to death for stealing[475]). The fact that decapitated individuals from attritional cemeteries were significantly less likely to have been buried in a coffin and significantly more likely to have been buried in a prone position than the wider cemetery population (the percentages of prone decapitated individuals in attritional and execution cemeteries are very similar), as well as having fewer objects in the grave (objects and coffins also being very rare amongst the execution and isolated burials), also suggests that they were being treated differently to the rest of the individuals in the cemetery, something which may also support the idea that decapitation was the mechanism of death. The possibility that individuals who were subject to decapitation may have been different to the rest of the population is also suggested by the evidence that they had poorer dental hygiene, a poorer health status in adult life, increased mechanical loading and more wear and tear on their joints, as well as a higher rate of fractures.

These differences could possibly be a reflection of the lower social position of those individuals generally subject to capital punishment (theft, fighting and attacks on property are all listed as capital crimes in the ninth- and tenth-century law codes[476]), although this is not to say that those amongst the higher social orders could not also have been decapitated[477]. However, in cases where kings and nobles were decapitated after they had been defeated in battle or murdered, bodies and heads appear to have been disposed of in marshes or rivers[478], in undergrowth[479], or fixed to posts[480], although a number were later retrieved for burial in churches or monasteries[481]. It is not known whether any such high-ranking individuals would have been decapitated and then buried at specific sites of execution.

The evidence obtained from the skeletal remains of decapitated individuals from this period, including those from mass graves, which has been discussed in detail above, will be compared with that from other periods in chapter 9. The possibility that the decapitations were the result of judicial execution will be discussed in the light of evidence from other periods in chapter 10.

Chapter 8

Decapitation in the Medieval and Early Post-medieval Periods

There were only a very small number of sites from these two periods that had evidence for possible or definite decapitation burials, with forty individuals from twenty-six sites dating to the medieval period, and thirteen individuals from ten early post-medieval sites. Of those individuals where a biological sex was assigned, thirty-three (just under ninety per cent of the total) were adult males, with two adult females and two non-adults also present. The cranium and mandible were found in correct anatomical position in twenty-three cases (just under forty-nine per cent of the total), with headless burials and burials with the cranium and mandible displaced representing just under twenty per cent each (nine in each case), with the remaining cases represented by isolated deposits of crania and mandibulae. Decapitated individuals were identified from within cemetery assemblages (twenty-nine individuals, and just under fifty-seven per cent of the total), from within church buildings (eight individuals, just under sixteen per cent), from isolated burials or deposits (six individuals, just under twelve per cent), and from mass graves (eight individuals, just under sixteen per cent).

Amongst these examples of decapitation, there are a number of interesting reports, written in the nineteenth and early twentieth centuries, of non-controlled excavations in which decapitated individuals were found, including a headless skeleton from beneath a brick floor in the Saracen's Inn, Salisbury, Wiltshire[482]; a skeleton found with the cranium and mandible between the lower limbs beneath a monumental brass at Freshwater Church, Isle of Wight[483]; a coffined skeleton from beneath the floor at the church of Hooton Roberts, South Yorkshire, with one of the neck vertebrae 'cut clean in half'[484]; and a skeleton from underneath Fordington Road, Winchester, that was dated to the thirteenth century from the associated artefacts, and that had the cranium, mandible and some cervical vertebrae absent[485]. The most interesting description provided in one of these reports is that given by 'L.M.M.R' about a lead-coffined burial found in Nuneham Regis, Warwickshire, with preservation of soft tissue, hair and clothing, who had been beheaded. The head (with a peaked beard and long brown hair) had been wrapped separately in linen and placed at the neck end of the post-cranial remains, which were dressed in a linen shirt (pulled up over the stump of the severed neck) with the initials 'TB' embroidered on the front[486]. Unfortunately, the nature of these reports means that more detailed examination of the remains was not carried out at the time and none of the burials were removed from their original burial locations, making it impossible to now verify whether there was evidence for decapitation-related peri-mortem trauma to any of the individuals.

Other interesting cases where no osteological analysis appears to have been carried out, or where this data is not available, include an isolated cranium and mandible found at the level of the foundations in the chancel of Lammana Chapel, Looe, Cornwall, and 'set upright' on the mandible[487]; and the burial of an adolescent female found just outside the boundary of the churchyard at Hoo St Werburgh, Kent, who had the cranium and mandible buried by the side of the torso[488]. Other cases are said to have had no evidence for peri-mortem trauma, including a medieval burial from Whithorn, Dumfries and Galloway, with the cranium, mandible and C1-C2 found beneath the left elbow[489]; the medieval burial of a juvenile from the cemetery of St Mary Spital, London, with the cranium and mandible found at the feet[490]; and a very interesting post-medieval adult male burial, found in an isolated grave adjacent to the church at Guestwick, Norfolk, who was buried in a contorted position with the left upper limb and both lower limbs flexed, and who had the cranium and mandible placed next to the right hand, which had copper-alloy eyelets on two of the digits[491]. Unfortunately, this burial cannot now be located in the archives and it was probably reburied soon after the original analysis.

A small number of other burials have limited information available on the evidence for peri-mortem trauma, including a post-medieval adult male burial from the prison cemetery at Oxford Castle, who had been subjected to a post-mortem craniotomy as well as having had the head removed with a saw cut through the cervical vertebrae[492], before the cranium was placed into the opened rib cage[493]; a poorly preserved skeleton from St Mary Graces, London, with a posteriorly directed chop through the superior of the body and arches of C4[494]; and the isolated deposit of an adult male cranium and C1-C3 from a gulley in the grounds of Basing House, Basingstoke, Hampshire, almost certainly dated to the Civil War siege of the house, that had evidence for a sharp-force injury to the right parietal and a penetrating injury crossing the left lambdoid suture, as well as possible peri-mortem damage to C2 and C3[495].

Osteological Data

More detailed osteological information was available for a sample of twenty-one individual skeletons from eight medieval sites, twelve of which were analysed as part of this research. Of the twenty-one individuals, only one was female (an adolescent/young adult), with the rest being adult males, including three young adults, fourteen middle adults and three mature adults. The percentages of males and females and the age distribution in this sample were compared with those obtained from the published reports of six different medieval cemetery populations[496]. It could be seen that, whilst there were significantly more males and fewer females amongst the decapitated sample than in the wider population, there were no significant differences in the age distribution between the two samples.

The stature could be calculated for 19 of the decapitated individuals and the mean stature was 172.8cm, which was not statistically significantly different from the mean stature of 171cm calculated from 8,494 individuals from 34 different cemetery sites by Roberts and Cox[497].

The rates of various pathological conditions amongst the individuals were compared with the rates in the sample of six cemetery sites, mentioned above, for fractures, Schmorl's nodes and *os acromiale*, and from a sample of individuals from sixty-three cemetery sites from the period for all other conditions, which included dental disease, *cribra orbitalia*, non-specific infection, sinusitis and osteoarthritis/degenerative joint disease[498].

It was found that there were statistically significantly more individuals with dental caries amongst the decapitated sample than in the wider population. This cannot have been biased by differences in the age distribution between the two samples, as there was no evidence for this. Therefore, there is a possibility that the decapitated sample may have had access to a diet with higher levels of sucrose than was the norm for the period. There is also the possibility that the decapitated individuals had subjected their joints to higher levels of stress than the rest of the population, as the rate of degenerative joint disease was significantly higher amongst the decapitated sample. Over ninety per cent of individuals also had evidence for enthesopathies, although the rate of Schmorl's nodes was not significantly different. There also does not seem to have been any evidence that the heavy use of muscles in the decapitated sample extended back into non-adult life, as the rate of *os acromiale* showed no difference to that in the wider population, whilst humeral asymmetry was also relatively rare. Health status in adult life seems to have been lower amongst the decapitated individuals, with a much higher rate of non-specific infection, whilst ante-mortem fractures were also significantly more common amongst this sample than in the wider population.

When the evidence for peri-mortem trauma amongst the sample was analysed, it was found that all but one of the individuals had evidence for chopping blows. There were also very high numbers of individuals with evidence for non-decapitation-related cranial and non-cranial peri-mortem trauma, and blows were most commonly made from a number of directions in the same individual.

Of those individuals with detailed information available on the nature of the peri-mortem trauma, four had evidence for trauma related only to decapitation (three of these were from cemetery assemblages and one was from a mass grave), whilst the remaining seventeen individuals had evidence for extensive peri-mortem trauma (fourteen from cemetery assemblages and three from a mass grave), including individuals with chopping blows, incised cuts and stabbing injuries, located on the cranium, vertebral column, ribs, pectoral girdles, upper and lower limbs, hands and pelvis.

Decapitation-Related Trauma Only
The individual from the mass grave with evidence for this type of trauma was a young adult male from Towton, North Yorkshire (SK28), who was buried in an extended position with the cranium and mandible in correct anatomical position and who had a single incised cut to the anterior of the body of C3[499], which is likely to be related to cutting of the throat rather than a definite attempt at decapitation and which should probably be considered to be the mechanism of death in this individual. The individuals from cemetery assemblages with this type of decapitation include a young adult male from Fishergate, York (SK50), buried supine and extended with the cranium and mandible absent, probably as a result of truncation[500], who had a chop to the anterior of the body of C5, a chop

into the left superior facet of C5 from the superior left, and a chop through the inferior arch of C5 and superior arch of C6 directed from the anterior (figure 42, plate 53); and an old middle adult male from St Michael's, Thetford, Norfolk (F62), with a single posteriorly directed chop through the odontoid process of C2 and inferior facets of C1 that also chopped into the posterior of the right mandibular ramus[501].

Extensive Peri-mortem Trauma

Individuals with this type of trauma included an old middle adult male from North Elmham, Norfolk (SK171), who had evidence for at least five separate injuries to the cranio-cervical skeleton, as well as seven separate post-cranial injuries. These include two chops to C4, one directed from the anterior and one from the posterior; a posteriorly directed chop through the inferior border of the mandible that completely bisected the element (the facial skeleton including the superior part of the mandible were not recovered from the grave, suggesting they may have been completely separated from the rest of the remains prior to

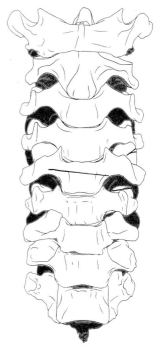

Figure 42: Chops to the cervical vertebrae of SK50 from Fishergate, York.

interment); chops to both temporals from the superior that may have been attempts to remove the ears; chops to the shaft of the left second metacarpal and corresponding proximal phalanx that are probably defensive injuries; two chops through the anterior of the manubrium; and a chop to the anterior of the distal left femur and proximal tibia with associated fracturing of the femoral shaft (figure 43, plate 54). There was also an old middle adult male from Fishergate, York (SK101), who was buried supine and extended with the cranium and mandible in correct anatomical position, and who had evidence for twelve separate injuries to the cranio-cervical skeleton, as well as two post-cranial injuries. Two of the chopping blows to the cranium cut through the maxillae and left zygomatic and the anterior left of the frontal. This part of the frontal, as well as the maxillary part of the facial skeleton, was not recovered from the grave, indicating that they had been completely separated from the rest of the individual at the time of burial (figure 44, 45).

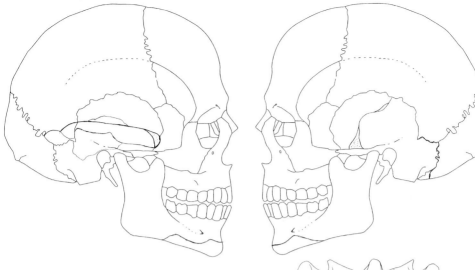

Figure 43: Chops to the cranium and mandible of SK171 from North Elmham, Norfolk.

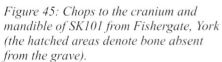

Figure 44: Chops to the cervical vertebrae of SK101 from Fishergate, York.

Figure 45: Chops to the cranium and mandible of SK101 from Fishergate, York (the hatched areas denote bone absent from the grave).

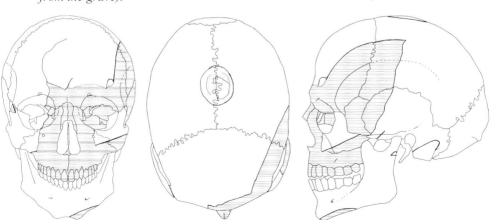

Other individuals with this type of trauma include a young adult from Fishergate, York (SK41), buried supine and extended with the cranium and mandible in correct anatomical position, who had evidence for two chops to C4 and C5; nine separate chops to the cranial vault, facial skeleton and mandible that were directed from the anterior, superior and left side; a chop to the midshaft of the left femur; a chop to the proximal shaft of the right femur; a chop to the dorsal side of one proximal hand phalanx that is probably a defensive injury; a stabbing injury to the lateral side of two left ribs; and a stabbing injury, directed from the anterior left, that penetrated through the anterior of the torso, nicked the anterior of the bodies of T4 and T5 and stabbed into the blade of the right scapula (figure 46, 47, 48, plate 55). There was also an old middle adult male from George Street, York (SK65), buried supine and extended with the cranium and mandible in correct anatomical position[502], who had three posteriorly directed chops to the arch of C2, three chops to the ribs, a chop to the transverse process of L3, a chop to the left

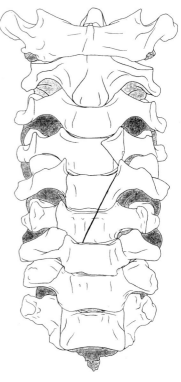

Figure 46: Chops to the cervical vertebrae of SK41 from Fishergate, York.

Figure 47: Chops to the cranium and mandible of SK41 from Fishergate, York.

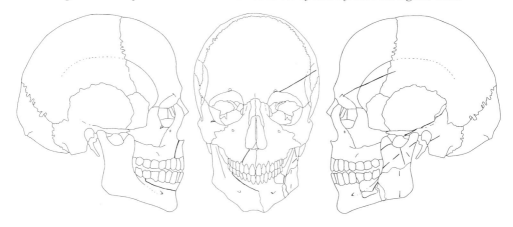

142

ilium, and peri-mortem fractures of the shaft of the right clavicle and right fifth metacarpal, likely to represent a defensive injury (plate 56). The only female from amongst the sample was an adolescent/young adult from Jewbury, York (SK2590), who was buried supine and extended with the cranium and mandible in correct anatomical position[503], and who had evidence for five separate chopping blows to the cranium and mandible, including a chop to the left mastoid and zygomatic that seems to have been an attempt to remove the ear, and a chop directed from the anterior right that cut through the maxilla and right mandibular ramus, severing the roots of the maxillary right second molar[504] and probably partially decapitating the individual.

The most interesting of the individuals with extensive peri-mortem trauma was the mature adult male from Hulton Abbey, Staffordshire (HA16), whose remains were found redeposited within the chancel of the abbey, and who had evidence for at least sixteen separate peri-mortem injuries, including chops through the body and arch of C3 and stabbing injuries to the anterior of the bodies of C7 and L2. There were also chops through the left pectoral girdle that separated the left upper limb from the torso, and chops through the distal radii, both proximal femorae and left distal fibula and tibia. There were also vertical chops through the bodies of the thoracic and lumbar vertebrae and a horizontal chop through the body of L1. These chopping

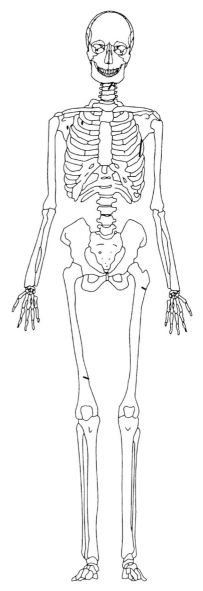

Figure 48: Peri-mortem injuries to the skeleton of SK41 from Fishergate, York

blows indicate that the individual was decapitated, and that the torso was separated into two sections, with the lower half of the body also being

143

separated from the upper half, the left upper limb and both lower limbs separated from the torso, and the hands and left foot severed from the limbs. It was interpreted as evidence for a hanging, drawing and quartering and seems to be an almost unique case[505].

Discussion

There are relatively few individuals from the medieval and early post-medieval periods with evidence for decapitation and the vast majority of these are adult males. There does not seem to have been any evidence for selection by age or stature as to who was subject to decapitation, although there is some suggestion that the decapitated individuals may have had access to a different diet and had a harder physical adult life, with more fractures and degenerative joint disease and a poorer adult health status. There seems to have been evidence for two distinctive types of decapitation in the sample, with decapitation seeming largely to have been an incidental part of the suite of peri-mortem traumata demonstrated by the majority of individuals from the period, whilst only a very small number of individuals had evidence for decapitation-related trauma with no other injuries. The fact that the cranium and mandible were found in correct anatomical position in the majority of individuals would also suggest that decapitation was incidental or, where it was the only form of trauma, that removal of the head was not an important part of the process. This may suggest that, as in the early medieval period (see chapter 7), decapitation may have been the mechanism of death, with it only being necessary to kill the individual, rather than completely separate the cranio-cervical skeleton from the rest of the remains.

In those individuals with extensive peri-mortem trauma, there were chopping blows (the most common type of cut), incised cuts and stabbing blows, with all areas of the skeleton potentially being affected. The high number of separate injuries to some individuals suggests that they were not purely defensive (although these type of injuries are present in some individuals) or incapacitating injuries, as, especially in individuals with multiple cranial injuries, it is very likely that they would have been successfully incapacitated by the first or second blow. The nature of these injuries in all individuals, regardless of their burial location, would suggest that they have a martial context, something that is confirmed by the burial location of four of the individuals, namely, in a mass grave of thirty-six adult males at Towton, North Yorkshire. These burials can safely be assumed to be directly associated with the Battle of Towton that took place in 1461 and claimed the lives of between twenty and thirty thousand combatants[506]. Very similar peri-mortem injuries were recorded in a group of twenty-two adult male individuals from the cemetery associated with the priory of St Andrew at Fishergate, York[507], nine of which were reanalysed as part of this research. In the past, these burials have been associated with the Battle of Fulford in 1066[508], although the original report does state that they are from at least three separate phases of burial[509]. They are, therefore, more likely to have been associated with smaller episodes of conflict between the later eleventh and fourteenth centuries, although it is possible that some of the burials from the earliest phase may indeed relate to the battle. The adult male individual from George Street, York, is also possibly a battle victim, as the traumata are located on the upper limbs, hands, vertebral column, ribs and pelvis, although there are no peri-mortem cranial injuries. This individual could also have been the victim of a less formalised type of interpersonal violence, which may also account for the cranial peri-mortem injuries in the adolescent/young adult female from Jewbury, York, further supported by the fact that the injuries in this individual were focused on the cranium[510]. In all these individuals with multiple peri-mortem traumata, it is probably safe to assume that the injuries were the mechanism of death, with decapitation being an incidental part of the act.

The only individual with extensive peri-mortem trauma for whom a different interpretation has been offered is the mature adult male from Hulton Abbey, Staffordshire, for whom the decapitation was a prelude to quartering, with the limbs being severed from the body, the hands and feet removed and the torso separated into vertical and horizontal segments[511]. The decapitation and the chopping injuries to the limbs could have been the result of some form of conflict, although the vertical chops through the vertebral column have only been recorded in one other individual from the entire decapitated sample (the adult male, Q1, from Maiden Castle) and seem to be the signature peri-mortem injuries for this type of judicial punishment.

Chapter 10 discusses all of the interpretations suggested for the different types of decapitation in the light of the evidence from the burials discussed above.

Chapter 9

Comparison between the Decapitated Individuals from the Iron Age, Romano-British and Early Medieval Periods

There has already been some discussion in this book about whether there may be evidence from the dating of some cemeteries and burials for continuity in the practice of decapitation, both between the Iron Age and Romano-British period, and between late Roman Britain and the early medieval period. This chapter aims to examine whether there is any possibility of continuity between the periods in terms of the demographic profile of those affected by decapitation, the burial practice and position of the head within the grave and the health status and evidence for peri-mortem trauma amongst the different samples.

Demographics

The numbers of adult males, adult females and non-adults represented in the decapitated samples from the Iron Age, the urban and rural/small-town Romano-British samples and the attritional cemetery and execution and isolated/mass-grave samples from the early medieval period were compared. It was found that there were no differences in the demographics of the Iron Age sample compared with the Romano-British urban sample, and also no differences between the Romano-British urban sample and that from the early medieval attritional cemeteries. However, there were statistically significantly more adult females and fewer adult males in the Romano-British rural and small-town sample when compared with the numbers in both the Iron Age and early medieval attritional decapitated samples. There were also statistically significantly more adult males and fewer adult females and non-adults in the early medieval execution/isolated-burial sample than in either the Romano-British urban or rural and small-town decapitated samples.

When the more detailed adult age-category data was analysed, from the sample for which detailed osteological information was available, it was found that, compared with the Iron Age and early medieval execution and isolated burial samples, the Romano-British samples had statistically fewer young adults and statistically more middle adults. It was also found that, whilst there were no differences between the numbers of mature adults in most samples, there were statistically more mature adults in the Romano-British rural and small-town sample when compared with the early medieval execution and isolated burial sample. The very small size of the early medieval attritional cemetery sample can probably account for the absence of any differences between this sample and either of those from the Romano-British period.

Burial Practice and Position of the Head
The decapitated individuals in the Romano-British urban sample and the early medieval attritional cemetery sample were significantly less likely to have been provided with a coffin than the wider population, whilst those in the former sample were also significantly less likely to have had objects buried with them (the decapitated individuals from the latter sample also had fewer objects than the wider population, although it was not statistically significant). Decapitations from both periods were also statistically significantly more likely to have been buried in a prone position than the rest of the population.

When the data on the position of the head was compared between the different groups, it was found that there were significantly more individuals with displacement of the head in the Romano-British samples compared to the sample from the Iron Age, whilst there were also significantly fewer individuals where the head was absent or where only the cranium and mandible were found in the Romano-British samples. The Romano-British groups also contained significantly more individuals with the head displaced, and significantly fewer individuals with the head absent than in those from the early medieval period. There were also some statistical differences between the Romano-British and early medieval samples in terms of how many individuals had the head in correct anatomical position. The Romano-British urban sample had statistically more individuals with the head in correct position than the early medieval attritional sample, with the Romano-British rural/small-town sample having statistically fewer individuals than the early medieval execution and isolated burial sample where this was the case. Both the Romano-

British urban and rural/small-town samples also had statistically significantly fewer individuals represented only by an isolated cranium and mandible than the early medieval execution and isolated burial sample.

Stature and Pathological Analysis

The males in both the Iron Age and Romano-British urban decapitated samples had a statistically significantly greater mean stature than individuals from the periods as a whole, with the other samples showing no differences between their average stature and that calculated for the wider population. The pathological analysis suggested that the individuals from both the Iron Age and Romano-British decapitated samples may have had access to a different diet, whilst the decapitated samples from all three periods had evidence for higher rates of degenerative joint disease, Schmorl's nodes and fractures than in the wider population, with those fractures recorded in the Iron Age and Romano-British samples having a high specificity for assault. The samples from the Romano-British and early medieval periods also had higher rates of non-specific infection than the wider population, suggesting they may have had a lower adult health status.

Evidence for Peri-mortem Trauma

The different types of peri-mortem trauma recorded in the decapitated samples from all three periods were compared, and it was found that there were significantly more individuals with chopping blows in the early medieval samples than in those from the Romano-British period, as well as significantly fewer individuals with incised cuts in the former sample when compared with the Romano-British rural and small-town sample. There were also more individuals in the Romano-British rural and small-town sample with evidence for both chopping blows and incised cuts than in the Iron Age and early medieval samples, as well as more individuals with multiple blows, and blows delivered from the anterior. The early medieval samples had significantly more individuals with decapitation-related peri-mortem injuries to the cranium, mandible, scapulae and claviculae than either of the Romano-British samples, whilst this sample also had more individuals with post-cranial non-decapitation-related trauma than the Romano-British rural and small-town sample.

Summary

In terms of the demographic profile of the samples, there were more differences between the Romano-British rural and small-town sample compared to those from the Iron Age and early medieval period than there were between those periods and the Romano-British urban sample. There were also more differences in the burial practice, with decapitated individuals from Romano-British rural and small-town cemeteries receiving the same burial treatment as the wider population, whilst Romano-British urban decapitations and those in the early medieval period were much less likely to have been provided with a coffin and much more likely to have been buried in a prone position. The position of the head showed a number of differences between the periods, with isolated crania and mandibulae being much more common in the Iron Age compared with the Romano-British samples, whilst displaced heads were more common in the Romano-British period, and individuals with the head absent much rarer than in the other two periods.

The taller-than-average stature of the individuals within the Iron Age and Romano-British urban decapitated samples, and the possibility that the individuals had access to a different diet than the rest of the population, the higher rates of degenerative joint disease, Schmorl's nodes and fractures amongst the samples from all three periods, as well as the higher rates of non-specific infection in the Romano-British and early medieval samples, compared with the wider population, suggests that there were differences between the decapitated individuals and the rest of the population in all three periods.

In terms of the peri-mortem trauma, there were more differences between the Romano-British rural and small-town sample compared to those from other periods, with more individuals having evidence for multiple blows, blows from the anterior and both chopping and incised cuts. The sample from the early medieval period had much more evidence for non-cervical decapitation trauma and post-cranial non-decapitation trauma than either of those from the Romano-British period.

Types of Decapitation

There were a number of different types of decapitation recorded amongst the samples from the three periods. In the Iron Age, the most common type of decapitation was a series of chopping blows directed to the posterior of the cervical column. Individuals with multiple peri-mortem traumata were rarer, as were isolated crania and mandibulae with non-

149

decapitation-related peri-mortem trauma, and individuals with incised cuts to the cervical vertebrae that seemed to be related to removal of musculature and connective tissue in order to remove the head from the post-cranial remains. There was also limited evidence for post-mortem and/or post-decompositional manipulation of the cranium for display or for use as a 'skull cup'. Evidence for cranial manipulation was also found in the Romano-British sample, although examples were very rare, suggesting that there may have been limited continuity of such practices between the periods.

The Romano-British sample also contained a small number of individuals where the cranium and mandible had been removed with incised cuts through the musculature and connective tissue, although the absence of any other evidence for peri-mortem trauma (unlike the Iron Age examples, where this trauma can probably be assumed to be the mechanism of death), and the possibility that these individuals were decapitated post-mortem, suggests that there was little continuity in this type of decapitation from the earlier period. There were a number of individuals from this period with posteriorly directed chopping blows, which may suggest some degree of continuity, although the additional chopping blows and incised cuts recorded in some individuals, performed in order to completely remove the cranium and mandible, are not seen in the Iron Age examples, suggesting that the motivation behind the act may have been different in the two periods (although there are a number of individuals in the Romano-British sample where the cranium and mandible were not completely removed). There is also an absence of individuals with multiple peri-mortem traumata in the Romano-British sample, although there are a few individuals who seem to have incapacitating and/or defensive injuries in addition to the decapitating blows. However, in the Romano-British period, the act of decapitation appears to have been the main focus, which was not necessarily the case in the Iron Age individuals.

The most distinctive form of decapitation recorded amongst the Romano-British cases, and not recorded at all in the earlier period, was slitting of the throat followed by complete decapitation, a type that was also not recorded amongst the decapitated sample from the early medieval period. There were also no individuals from the later period with evidence for incised cutting of soft tissues and disarticulation of the cervical column, suggesting that this was also a uniquely Romano-British type of decapitation. Single or multiple posteriorly directed chopping blows were the most common form of decapitation recorded amongst the early medieval sample. The fact that evidence for this type was also seen in the Iron Age and Romano-British periods suggests that there may have been some degree of continuity, although, again, there was no evidence for additional chopping blows and/or incised cuts to ensure the complete removal of the head in the individuals from the early medieval period. This period also sees a re-emergence of decapitation associated with extensive peri-mortem trauma in which the decapitation appears to have been an incidental part of the process, rather than, as in the Romano-British period, its main focus.

Discussion

The most obvious form of continuity observed between the three periods in the decapitated samples was in the lower health status, higher levels of activity-related changes and the possibility of access to a different diet than was the norm in the wider populations. It is also very noticeable that there were higher numbers of adult males affected by decapitation in the Iron Age, Romano-British urban, and early medieval samples. The individuals in the Iron Age and Romano-British urban male samples were also taller than was the average for the rest of the population. This suggests that there may have been continuity in the concept that decapitated individuals were somehow different to the wider population, although it was not possible to determine whether this was due to a deliberate selection of individuals based on their health status, or whether these differences during life were a result of specific roles and activities undertaken by the individuals, which then predisposed them to decapitation.

There also appears to be continuity in the 'poorer' burial practices accorded to decapitated individuals in the Romano-British urban and early medieval samples and in the higher numbers of individuals who were buried prone. Burial in a prone position is often interpreted as a show of disrespect or fear of the buried individual[512], although it has also been argued that, whilst it is certainly a minority burial rite, it does not necessarily have negative connotations[513] and may, in some cases, have been the accidental inversion of a coffined corpse[514]. However, the association of poorer burial practices and prone burial amongst decapitated individuals does indicate that there were differences, in both life and death, between those individuals and the rest of the population and this concept seems to have continued from the Iron Age, through the Romano-British period, and into the early medieval period.

However, in terms of the placement of the head, the sample from the Iron Age had many more individuals represented by only the cranium and mandible (sometimes with associated cervical vertebrae), whilst individuals with the head absent were also much more common in this period, as well as in the early medieval period, than amongst the Romano-British decapitations, where displacement of the head was the most common form. The Romano-British period was also the only one in which chopping blows associated with additional chops and incised cuts, performed in order to separate the cranio-cervical skeleton from the rest of the remains, were recorded, which suggests that the act of complete decapitation was much more important in this period than in either of the other two. There was also no evidence in the Romano-British sample for individuals with multiple peri-mortem traumata where the decapitation appears to have been simply part of the suite of injuries rather than the main aim. Where non-decapitation-related trauma does exist in the Romano-British sample, its sole intention seems to have been to subdue the individual in order to allow the head to be severed.

The possibility of continuity between the Iron Age, Romano-British and early medieval samples was also suggested by the presence of individuals with chopping blows directed to the posterior of the neck. Some of these individuals had only one or two chopping blows and it appears that, in these cases, the removal of the head was not necessarily an important part of the process, as it was sometimes found in correct anatomical position. It seems, therefore, that in these individuals, the aim was to kill rather than remove the head and, in that sense, there was continuity in the motivation behind decapitation across the three periods.

There was also evidence for limited continuity between the Iron Age and Romano-British periods in manipulation of cranial remains, with crania being worked and altered, as well as probably being displayed, in both periods. This does suggest that this aspect of decapitation-related activity was associated with a 'Cult of the Head', although the evidence for it is relatively rare compared with other forms of decapitation in both periods. Isolated crania and mandibulae were also found in both periods, with chopping blows being the most common type of decapitation-related peri-mortem trauma. However, these types of deposit were very rare in the Romano-British period, suggesting that, if they were related to a head cult, it had largely disappeared by the later period, whilst it was never as prevalent during the Iron Age as previously assumed.

The only sample in which adult females were more likely to have been decapitated was the Romano-British rural and small-town sample. This sample also had more anteriorly directed blows than seen in either the Iron Age or early medieval periods, as well as more individuals with multiple cuts and chops to the cervical vertebrae. There were also no differences in the burial practice accorded to decapitated and non-decapitated individuals in this sample, and there were more individuals with cutting of the throat associated with decapitation than in the urban sample. This form of decapitation, along with anteriorly directed incised cuts performed in order to sever the soft tissues of the neck (and not associated with other peri-mortem trauma, as seen in two crania and mandibulae from the Iron Age) was restricted to the Romano-British period, suggesting that some forms of the practice, both in terms of who was subject to it and the manner in which it was performed, were a purely Roman type with no continuity from earlier, or into later, periods.

Decapitations in the early medieval period were the least variable in terms of the types of cuts, with nearly all individuals having evidence for chopping blows delivered from the posterior, indicating that other forms of decapitation utilising incised cuts showed no continuity from the earlier period. There were also many more individuals with decapitation-related chops to the cranium, mandible, scapula and clavicle than in the earlier period, suggesting a certain imprecision in the way decapitations were performed that was not common in the earlier period.

In summary, there was some evidence for continuity between the three periods in the types of individual who were most likely to have been subject to decapitation and in how the decapitation was performed. Adult males with evidence for higher activity-related changes and a lower health status were the most common victims, with chopping blows being the most common type of peri-mortem trauma, the individuals then being subjected to 'poorer' burial practices than was the norm for the rest of the population. However, individuals with evidence for extensive peri-mortem trauma were restricted to the Iron Age and early medieval period, whilst there was also much less variety in the methods of decapitation used in the latter sample. An absence of continuity in certain aspects of the practice was also indicated by distinctive types of decapitation being restricted to certain periods, with at least one type being found only in the Iron Age (non-decapitation trauma with incised cuts to the cervical vertebrae), whilst the Romano-British period had at least four distinctive types (incised cutting and disarticulation of the cervical vertebrae; cutting of the throat associated with decapitation; decapitation associated with additional chops and cuts in order to completely remove the head; and complete decapitation associated with incapacitating and/or defensive injuries), suggesting that decapitation in the Romano-British period may have been, at least in part, a distinctly different phenomenon to that recorded in other periods.

Chapter 10

Interpretations of the Practice of Decapitation

This chapter will re-examine the different interpretations that have been given for the practice of decapitation in different periods (outlined in chapter 1) in light of the intervening evidence that has been described and discussed in previous chapters.

Cult of the Head
There appears to be limited evidence for the Cult of the Head amongst Iron Age and Romano-British examples of decapitation. In the cases of the isolated head deposits from Stanwick and Heslington, North Yorkshire, the head was removed from the post-cranial remains with incised cutting, which may suggest that it was performed in a ritual context after death (in the case of Stanwick, the mechanism of death was almost certainly a number of sharp-force injuries to the cranial vault and facial skeleton, performed with a heavy blade, although the same weapon was not used to perform the decapitation). The possible ritualistic nature of the head removal may suggest that this is related to a head cult, although the heads were (definitely, in the case of Heslington, and probably, in the case of Stanwick) not displayed, at least for any length of time, after decapitation had taken place.

There is more evidence for the Cult of the Head in the examples of drilled crania and possible skull cups from Iron Age Britain, and similarly modified cranial remains from Romano-British contexts, as well as in isolated cranial remains (a number of which have evidence for peri-mortem trauma although not necessarily decapitation) from settlement and temple sites. This may indicate that there was limited continuity in the practice (which was already rare) into the Romano-British period, although Roman literary sources contain much more evidence for decapitation and display of heads by the Romans themselves, particularly the military, than by Northern European Iron Age tribes. Evidence of long-term curation of cranial remains from the Cladh Hallan Bronze Age burials suggests that a head cult may have existed in earlier periods in Scotland, although evidence that the post-cranial remains were also being preserved and curated in similar ways suggests that it was not purely the head that was the focus for cultic activities at this site.

There is very little evidence to suggest that the 'typical' Romano-British decapitation burial is related to a head cult, as there are very few parallels for this specifically Roman type of practice in preceding periods, either in Britain or Northern Europe, and there is a gap of at least a century (the majority of Romano-British decapitations dating to the mid-second century or later) between the Iron Age practices and those seen in the following period. There is also very little evidence that the heads of these decapitation burials were used in any form of display, as the crania usually remained articulated with the mandible and cervical vertebrae and the post-cranial remains were almost always fully articulated, indicating a single episode of burial of the cranio-cervical and post-cranial remains in the immediate post-mortem period[515].

Aiding Passage to the Afterlife

This interpretation has been suggested for post-mortem decapitations in cases where individuals were believed to have died before their time or in unusual circumstances. The demographic profile of the complete decapitated sample when compared with wider cemetery populations indicated that there were significantly fewer non-adults amongst the decapitations than would be expected, suggesting that individuals subjected to decapitation were not dying at a younger age, whilst the demographic profile of the rural and small-town decapitated samples mirrored that of the wider population, again suggesting that selection for decapitation was not based on an unusual age profile. There was significantly more evidence for non-specific infection amongst the rural and small-town decapitated sample than in the wider population, which could be evidence for disease processes that may have led to premature death. However, the presence of skeletal responses to disease indicate that the conditions were chronic and those suffering with them were 'survivors', whilst acute illness would have killed individuals before bony changes could manifest, leaving no evidence on the skeleton[516]. This, coupled with the similarities between the adult demographic profiles in the decapitated and wider populations, would suggest that there was little evidence from the sample of burials to support this interpretation.

There was also little evidence from either sample for peri-mortem trauma not directly related to the practice of decapitation and, where this was present, it was in the form of single sharp-force traumata in locations commensurate with incapacitating or defensive injuries that probably occurred at the same time as the act of decapitation, rather than being related to accidental or violent deaths. However, the urban decapitated sample, particularly the adult males, contained significantly more middle adults and fewer mature adults than the wider cemetery population, suggesting that there was an age bias for those selected for decapitation in this sample, potentially adding to suppositions that this interpretation could be correct for a number of individuals. It is also a possibility that the visible deformities and disabilities recorded in a number of individuals may have led to beliefs that they would find it difficult to enter the afterlife because of their visible imperfection[517], although it is then difficult to see how and why another physical mutilation in the form of decapitation could have aided their passage. There also does not seem to be any obvious evidence as to which members of the community with disabilities and deformities may have been selected for decapitation, as individuals of both sexes and all ages were decapitated, whilst both sexes and a wide variety of ages were represented amongst individuals with disabilities who were not subjected to decapitation.

Preventing the Dead from Returning
The presence of individuals amongst the decapitated sample with visible deformities and disabilities could also support this interpretation, as it may have been thought to lead to the dead being restless, or in a state of limbo, as they were unable to enter the afterlife successfully (see above, this page), with decapitation being believed to prevent, or end, this liminal state. However, as previously stated, not all individuals with disabilities were decapitated, so presumably not all these individuals were thought to automatically return to haunt the living. The presence of decapitated individuals within the rural and small-town samples who had higher rates of infectious disease, which may have led to unusual deaths and restless corpses (although see above, p.156), could also support this interpretation. The fact that prone burial is much more common amongst decapitated burials than amongst the wider cemetery population, with burial in a prone position suggested to relate to attempts to keep the corpse in the grave and prevent haunting[518], may suggest that decapitation was performed for similar reasons[519].

However, there is very little evidence amongst decapitated burials for other methods that attempted to keep the individual in the grave, such as placing heavy stones on the body, although there are two adult females (from Dunstable, Bedfordshire, and Tubney Woods Quarry, Oxfordshire) who, as well as being decapitated, had had their distal lower limbs removed (by peri-mortem chopping blows and incised cuts in the case of the individual from Dunstable) and replaced beside their upper limbs. This could have been an attempt to prevent their corpses from 'walking', and its association with decapitation in these cases could also suggest that head removal was supposed to have the same effect. As the occurrence of this type of mutilation is very rare, both in decapitated and non-decapitated burials (a non-decapitated adult male from Dunstable had a peri-mortem severance through the right distal tibia and fibula, with the severed elements being placed under the left distal limb[520], whilst a young adult male from Alington Avenue, Dorset, demonstrated evidence for a peri-mortem amputation of the right upper limb[521] with the severed elements being absent from the grave), presumably decapitation on its own was assumed to keep the individual in their grave.

There is better evidence from the medieval and later ethnographic sources that this interpretation could account for a number of decapitated burials, as the only reason ever given for post-mortem decapitation is as a method of preventing the dead from returning to haunt the living, bringing episodes of haunting to an end, or ending the return of individuals believed to be revenants. However, there are no similar written sources for the Roman period and there is a danger of projecting medieval and post-medieval ideas back into the ancient past, a problem very similar to those assumptions that have been made about the prevalence of the Cult of the Head in Northern Europe being based on literary sources that refer specifically to Mediterranean tribes.

Poena Post Mortem

The evidence that the urban Romano-British decapitated sample, and particularly the adult males, were significantly less likely to have been provided with a coffin or objects than the wider urban cemetery population, and more likely to have been buried in a prone position (although see above, p.157, for the arguments about what prone burial may signify), may suggest that the decapitation and associated burial practice was some form of *poena post mortem*. This may also be the explanation for the two adult female burials (previously mentioned, this page) with their lower limbs removed and rearranged in the grave, as well as a non-adult from Stanground, Cambridgeshire, whose body had been dismembered and decapitated[522]. Early medieval decapitated burials were also significantly less likely to have been provided with a coffin and more likely to have been buried prone than the wider cemetery population, which suggests that this may also provide an explanation for decapitated burials in this period.

There is a body of evidence from Roman literary sources and material culture for *poena post mortem* in the form of decapitation of the statuary of deposed and hated rulers, with the decapitation of corpses also being recorded; in one case the head was subsequently carefully buried with the rest of the remains. However, it was usually the case that heads, and sometimes bodies, were displayed and then disposed of, rather than being formally interred (this may account for the isolated cranial remains found in pits and ditches on Romano-British settlement sites), and the majority of the surviving statuary show evidence for extensive mutilation of the face, something that is also recorded in the sources but is not generally recorded in decapitated burials (with the possible exception of an individual from Lankhills, Winchester, with a single sharp-force injury to the anterior of the maxilla and mandible, and a small number of individuals from Dunstable and Driffield Terrace, York, with multiple chop marks to the mandible).

The evidence from the sources as regards the extensive nature of post-mortem mutilation and display, and the casual way in which bodies and heads were subsequently disposed of, does not, therefore, find a reflection in the formal manner in which Romano-British decapitated burials were interred, whether or not they were accorded the same types of funerary equipment as the majority of the population. There is also almost no evidence amongst these burials for display of the head (there were no penetrating injuries and the mandible and cervical vertebrae remained in complete articulation with the cranium, although display of the head on top of the coffin may have occurred in a very small number of cases, see endnote 515), with a number of burials showing evidence that the cranio-cervical remains had been placed into the grave before the post-cranial remains.

Human Sacrifice

This may be the interpretation for the small group of isolated head deposits from the Bronze and Iron Ages that display evidence for peri-mortem trauma in addition to decapitation with incised cuts to the cervical vertebrae, as they may be examples of the 'overkill' that is often recorded in Iron Age bog bodies, also often assumed to have been sacrificial victims[523]. The rapid burial in a small pit of the head from Heslington, North Yorkshire, and the deposition in a palaeochannel of the head from Birstall, Leicestershire, may be evidence for burial in liminal locations (usually watery), something that also occurred with bog bodies, as well as with deliberate deposits of metalwork that are also suggested to have been sacrificed, with items being deliberately broken or bent before deposition[524].

In the Romano-British period, there are a number of decapitated burials, with significantly more found in rural and small-town cemeteries than in urban areas, with evidence for slitting of the throat, something that is also recorded in a number of bog bodies, and is commonly associated with human sacrifice in a number of different cultures (although cutting of the throat is also recorded in cases of murder and judicial execution), with the release of blood being an important part of the sacrificial process. These individuals are assumed to have been live human sacrifices (as there does not seem to be any motivation for specifically cutting the throat of a corpse during the process of decapitation), something that is supported by the presence of peri-mortem incapacitating injuries in some of the individuals, as well as evidence for dental trauma, flexion of the neck at the time the decapitating blows were delivered, and restraint of the limbs in the grave.

There does not seem to have been a particular group of individuals who were selected for sacrifice, as adult males and females, as well as a small number of non-adults, displayed evidence for this type of decapitation, and it is interesting that a number of individuals thus selected demonstrated visible deformities and disabilities (hand trauma and amputations, for example). This seems to be in complete contrast to the perfect and unblemished nature of the animals selected for Roman religious sacrifice, something that was also expected of the priests who would have carried out the sacrificial rites[525]. However, there is evidence that a number of Iron Age bog bodies also had disabilities and deformities of various kinds, including polydactyly (extra fingers), fractured limbs with shortening, limited mobility, scoliosis and dyschondrosteosis[526], and it has been suggested that this contributed towards their selection for sacrifice[527]. It is therefore possible that Romano-British decapitated burials with slitting of the throat are a continuation, with major modifications in terms of burial practice and location, of this practice.

It is also interesting that significantly more individuals with this type of decapitation were found in rural and small-town cemeteries, which may suggest that human sacrifices were largely performed in areas where centralised control and influence were weaker, although there are examples of individuals with cut throats from extra-mural cemeteries in Winchester (Venta Belgarum) and York (Eboracum). This either suggests that it was still possible to carry out human sacrifices in areas where Roman influence and control was, arguably, at its peak (although the burials from Winchester date to the third and fourth centuries, when this influence may have been waning, even in urban areas[528]), possibly indicating complicity, if nothing else, by the authorities. The number of examples with this type of decapitation was, however, small, indicating that if they are cases of human sacrifice, it was a rare event in Roman Britain.

Execution
The demographic profile of the decapitated sample from the Romano-British urban cemeteries, with fewer mature adults than would be expected, suggests that these individuals were not necessarily dying natural deaths, and this, coupled with the fact that there were significantly more adult males amongst the sample, may suggest that these decapitations are examples of judicial execution. It is known from Roman sources that decapitation was used as a military punishment, and a military context for at least some of the individuals may be suggested by the taller-than-average adult male stature (the Roman army had height restrictions for recruits[529]), as well as the evidence for activity-related skeletal changes and patterns of ante-mortem trauma that suggest an involvement in low-level interpersonal violence.

Judicial execution could also be suggested for those Romano-British decapitated burials where there was evidence for single posteriorly directed chopping blows, especially where the neck was flexed, and/or where there was evidence for dental trauma, bodily restraint or the head not being completely removed, suggesting that the aim of the decapitation was not to separate the cranio-cervical skeleton from the post-cranial remains but to kill (a number of these examples were from within the urban sample). It should not necessarily be seen as a problem that there were some adult females and non-adults included amongst this number, as the age of criminal responsibility in Roman law was seven, with boys over fourteen and girls over twelve considered to be adult for this purpose[530]. No distinction was made between adult males and females in terms of the types of punishment that could be meted out[531], although decapitation does seem to have been more commonly performed on males[532]. The literary evidence for decapitation as a method of execution states that it was initially reserved for citizens, although this does not necessarily preclude Romano-British decapitated burials from being executions, as universal citizenship was introduced in the early third century, whilst the majority of decapitated burials date to the later third and fourth centuries. The formal burial accorded to decapitated burials is also not necessarily to be seen as an argument against judicial execution, as the families of the executed were permitted to recover the body for burial.

The evidence that execution could account for a number of the decapitated burials in the early medieval sample is very similar in nature to that seen in the preceding period. Nearly all individuals were adolescent or adult males with posteriorly directed chopping blows, and with evidence for flexion of the neck, bodily restraint, and heads often remaining in full or partial articulation with the rest of the body, being common; furthermore, unlike the preceding period, the majority of individuals are buried in isolated locations (in earlier centuries) or specific burial areas (from around the ninth century onwards), rather than in community cemeteries. This may represent a change in attitude about who could be buried in these cemeteries and/or greater control by the authorities in how and where executed individuals could be interred. The very small number of decapitated individuals that are found in community cemeteries (which have skeletal evidence very similar in nature to those from the other types of burial location) may represent less formalised/extra-judical executions conducted and controlled by local communities, possibly with the family later being allowed to recover the body for formal burial. The display of heads of the executed also seems to have occasionally occurred in this period, with some cranial remains recovered separately from post-cranial skeletons in execution cemetery assemblages, and isolated cranial remains that show possible evidence for display also receiving final interment in pits on settlement sites.

Warfare/Interpersonal Violence
The presence of significantly more adult males amongst the decapitated samples from the Iron Age, and urban Romano-British, early medieval and medieval periods, might suggest that they represent deaths as a result

of warfare or less formalised interpersonal violence. Active participants in warfare in the majority of periods and cultures are much more likely to have been adult males[533], although Rebecca Redfern[534] has demonstrated that adult females were actively engaging in interpersonal violence during the Iron Age in Dorset. In contrast, skeletal remains that seem to relate to massacres are much more likely to have been composed of adults of both sexes and non-adults[535]. The decapitated samples from the Iron Age and early medieval periods either derived from single graves in cemetery locations, isolated burials, or multiple interments in a single pit or grave, whilst all those from the Romano-British and medieval periods were recovered from single graves, a finding that may reflect differences in whether it was friendly or hostile forces who undertook the burial. It may also be a reflection of how many individuals were involved in a conflict, as large numbers of casualties may have been easier to inter in a single pit close to the site of the battle[536].

The taller-than-average stature of the individuals in the Iron Age and urban Romano-British decapitated samples, plus the prevalence of activity-related skeletal changes and ante-mortem traumata with a high specificity for assault, may also indicate a military context for the burials. However, it is interesting that those individuals from the medieval period who were from a definite military context were not statistically taller than the wider adult male population, suggesting there may have been more selection on the basis of stature in earlier periods.

The multiple cranial and post-cranial peri-mortem traumata recorded in a number of individuals from the Iron Age, early medieval and medieval periods, with decapitation almost appearing to have been an incidental part of the suite of traumatic injuries, would suggest that they resulted from warfare or less formalised interpersonal violence rather than from an act focused on decapitating the individual. This is also suggested by the fact that the cranium and mandible were found in correct anatomical position in a number of these individuals, indicating that complete removal of the head was not achieved, and suggesting that it was not an important part of the mechanism of death in these individuals. However, the pattern of peri-mortem trauma in the Romano-British examples is very different, with the majority of injuries being concentrated on the cervical vertebrae and associated areas of the skeleton. In individuals with evidence for non-decapitation-related trauma, the injuries were usually restricted to one or two separate traumata that seemed to be incapacitating or defensive injuries. Some of the cranio-cervical injuries in these individuals were probably associated with the removal of remaining soft tissue in cases where the decapitation was not successfully completed with the initial blows. This indicates that head removal was an important part of the process and suggests that decapitation was the sole aim and purpose of the act. Therefore, in the Romano-British period, warfare is probably not the most convincing interpretation for any of the decapitated burials.

Live or Dead?
The preceding discussion has suggested that there is some evidence that could be used to support each of the different interpretations that have previously been suggested for the act of decapitation, with the same evidence often used to argue for at least two separate (and often vastly different) interpretations ('equifinality'). The differing nature of the evidence from the burial practices, demographic profiles, health status and peri-mortem trauma amongst the sample of decapitated burials also suggests that there are a number of different types of decapitation that probably resulted from very distinct and different motives, although it may be impossible to ever definitively say what these were, particularly for the examples from the Romano-British period.

However, there is more definite evidence from a number of individuals as regards whether they were already dead at the time of decapitation or whether the decapitation was the mechanism of death. A small number of individuals from the Romano-British period, as well as a group of isolated head deposits from the Bronze and Iron Ages, had evidence for incised cut-marks on the anterior of the cervical vertebrae, including some that were positioned in locations that would have been inaccessible unless the intervertebral connective tissues had already been partially severed. The precise nature of these cuts would suggest that decapitation was performed on a corpse, although there is evidence that the Iron Age individuals were killed immediately prior to decapitation (by hanging and multiple cranial sharp-force injuries). There was no similar evidence of trauma on the Romano-British examples, suggesting a non-violent mechanism of death in these cases and probably indicating decapitation as some form of post-mortem ritual.

A second group of individuals from the Romano-British period had evidence for slitting of the throat and/or flexion of the neck when decapitation was performed, peri-mortem dental trauma, incapacitating or defensive injuries, or evidence for restraint of the upper limbs. All of this evidence, particularly that for flexion of the neck, suggests that decapitation (or slitting of the throat as part of the decapitation process) was the mechanism of death in these individuals and therefore an interpretation of human sacrifice or judicial execution can be favoured in these cases.

Conclusion

This book has demonstrated that the practice of decapitation in Britain is much more varied than previously assumed, with a number of distinct decapitation types identified in burials from the Neolithic to the post-medieval period. The research has demonstrated the importance of the reanalysis of the skeletal remains in cases where decapitation is assumed, as a number of burials not previously reported to demonstrate any evidence for peri-mortem trauma were found to display very clear signs of trauma, both directly and indirectly related to the act of decapitation. Nearly without exception, where decapitated burials were subjected to detailed analysis during this research, such evidence for trauma was found, suggesting that this was the norm and that the act was one generally performed in the peri-mortem period, rather than being aided by the decomposition process, as has previously been stated for a number of such burials from the Romano-British period[537]. The book has also demonstrated that there is strong evidence that decapitation was the mechanism of death in a number of individuals from this period, in contrast to nearly all previous commentaries, which have seen the practice as only ever being performed on a corpse.

The book has demonstrated that a small number of those individuals for whom decapitation was the mechanism of death may have been the victims of live human sacrifice during the Romano-British period. This is in stark contrast to previous assumptions that no decapitated Romano-British burials can have been the product of sacrifice, as it was a practice that had been banned throughout the empire in 97 BC (see chapter 1). However, the ban was restated in the *Lex Cornelia de sicariis et veneficiis* of 81 BC[538], and it was also necessary for the Druidic religion, and its practice of human sacrifice, to be suppressed in Gaul and Britain during the first century AD[539]. There is also a reference to a human sacrifice to Jove being carried out on Cyprus in the second century AD, with the practice only being abolished during the reign of Hadrian[540], all of which suggests that it continued despite official proscriptions. Bog bodies, such as Worsley Man, and the discovery of a fourth-century *defixio* from Brandon, Suffolk, wishing for the sacrifice to Neptune of a thief who stole an iron pan[541], also indicate that the practice may have continued into the

Romano-British period. The possibility that some decapitated burials from Roman Britain were the result of such live human sacrifice should, therefore, be reconsidered.

The book has shown that there do seem to be differences between the types of individuals on whom decapitation was performed in the Romano-British urban extra-mural cemeteries and those buried in small-town and rural cemetery sites, in terms of the demographic profile, health status, prevalence of ante-mortem trauma and burial practices. There were also differences between decapitated individuals and the wider cemetery population, especially in urban areas, which suggests that there was a degree of selection as to who was subjected to decapitation, contrary to previous statements that the act of decapitation itself was the only aspect of the burial that distinguished it from the rest of the cemetery population[542].

The book has also demonstrated that there seems to be very little evidence, either from the archaeological, literary or ethnographic record, to support the majority of interpretations that have been used to explain the occurrence of decapitated burials in the Romano-British period, all but two of which (execution and warfare) are dependent on decapitation being a purely post-mortem act. Only one post-mortem interpretation, namely that decapitation was performed in order to prevent the dead returning to haunt the living, is supported by any evidence.

There appears to be limited evidence for the Cult of the Head in Britain during the Iron Age, with little evidence for continuity into the Romano-British period, and, where it does appear to have been a motivation for ritual practices, it resulted in post-mortem manipulation of cranial remains, rather than being the motivation for the 'typical' type of decapitated burial where the cranium and mandible are interred with the post-cranial remains. This 'typical' decapitation burial has been demonstrated to be largely limited to Roman Britain, with a very small number of such burials found elsewhere in the empire, the majority of which, where evidence is available, seeming to display evidence for very similar peri-mortem trauma to those examples from Britain where it has been demonstrated that decapitation was probably the mechanism of death.

The existence of individuals on whom the decapitation was carried out post-mortem, or as a possible human sacrifice, therefore seems to be restricted to Britain, with the numbers of individuals for whom decapitation was probably the mechanism of death also being far in excess of anything seen elsewhere in the empire. Although a limited number of the burials have been shown to date to between the first and second centuries AD, the majority of decapitated individuals seem to belong to the third and fourth centuries AD, a period which, it has been argued, shows a greatly increased regionalisation across the empire in terms of trade[543] and building styles[544]. It would seem to be the case that decapitated burials were another form of this regionalisation in Roman Britain. It could be argued that this was influenced by the Celtic head cult traditions of Ireland and Scotland, although, as this research has shown, there is as limited evidence for the Cult of the Head in the predominately Celtic areas of Britain as there is in England and Wales, suggesting that a different explanation needs to be sought.

By contrast, the book has largely confirmed interpretations previously proposed for decapitations in the early medieval and medieval periods, namely execution and warfare, whilst providing striking evidence that a large number of Romano-British decapitated burials look very similar, in terms of the nature of the peri-mortem trauma, to burials from early medieval execution cemeteries. However, medieval victims of warfare had entirely different peri-mortem traumata signatures to Romano-British decapitations, indicating that this is unlikely to provide an explanation for such burials. The book has also provided further evidence to support Andrew Reynolds's assertion that specific execution cemeteries were a largely pre-Conquest phenomenon, with no such sites being identified that definitely date to the later medieval period[545]. The book has, however, identified a small number of burials from parish church cemeteries and abbeys that showed evidence for decapitation as the mechanism of death (or, in the case of the adult male from Hulton Abbey, Staffordshire, as part of a much more complicated process). This demonstrates that victims of judicial execution were no longer being buried in separate and specific locations, but had returned to being interred in community cemeteries, as was the case in the earlier centuries of the early medieval period. Andrew Reynolds also noted this change in burial location, as well as a decrease in the number of executed criminals recorded in later medieval written sources[546], something that was also supported by the low numbers of decapitated burials from the period that have been identified in this book.

The variety of different types of peri-mortem signatures of decapitation demonstrated in this book (see appendix 2) suggest that the act may have been performed for a number of different reasons, and that no single explanation can account for all such burials in any one period, although different interpretations should probably be given more weight in certain periods than others. Importantly, although equifinality may preclude decapitation burials that resulted from live human sacrifice being completely separated from those produced by judicial and extra-judicial execution, the fact that decapitation has been demonstrated to have been the mechanism of death in a number of individuals argues that these interpretations should be given much more weight in any future discussion of Romano-British decapitated burials.

Directions for Future Research
The identification of so many distinct types of decapitation was not anticipated during the data collection phase of this research and the sample size was, therefore, not sufficient to allow for separation into these different types for data analysis. A detailed osteological analysis of a larger sample of each type of Romano-British decapitation burial would provide data on whether there were any statistical differences, in terms of the demographic profile, stature, health status, ante-mortem trauma and burial practices, between individuals subjected to each different type.

Only a limited sample of non-adult Romano-British individuals was available for the present research, a result of the cemetery sites selected for analysis having small numbers of such individuals, which made detailed discussion of the act of decapitation in such individuals impossible. A detailed osteological analysis targeted at decapitated non-adults would enable this discussion, based on the demographic profile, health status, ante-mortem trauma and the different types of decapitation-related peri-mortem traumata observed in such individuals, to take place.

The book identified specific geographical areas within Britain, such as Lincolnshire and South-East England, where there were high levels of Romanisation but very few decapitated burials, and further research is needed to try and provide explanations for why this may be the case.

Only a very small number of decapitated burials from early medieval attritional cemeteries were available for analysis as part of this research, which precluded detailed comparisons, both between the types of individuals affected and the types of decapitation performed, for this period. This comparison needs to be undertaken in order to illuminate the possibility of continuity of burial practices, including decapitation, between the Romano-British and early medieval periods, which has already been suggested by the existence of cemeteries such as Wasperton, the use of which spans the fourth to seventh centuries AD. The analysis of a much larger sample of decapitated early medieval burials and their comparison with the Romano-British evidence would help to determine how prevalent this continuity actually was.

Appendix 1

Materials and Methods Used
in the Research

The initial stages of the research involved an in-depth literature search through published monographs, national and local journals and unpublished grey literature to identify sites where decapitation was recorded as occurring or where, although the specific word was not used, the descriptions of skeletons suggested that decapitation may have occurred, such as a recorded absence or displacement of the cranium and mandible or the presence of an isolated cranium and mandible. The search was restricted to sites from England, Wales and Scotland, but a long time period, from the Neolithic through to the early post-medieval period, was examined. This was in order to place decapitations from the Roman and early medieval periods into a wider temporal context, and to assess whether there were continuities from earlier periods in the manner and geographical distribution of the practice, as suggested by the 'Cult of the Head' theory (see chapter 1). Literature from later historical periods was examined in order to identify sites where decapitations existed that could be ascribed to a more definite motive, such as known executions and battle victims, in order to compare the manner of the decapitations to those from earlier periods.

Once suitable sites were identified, a number of pieces of data were collected for each individual, including the presence or absence of a body container, clothing and deliberate grave inclusions; body position; placement of head; age and sex; and presence or absence of osteological evidence for decapitation. This data was inputted into a database along with other details of the site, such as the National Grid reference, county, site name, date, total number of burials and their demography, number of decapitations and the bibliographic references for the site.

A number of sites were then selected from this database and the skeletal remains therein subjected to a full osteological examination. The selections were based on a number of criteria, including the date and type of the assemblage and how well preserved the skeletal remains were, in order that as large a variety of samples as possible could be examined and the maximum amount of osteological data obtained from them. However, the selection of samples was ultimately determined, in a number of cases, by the availability of the remains for study, as some samples, especially those excavated in the nineteenth and earlier twentieth centuries, were either not retained for study or could not now be traced.

Once collections had been identified and located, osteological analysis took place at various holding institutions and, in rare cases where the institutions gave permission for the remains to be removed from their premises on loan, in the laboratories of the University of Winchester. As the collections to be examined comprised the remains of once-living people, there were specific ethical considerations that had to be taken into account that would not have applied to other classes of archaeological material. Skeletal remains were handled with care and respect at all times in accordance with the British Association of Biological Anthropologists and Osteoarchaeologists (BABAO) Code of Ethics.

For a number of collections where time and space allowed, or where cemeteries were within certain study areas, all individuals within the collection were subjected to a visual assessment of the cervical vertebrae, cranium and mandible to determine the existence of decapitations not previously recognised during excavation, either because the position of the head within the grave did not suggest decapitation had occurred and therefore the vertebrae were never previously examined in detail, or because of poor original site recording which did not allow body positions to be determined. Any individuals who were then found to have osteological evidence for decapitation were subjected to a full skeletal analysis in the same manner as the already-identified decapitations.

The skeletal analysis involved each individual being laid out in anatomical order with an inventory of dentition and skeletal elements then being completed, both on written and diagrammatic pro forma. This allowed the presence or absence of each skeletal element to be taken into account during the data analysis where it could have an effect on the diagnosis of pathological conditions or trauma. The individual was then subjected to a range of osteological techniques used to determine age at death, sex, metric and non-metric data, as well as a detailed examination of pathological changes and trauma. The methods used for each of these aspects of the analysis are detailed below.

A total of 170 decapitated individuals from 53 different sites were osteologically examined for the purposes of this research. A number of other individuals were subjected to a visual examination in order to assess whether they had been decapitated but were not subjected to a more detailed analysis when no such evidence could be found, either because of missing skeletal elements, poor skeletal preservation or a lack of bony trauma. The sites from which decapitated individuals were selected and the numbers of such burials osteologically analysed are tabulated in appendix 3 and all skeletal data on these individuals included in this book derives from this analysis. Where the skeletal analysis undertaken by other researchers on further individuals was deemed to be of sufficient quality (i.e. where they determined age and sex, calculated stature, and recorded information on pathological changes and decapitation trauma) this data was also used in the detailed analysis. This was the case for a further 200 individuals and these are also tabulated in appendix 3.

Age Determination

There are two distinct types of age determination from the human skeleton, with age determination in non-adults being dependent on measuring the growth and development of the skeleton, whilst in adult individuals it records the degeneration of certain elements. The age of non-adult skeletons in this project was assessed by the development of the dentition, long-bone length and fusion of ossification centres. The dentition is commonly used for age determination of non-adults, as it survives the burial environment well and the development of the teeth takes place over the whole of the non-adult age range, although there are periods, especially in the older age stages, when there is little change in the dentition, making accurate determinations of the age at death difficult. Dentition is also used as, in skeletal collections of documented sex and chronological age, it was found to vary less from the chronological age than did the skeletal age[547]. The methods of dental age determination used in this research were based on the visual charts of Douglas Ubelaker, which were originally developed from Native American samples but are widely used for archaeological populations from many parts of the world, and were used for more complete dentitions where teeth were *in situ* in the alveolar bone and the root formation could not be assessed[548]. In cases where the roots were observable, the charts devised by Moorrees *et al.* and revised by Smith were used[549]. This is the most commonly used method for archaeological material, but it has been argued that the times for M1 (first molar) crown completion and M1 root formation are too low[550].

Long-bone length is used in non-adult age estimation as it records the linear growth of the individual, which advances during the same period as dental development and skeletal maturity but not necessarily in synchrony, as factors such as poor nutrition and exposure to disease can have a greater adverse effect on long-bone length[551]. Measurements were taken of the diaphyseal lengths (the shaft of the bone excluding the unfused ends) of all complete non-adult long bones and these were compared against the standards for age estimation from long-bone lengths as given in Scheuer and Black, as adapted from the work of Maresh for older non-adults and from Scheuer *et al.* for very young individuals[552]. Both these sets of standards were devised using living populations and are commonly used for archaeological samples. Where dentition was also available for the same individual, the age from the dentition was preferred for the reasons given above but, by comparing both sets of data, any degree of delayed skeletal growth could be assessed.

The fusion of skeletal ossification centres is a process that occurs between one or more primary centres, such as between the ilium, ischium and pubis in the pelvis, or between a primary centre and its epiphyses, such as in the long bones, and is the final stage of bone growth at those centres. The age at which it occurs varies greatly between different centres, with the vertebrae completing fusion between the centra and neural arches by around the age of six years, whilst the sternal end of the clavicle does not completely fuse until around thirty years of age[553]. However, the majority of ossification centres complete fusion during adolescence and the age at which this occurs differs between males and females, with the bones of females generally fusing around two years earlier than males[554]. This method was, therefore, very useful for age determination of older non-adults during the period of static dental development. The method was also used to assess age in individuals where long-bone lengths and dentition were not obtainable due to poor preservation and was used as a comparison for the ages obtained from dental development and long-bone length for other individuals.

For adult individuals, age was assessed from two areas of the *ossa coxae* (pelvis), namely the pubic symphysis and the auricular surface. Assessments were made from both left and right sides and an age estimation was made based on the most common age category and taking into account any evidence for pathological alteration of the area. Standards for age determination from the pubic symphysis were first devised by Todd in the 1920s[555], and there were a number of later

174

revisions of the method, including that devised by Brooks and Suchey in 1990, which was the technique employed in this research and which has recently been further revised by Hartnett in 2010, although this has so far only been tested on North American samples[556]. There are a number of problems with this method of age estimation, including the fact that the pubic symphysis is very prone to fragmentation and post-mortem loss because of its anterior position and thin cortical bone. This reduces the number of skeletons on which the method can be employed. More importantly, the published standards have very wide age ranges for each stage, with a large overlap; for example, Stage 4 of the Brooks and Suchey method has a range of twenty-six to seventy years for males and twenty-three to fifty-seven for females, whilst Stage 5 has ranges of twenty-five to eighty-three and twenty-seven to sixty-six for males and females respectively. All of the methods also seem to have the same problem in tending to over-age younger individuals whilst under-ageing older ones[557]. This method was therefore employed in conjunction with that for the auricular surface. This area of the *ossa coxae* tends to survive very well, increasing the number of individuals on which it can be used. The method employed for this research was that of Lovejoy *et al.* devised in 1985[558]. The method has been tested on a number of other samples, although it has received less attention than the pubic symphysis technique, and, like the aforementioned method, has been found to over-age younger individuals and under-age older ones, with less than forty per cent of individuals in one sample being assigned the correct age range[559]. However, its survivability in archaeological and forensic contexts has led to an attempt to increase its use, with recent refinements and tests of the new methods suggesting that the Lovejoy *et al.* method is more accurate for most age categories but is more difficult to apply[560]. Despite the inherent problems with both of these methods of age determination, in combination they are the most commonly used on archaeological material, and therefore the age estimations obtained from them during this research will be comparable to those reported for the wider archaeological populations of the same periods.

The final technique used to determine the age at death for younger adults was the recording of a number of late fusing ossification centres, such as the iliac crest and vertebral endplates (which complete fusion at around the age of twenty to twenty-five years) and the sternal end of the clavicle (which, as already stated, completes fusion by around thirty years). The degree of fusion of the sternal end of the clavicle was particularly useful in adult individuals where other ossification centres had completed fusion but where no pelvis had survived.

There are a number of other age determination techniques that have been devised for adult skeletons, including the morphology of the sternal end of the rib[561]. The fourth rib was used in developing the technique, which means it can be a problematic technique to apply to archaeological samples as the ribs are often fragmentary, making it difficult to identify the correct bone. This technique was not used in the current research for this reason, although there has been a recent attempt to devise standards for the first rib, which is much more easily identified in archaeological samples[562].

Cranial suture closure was one of the first methods used to try to determine age at death in adult individuals, a result of the predominance of studies of the cranium in early physical anthropology[563]. From as early as the mid-twentieth century, the technique has been found to be unreliable and erratic (a finding that more modern studies have only confirmed[564]), as well as being very time consuming; for these two reasons it was not employed during this research.

The final technique often used to determine age at death in adults is the degree of dental attrition (dental wear). Miles was the first to devise a standard for this technique in 1963, which was then adapted by Brothwell in 1981[565]. A number of studies have found that for a wide range of archaeological and modern populations the technique was relatively accurate in predicting the age at death[566]. However, dental attrition is affected by differences in diet and the use of teeth as tools, and in one Roman population previously examined by the author and which formed part of the data set used in this research, sixty-two per cent of individuals had lower rates of dental attrition than expected for their age as assessed from the pubic symphysis and auricular surface.

Once age had been estimated using the above techniques, each individual was placed into a specific age category, as used by the Biological Anthropology Research Centre at the University of Bradford and advocated by Falys and Lewis in 2011[567]. These categories are as follows:

- foetal (up to forty weeks gestation)
- neonate (forty weeks gestation to one month post-natal)
- infant (one month to one year)
- younger child (one to six years)
- older child (seven to twelve years)

- adolescent (thirteen to eighteen years)
- young adult (nineteen to twenty-five years)
- young middle adult (twenty-six to thirty-five years)
- old middle adult (thirty-six to forty-five years)
- mature adult (forty-six years and above)

Where poor skeletal preservation did not allow for accurate age determination, or where the ages determined from the pubic symphysis and auricular surface were vastly different, wider age categories were used, such as middle adult (twenty-six to forty-five years), or skeletons were described as non-adult (under nineteen years) or adult (over nineteen years). However, the nature of the research, with a focus on more complete and relatively well-preserved individuals, meant that this was a rare occurrence.

Sex Determination

The determination of biological sex from the skeleton is dependent on the assessment of a number of sexually dimorphic features which reflect hormonal differences between males and females, with the features found in male individuals being dependent on the production of androgens, whilst the female phenotype is the 'default setting' into which all foetuses will develop if not directed otherwise by these male hormones[568]. Although the terms 'sex' and 'gender' are often used interchangeably, including in scientific publications[569], the two terms do not describe the same thing, with 'gender' being a social construct that may or may not depend on the biological sex of the individual. There are many cultures, both ancient and modern, where sex and gender are regarded as being entirely independent from one another and there are accepted sexes that are neither biologically male nor female and genders that are neither masculine nor feminine[570].

The sexually dimorphic features that are apparent in adult skeletons do not truly manifest themselves in younger individuals as the levels of androgens in the male body are much lower before puberty, and therefore the determination of sex in non-adult individuals is much more difficult[571]. There have, however, been a number of attempts to devise methods for assigning sex in neonates and infants that usually use the same morphological indicators applied to adult individuals[572]. However, there have been mixed results using these methods, with some studies confirming sexual dimorphism in neonates and infants, and others finding

177

no differences. For this reason, no attempt was made during this research to assess sex in non-adult remains.

Sex determination of adults employed an examination of sexually dimorphic features of the pelvis and cranium and mandible. Those in the pelvis reflect a combination of functional and evolutionary adaptations, with the female pelvis being a compromise between successful bipedalism and delivery of offspring[573]. The methods used during this research to assess sex from the pelvis were a combination of those devised by Phenice in 1969 for the ventral arc, sub-pubic concavity and ischio-pubic ramus ridge, and Buikstra and Ubelaker in 1994 for the greater sciatic notch[574]. In three different tests of the Phenice method on documented skeletal collections, it was found to have accuracies of ninety-six per cent, eighty-three per cent and fifty-nine per cent, although in 2002, Bruzek suggested it had an average accuracy of around eighty per cent[575]. This method also has the disadvantage, like the age determination method employing the pubic symphysis, of being reliant on the preservation of the pubic bone.

Sex determination from the greater sciatic notch, which tends to survive better than the pubic bone in archaeological samples, was found to have an accuracy of eighty per cent in one recent study, whilst a separate study was able to correctly sex sixty-eight per cent of females and seventy-four per cent of males from the greater sciatic notch alone[576]. Combined methods, using a number of features, including the greater sciatic notch and features of the pubic bone, were found to have an accuracy rate of around ninety-five per cent[577].

Sexually dimorphic features of the cranium and mandible are a reflection of the extra somatic growth that males experience before their later puberty and the acceleration in muscle mass that occurs during this period, whilst females retain the more gracile juvenile form[578]. The method of sex determination from the cranium and mandible used during this research was that devised by Buikstra and Ubelaker, which scores the size and shape of five different features (the nuchal crest, glabella, mastoid process, orbital ridge and mandible)[579]. Tests of the visual sexing method for the cranium have reported accuracies of seventy per cent and eighty per cent, with an increase to ninety per cent when the mandible is included, although another study has found mandibles of individuals otherwise sexed as female were incorrectly assigned the male sex in fifty-one per cent of cases[580]. When sex determination methods from the pelvis and cranium and mandible are combined, the accuracy rates have been reported to increase to over ninety-seven per cent[581].

Once the sexually dimorphic features of the pelvis and cranium and mandible of the individuals in this research had been assessed, they were placed into one of five categories, dependent on their combined scores, namely:

Definite female   F, or female
Possible female   ?F, or ?female
Indeterminate   ?
Possible male   ?M, or ?male
Definite male   M, or male

Individuals of indeterminate sex were those where the features of the pelvis and cranium and mandible were either individually intermediate between male and female or where there was a strong disagreement between the sex determination from the cranium and mandible and that from the pelvis. However, in most cases, the sex from the pelvis was preferred to that from the cranium and mandible due to the higher accuracy rates, and also because it has been suggested that older females can have more masculine crania, whilst the crania of younger males tend to look more feminine, which reflects the hormonal changes taking place in post-menopausal females and the weaker androgen influence in younger males[582]. For poorly preserved individuals where very few or none of the sexually dimorphic features could be assessed, the sex may have been recorded as 'unknown', which does not mean the same as 'indeterminate'. However, the nature of the research meant that this term was very seldom used.

Metrical Analysis

A number of measurements from the cranium, mandible and post-cranial skeleton were recorded from non-adult and adult individuals. They were taken using an osteometric board, spreading calipers, linear calipers and a tape measure where appropriate. Measurements from the long bones were used to estimate stature for adult individuals using the formulae devised by Trotter in 1970[583]. These were based on modern North American samples, so there is doubt about their validity for use on European archaeological populations; however, at present, they are the formulae most commonly applied to archaeological samples, making it possible to compare the present sample with larger datasets from the periods under study.

Adult stature is a combination of genetic and environmental factors, with environmental stresses (such as poor nutrition) preventing individuals from fulfilling their genetic growth potential and resulting in reduced skeletal growth and a reduced terminal (adult) stature[584]. Therefore, if the average stature of a specific group within a genetically homogenous population is lower than the average for that population, this may imply higher levels of environmental stress amongst that specific group[585].

Measurements from the cranium and mandible were also used to aid in the assessment of the ancestry of individuals. Ancestry from the human skull has long been a controversial subject due to its use in the nineteenth and earlier twentieth centuries to produce typologies of 'higher' and 'lower' races[586]. However, it is generally accepted that there are three broad categories of skull type amongst modern populations, although with much admixing amongst certain populations – namely, European, sub-Saharan African and South East Asian (formerly known as caucasoid, negroid and mongoloid, respectively), which all have a number of distinct cranial features[587]. The crania of all individuals in this research were subjected to a visual assessment of their ancestry based on the criteria recorded by William Bass in 1995, with complete skulls having photographs taken of their anterior and lateral view to aid in later analysis. If any distinctly non-caucasoid features were noted on a skull, these were recorded and an assessment of ancestry was made. These visual assessments were then checked by the inputting of cranial measurements into FORDISC 3.0, a discriminant functions software program based on William Howells's worldwide reference populations[588]. This assesses how similar the sample skull is to each of the reference populations in the program and allows a skull to be identified as belonging to one specific population, a mix of different populations or as having no affinity with any known population.

Metrical analysis was also used in the assessment of long-bone asymmetry, which is more commonly found in the upper limb as a result of increased mechanical loading of the dominant side. Increases in bone length and dimensions of articular surfaces are often a result of large mechanical loads being placed on the dominant limb during adolescence whilst the long bones are still growing, whereas increases in diaphyseal cross-sectional shape and area, due to loading, are more common in adults[589].

Non-metrical Analysis
A number of non-metric traits were recorded on each skeleton, most on

the cranium and mandible but also some on the post-cranial skeleton, and these were taken from the list given in Buikstra and Ubelaker. In cases where two or more skeletons from a given population demonstrated a particular non-metric trait that was not listed on the recording form, this was also recorded. Non-metric traits are 'minor variants of phenotypic expression'[590], with some believed to have a genetic basis, whilst others may reflect environmental and activity-related pressures[591].

Musculo-skeletal Stress Markers

Musculo-skeletal stress markers, otherwise known as enthesopathies or entheseal changes, are expressions of stress at muscle attachment sites on the skeleton in the form of enthesophytic bone formation around the margins of an attachment site, or roughening, porosity or cortical defects of the surface of the attachment[592]. Their formation has been linked to patterns of activity amongst certain populations[593], although a number of recent studies have advised caution as to their use as they have found that body size and age have a significant effect on their expression[594]. However, one recent study has confirmed that stress markers on the humerus correlated with activity patterns in a sample of populations of known occupation, with age not significantly affecting their presence and severity, and the study suggested that they could be used to reconstruct past lifestyles as long as the appropriate muscle attachment sites were properly recorded[595]. For this research, the presence of stress markers and at which muscle attachment site they occurred were recorded, as well as the nature of their expression (i.e. whether enthesophytes, roughening, porosity or cortical defects).

Pathological Changes

Any pathological changes to the skeleton were described in detail and, where necessary, photographed to aid in their diagnosis. Diagnoses were usually made with reference to the descriptions and photographs in the volumes produced by Aufderheide and Rodríguez-Martín, and Ortner, although other texts were used where necessary[596]. All reference material used to aid in diagnosis are discussed and acknowledged at the appropriate places in the text.

Trauma Analysis

As one of the major aims of this research was to assess the manner of the decapitations through an analysis of the osteological evidence for the practice, evidence for cut marks and other peri-mortem trauma, both directly and indirectly related to decapitation, were very carefully examined, described and photographed, as well as being visually recorded on pro forma. Those for the cervical and upper thoracic vertebrae were specially designed for the project by Caroline Needham from the Centre for Anatomy and Human Identification, University of Dundee.

It was vital for this research that peri-mortem cut marks and fractures were distinguished from those sustained ante-mortem and demonstrating healing, indicating the individual survived the injury for some time before death, or post-mortem, either by ancient disturbances and truncations of the skeletal remains or by modern excavation damage.

Fresh bone – which retains its collagen content for a number of weeks after death, depending on the conditions of the burial environment, and is therefore more pliable – will fracture differently to dry bone, which has lost this collagen content and become more brittle[597]. This difference in response to the application of force is the main factor used to distinguish between peri- and post-mortem fractures. The brittle nature of dry bone means that it tends to present with roughened fracture surfaces, undulating or jagged fracture margins and a tendency to produce fracture lines that run perpendicular to the long axis of the element. However, fractures that occur in the earlier dry-bone stages can produce spiral or helical fracture outlines that resemble peri-mortem fractures in this regard, although not in the appearance of the fracture surface, a feature that can be used to distinguish fractures that are generally indicative of post-depositional disturbance and may have occurred as part of a secondary burial ritual[598]. Post-mortem cranial fractures were distinguished by their slightly roughened broken edges and their linearity, with fractures often crossing cranial sutures and producing sub-rectangular and diamond-shaped broken fragments[599]. Broken surfaces that are paler than the rest of the bone are also a distinguishing feature in post-mortem fractures of more modern origin, as, unlike the surrounding bone, the broken surface has not been exposed to staining by water, soil and vegetation[600]. Excavation damage can also be identified as fractures with pale edges and with crushed bone and soil smeared across the broken surface, which are often the result of blows with a mattock or shovel, or by small penetrating marks with pale crushed edges, which are caused by the point of archaeological trowels.

Ante-mortem sharp-force and blunt-force trauma and fractures were distinguished by the presence of actively remodelling bony calluses around the area of the trauma or by healing having been completed. Studies by Sledzik and Kelly[601] on soldiers of the American Civil War who had survived injuries for varying lengths of time, and for whom the type of injury, the length of time survived and the medical treatment received were known, found that osseous remodelling, in the form of periosteal woven bone, was seen, on average, thirteen days after the injury was sustained, with some individuals demonstrating changes after seven days. Therefore, trauma with evidence for healing can be assumed to have occurred at least seven days ante-mortem. A bony callus will then start to appear around the site of the fracture, usually distinguishable on radiographs from two to three weeks after the injury is sustained[602]. Consolidation of this woven bone callus into compact lamellar bone then occurs within weeks or months, depending on the element affected, and bony remodelling of the site then takes place over the following years until the fracture becomes indistinguishable from the surrounding bone in around ten years[603].

All evidence for ante-mortem trauma was described in detail and photographed where appropriate. This included ante-mortem blunt- and sharp-force trauma and fractures of the cranial and post-cranial skeleton, with the descriptions of different types of fractures – including linear, comminuted, crush, compression, avulsion, greenstick and impaction – applied as defined by Lovell in 1997[604]. For cranial vault depressed fractures, features such as size, degree of healing and any associated infection were recorded, whilst for other types of fracture, the degree of angulation, misalignment and shortening, as well as the amount of healing and any associated infections, were recorded as described by Lovell in 1997 and Roberts in 2000[605].

Peri-mortem fractures were distinguished by their smooth un-stepped fracture surface with obliquely angled edges[606]. Long bones and other elements, such as the mandible, tend to splinter, with fragments often remaining attached to one another and with sharp and irregular fragments of bone[607]. Elements can also present with 'butterfly' fractures, so called because of the shape of the bone fragment produced, which often result from bending forces that cause fractures along the shear planes within the bone structure that run at 45-degree angles to the compressive stress[608] (plate 57). Peri-mortem fractures to the cranium present with a different appearance due to the spherical shape of the vault and often exhibit concentric fractures around the point of impact and/or linear, radiating fractures from the point of impact of the blow that commonly extend to the cranial sutures and then follow the line of the less resistant and weaker suture rather than crossing it[609]. The point of impact on the ectocranial surface is often compressed, which can also produce an equivalent bowing of the endocranial surface, or the force of the blow can fracture both tables of the vault and push the resulting fragments into the intra-cranial space. These fragments can remain attached to the vault or can separate at the endocranial concentric fracture lines, producing an internal 'bevel', with or without the detached fragment being preserved[610] (plate 58).

Peri-mortem sharp-force injuries were distinguished from peri-mortem fractures by their linearity, well-defined clean edges, and flat, smooth, polished cut surfaces[611]. There are a number of different classes of sharp-force injury, including chopping blows, incisions and stab wounds, all of which produce different signatures on bone.

Chopping blows were distinguished by their linear and broad appearance, with their width and depth being very similar, and sometimes presenting with striations running parallel to the short axis of the cut surface, which are presumed to be produced by blades with defects in their cutting edge[612] (plate 59).

Incised cuts were distinguished by their narrow and fine appearance, with striations often present which run parallel to the long axis of the cut, a result of the blade being drawn across the bone surface rather than through it. These striations are particularly apparent in slicing/incised wounds inflicted by lithic tools and are considered to be one of the characteristic features of lithic as opposed to metal weapons, along with curvature of the walls of the cut[613], although striations have also been noted in incised cuts made with metal tools[614] (plate 4).

Stabbing injuries were distinguished by being deeper than they are wide, and manifested as punctures into or through the bone with polished margins[615] (plate 60).

The angle of the cuts was recorded visually, as well as being described; for example, a cut could be described as being angled right-superior to left-inferior and postero-superior to antero-inferior, and the direction could usually be determined by the presence of small amounts of crushing of the cortical and trabecular bone on the margin facing the direction of the blow, and/or peeling of the bone surface on the far margin of the cut if the bone was bisected, or lifting of the bone on the far margin if the cut nicked into the bone[616].

Various studies have attempted to identify the distinguishing features of sharp-force injuries produced by different types of metal instrument, including heavy and thick-bladed tools such as machetes and axes, and lighter and finer swords and knives[617]. In 2005, Alunni-Perret *et al.* compared the features of experimentally produced knife marks on defleshed human bone to those produced by an axe and found that axe marks were characterised by smooth cut surfaces, a characteristic of sharp-force injuries, as well as the pushing back of the edges of the adjacent bone that are indicative of a blunt-force mechanism[618], although, as Lewis pointed out in 2008, it is not known how the absence of soft tissue overlying the bone may have affected the results[619]. Lewis also demonstrated clear differences between sharp-force injuries made with swords compared to those produced by knives on bovine femorae. Sword injuries demonstrated deeper and wider cuts with a straight floor and either a V-shaped section or a flat-bottomed one, depending on how sharp the sword was, and had one smooth, vertically curved wall and one rougher, vertically straight wall. Knife wounds, on the other hand, were shallower and thinner, with a meandering floor that was always V-shaped in section and with both walls presenting as vertical. Sword cuts also demonstrated more damage to the surrounding bone than those produced by knives. Lewis concluded that it was possible to easily distinguish between marks produced by swords as opposed to knives, although he did seem to suggest that during the experimental study, the swords had been used to chop, whilst the knives had been used to slice. This, therefore, does not really assist in distinguishing slicing (incised) cuts made by swords from those produced by knives. The study also attempted to distinguish between the cuts made by different types of sword, including machetes, broadswords, katanas and scimitars, and determined that the differences seen were dependent on how heavy and sharp the blades were, as well as whether they were wielded with one or two hands. Heavier weapons tended to produce more breakage of the bone surrounding the cut, sharper weapons produced unilateral flaking of the sides of the cut, as did weapons wielded single-handed, whilst bilateral flaking of the sides was produced by blunter weapons and those wielded with two hands. This analysis was used during the present study to aid in the differentiation of slicing/incised knife marks and hacking/chopping blows made either by an axe or sword, but the types of sword used during the study and their characteristics are not particularly applicable to the periods under study in the present research.

Peri-mortem trauma that was recorded as being directly related to the act of decapitation was restricted to the area from the mid- to inferior part of the cranium down to the shoulders, and included trauma seen on the cervical vertebrae, the claviculae, the superior part of the scapulae and manubrium, the mandible, and the mastoid processes, occipital and cranial base. Trauma recorded on any other elements were assessed as to their likely aetiology; for example, peri-mortem trauma of the distal upper limbs, metacarpals and manual digits are most commonly recorded in individuals who have been the victims of assault and are related to attempts to ward off blows – so called 'defensive injuries' – whilst cuts to areas of significant soft tissue (cuts to the anterior of the *ossa coxae* or sacrum probably originated as blows into the abdomen), musculature or ligament attachments (such as the rotator cuff of the shoulder or the distal femur) might have been attempts to incapacitate the individual by immobilising them[620].

Statistical Analyses

Statistical analysis was employed to make full use of the data where the sample size was judged to be large enough for such tests to be meaningful. Fisher's exact test for small samples was used for the majority of statistical analyses of categorical data, whilst the chi-square test was used for larger sample sizes, and the *t*-test and one sample *t*-test were used to compare the means of continuous data. The tests were performed using the GraphPad Quick Calcs Online Calculator[621]. The text does not include the full details of the results of the statistical analyses, but the result was judged to be statistically significant when the '*p* value' was smaller than 0.05.

Appendix 2

Identifying Decapitations – A Signature List

A number of different types of decapitation have been identified and described in this book, with data presented on the nature of the associated peri-mortem trauma, the periods and types of site in which the type of decapitation was found, the types of individuals affected, the associated burial practice and body position, and the possible interpretations for each type. Each of these different types is summarised below and it is hoped that this may be used to provide better descriptions of decapitated burials excavated and analysed in the future.

Type 1: Incised cutting to the cervical vertebrae
Type 1a
• Peri-mortem decapitation trauma: multiple incised cuts to the bodies, arches and facets of the cervical vertebrae
• Other peri-mortem trauma: none
• Frequency: rare
• Periods found: Bronze Age, Romano-British
• Types of sites: palaeochannels, urban cemeteries, rural and small-town cemeteries
• Individuals affected: adult males, adult females, non-adults
• Position of head: isolated, displaced
• Ante- or post-mortem: post-mortem
• Possible interpretations: Cult of the Head (prehistoric examples), *poena post mortem*, preventing dead from returning

Type 1b
• Peri-mortem decapitation trauma: multiple incised cuts to the bodies, arches and facets of the cervical vertebrae
• Other peri-mortem trauma: cranial sharp-force trauma, peri-mortem vertebral fractures
• Frequency: rare

- Periods found: Iron Age
- Types of sites: settlement sites, hills forts
- Individuals affected: adult males
- Position of head: isolated
- Ante- or post-mortem: ante-mortem
- Possible interpretations: Cult of the Head, warfare

Type 2: Incised cutting to the anterior of the cervical vertebrae
Type 2a
- Peri-mortem decapitation trauma: incised cut to the anterior of the cervical vertebrae associated with additional incised cuts to the cervical column
- Other peri-mortem trauma: none
- Frequency: rare
- Periods found: Romano-British
- Types of sites: rural and small-town cemeteries (statistically more for whole of Type 2), urban cemeteries (rare)
- Individuals affected: adult males, adult females, non-adults
- Position of head: displaced
- Ante- or post-mortem: probably ante-mortem
- Possible interpretations: human sacrifice

Type 2b
- Peri-mortem decapitation trauma: incised cuts to the anterior of the cervical vertebrae associated with additional incised cuts and/or chopping blows to the cervical column
- Other peri-mortem trauma: possible (blunt-force cranial injury)
- Frequency: rare
- Periods found: Romano-British
- Types of sites: rural and small-town cemeteries, urban cemeteries
- Individuals affected: adult males, adult females
- Position of head: displaced
- Ante- or post-mortem: probably ante-mortem, certain in cases where neck flexed, probable in cases with incapacitating injuries or restraint of body
- Possible interpretations: human sacrifice, execution

Type 2c
- Peri-mortem decapitation trauma: incised cuts to the anterior of the cervical vertebrae associated with additional chopping blows

• Other peri-mortem trauma: possible (sharp-force cranial injuries, incapacitating injuries)
• Frequency: rare
• Periods found: Romano-British
• Types of sites: urban cemeteries, rural and small-town cemeteries
• Individuals affected: adult males, adult females
• Position of head: displaced
• Ante- or post-mortem: probably ante-mortem, certain in cases where neck flexed, probable in cases with incapacitating injuries or restraint of body
• Possible interpretations: human sacrifice, execution

Type 3: Chopping blows to the cervical vertebrae
Type 3a
• Peri-mortem decapitation trauma: multiple chopping blows to cervical vertebrae with no additional chops or cuts
• Other peri-mortem trauma: none
• Frequency: relatively common
• Periods found: Romano-British, early medieval, medieval
• Types of sites: urban cemeteries, rural and small-town cemeteries, attritional cemeteries, isolated burials, execution cemeteries, priory cemeteries
• Individuals affected: adult males, adult females, non-adults
• Position of head: displaced, correct anatomical position, absent, isolated
• Ante- or post-mortem: unknown, ante-mortem where neck flexed, possible ante-mortem in cases with dental trauma or evidence of restraint of the body
• Possible interpretations: execution, *poena post mortem*, preventing dead from returning

Type 3b
• Peri-mortem decapitation trauma: chopping blow to cervical vertebrae with associated additional chopping blows or incised cuts
• Other peri-mortem trauma: none
• Frequency: relatively common
• Periods found: Iron Age, Romano-British, early medieval
• Types of sites: settlement sites, urban cemeteries, rural and small-town cemeteries, execution cemeteries
• Individuals affected: adult males, adult females

• Position of head: isolated, displaced
• Ante- or post-mortem: unknown, ante-mortem where neck flexed, possibly ante-mortem in cases with evidence of restraint of the body
• Possible interpretations: Cult of the Head, execution, *poena post mortem*, preventing dead from returning

Type 4: Single chopping blow to the cervical vertebrae
Type 4a
• Peri-mortem decapitation trauma: single chopping blow to cervical vertebrae delivered from the anterior
• Other peri-mortem trauma: none
• Frequency: relatively common
• Periods found: Iron Age, Romano-British, early medieval
• Types of sites: settlement sites, hill forts, urban cemeteries, rural and small-town cemeteries, execution cemeteries
• Individuals affected: adult males, adult females, non-adults
• Position of head: displaced, correct anatomical position, absent
• Ante- or post-mortem: unknown, possibly ante-mortem in cases with evidence of restraint of the body
• Possible interpretations: Cult of the Head, execution, *poena post mortem*, preventing dead from returning

Type 4b
• Peri-mortem decapitation trauma: single chopping blow to cervical vertebrae delivered from the posterior
• Other peri-mortem trauma: none
• Frequency: common
• Periods found: Iron Age, Romano-British, early medieval, medieval
• Types of sites: settlement sites, hill forts, urban cemeteries, rural and small-town cemeteries, attritional cemeteries, execution cemeteries, isolated burials, church cemeteries
• Individuals affected: adult males, adult females, non-adults
• Position of head: isolated, displaced, correct anatomical position, absent
• Ante- or post-mortem: unknown, ante-mortem where neck flexed, possibly ante-mortem in cases with evidence of restraint of the body, dental trauma or head retained in correct anatomical position
• Possible interpretations: execution, *poena post mortem*, preventing dead from returning

Type 4c

• Peri-mortem decapitation trauma: single chopping blow to the cervical vertebrae delivered from a lateral direction
• Other peri-mortem trauma: none
• Frequency: rare
• Periods found: early medieval
• Types of sites: execution cemeteries
• Individuals affected: adult males
• Position of head: correct anatomical position, displaced, absent
• Ante- or post-mortem: unknown, ante-mortem when neck flexed, probably ante-mortem when evidence of restraint of the body
• Possible interpretation: execution

Type 5: Chopping blows associated with non-decapitation related trauma
Type 5a

• Peri-mortem decapitation trauma: chopping blows to the cervical vertebrae sometimes associated with additional chops or cuts
• Other peri-mortem trauma: sharp-/blunt-force cranial injuries
• Frequency: rare
• Periods found: Romano-British
• Types of sites: urban cemeteries, rural and small-town cemeteries
• Individuals affected: adult males, adult females
• Position of head: displaced, correct anatomical position
• Ante- or post-mortem: ante-mortem
• Possible interpretations: execution

Type 5b

• Peri-mortem decapitation trauma: chopping blows to the cervical vertebrae sometimes associated with additional chops or cuts
• Other peri-mortem trauma: post-cranial sharp-/blunt-force injuries (defensive or incapacitating injuries)
• Frequency: rare
• Periods found: Romano-British
• Types of sites: urban cemeteries, rural and small-town cemeteries
• Individuals affected: adult males, adult females
• Position of head: displaced, correct anatomical position
• Ante- or post-mortem: ante-mortem
• Possible interpretations: execution

Type 5c
• Peri-mortem decapitation trauma: unknown
• Other peri-mortem trauma: chops and cuts to remove lower limbs at the knee
• Frequency: very rare
• Periods found: Romano-British, early medieval
• Types of sites: rural and small-town cemeteries, attritional cemeteries
• Individuals affected: adult females
• Position of head: displaced
• Ante- or post-mortem: unknown
• Possible interpretations: *poena post mortem*, preventing dead from returning

Type 6: Extensive trauma with incidental chopping blows to cervical vertebrae
Type 6a
• Peri-mortem decapitation trauma: chopping blows to the cervical vertebrae (incidental)
• Other peri-mortem trauma: extensive cranial and post-cranial sharp-force injuries
• Frequency: common
• Periods found: Iron Age, medieval
• Types of sites: isolated burials, settlement sites, church cemeteries, priory cemeteries
• Individuals affected: adult males
• Position of head: absent, correct anatomical position
• Ante- or post-mortem: ante-mortem
• Possible interpretation: warfare

Type 6b
• Peri-mortem decapitation trauma: chopping blows to the cervical vertebrae (incidental)
• Other peri-mortem trauma: extensive cranial and post-cranial sharp-force injuries (restricted to defensive and incapacitating injuries)
• Frequency: relatively rare
• Periods found: early medieval
• Types of sites: attritional cemeteries, isolated burials, mass graves
• Individuals affected: adult males
• Position of head: correct anatomical position

• Ante- or post-mortem: ante-mortem
• Possible interpretation: warfare, massacre

Type 7: Extensive dismemberment trauma with single chop to neck
• Peri-mortem decapitation trauma: single chop to posterior of mandible or cervical vertebrae
• Other peri-mortem trauma: extensive chopping blows to all parts of the skeleton with separation of elements and vertical chops to vertebral arches and bodies
• Frequency: very rare
• Periods found: early medieval, medieval
• Types of sites: isolated burials, abbey cemeteries
• Individuals affected: adult males
• Position of head: absent, displaced
• Ante- or post-mortem: ante-mortem
• Possible interpretation: execution

Type 8: Incised cutting of the clavicle
• Peri-mortem decapitation trauma: incised cuts to the clavicle
• Other peri-mortem trauma: none
• Frequency: very rare
• Periods found: Neolithic
• Types of sites: long barrows
• Individuals affected: adults
• Position of head: disarticulated
• Ante-or post-mortem: probably post-mortem
• Possible interpretation: unknown

Appendix 3

Skeletons Analysed as Part of the Research

Skeletons Analysed by the Author

Site name	County	Period	No. individuals
Birstall	Leicestershire	Bronze Age	1
Maiden Bower	Bedfordshire	Iron Age	1
Prebendal Court, Aylesbury	Buckinghamshire	Iron Age	1
Sovell Down	Dorset	Iron Age	1
Danebury	Hampshire	Iron Age	3
Old Down Farm, Andover	Hampshire	Iron Age	1
Suddern Farm	Hampshire	Iron Age	1
Winklebury	Hampshire	Iron Age	1
Stanwick	North Yorkshire	Iron Age	1
Dunstable	Bedfordshire	Romano-British	13
Friary Fields, Dunstable	Bedfordshire	Romano-British	3
Gayhurst Quarry	Buckinghamshire	Romano-British	1
Yaxley	Cambridgeshire	Romano-British	1
Alington Avenue, Dorchester	Dorset	Romano-British	1
Little Keep, Dorchester	Dorset	Romano-British	5
Maiden Castle Road, Dorchester	Dorset	Romano-British	1
Old Vicarage, Fordington	Dorset	Romano-British	1
Southfield House, Dorchester	Dorset	Romano-British	1
Woodcutts	Dorset	Romano-British	2
Woodyates	Dorset	Romano-British	1
Carfax, Winchester	Hampshire	Romano-British	1
Cowdery's Down	Hampshire	Romano-British	1
Eagle Hotel, Winchester	Hampshire	Romano-British	1
Hyde Street, Winchester	Hampshire	Romano-British	1
Lankhills, Winchester	Hampshire	Romano-British	13
Northbrook Avenue, Winchester	Hampshire	Romano-British	1
St Martin's Close, Winchester	Hampshire	Romano-British	1
Victoria Road East, Winchester	Hampshire	Romano-British	1
Winchester Street, Andover	Hampshire	Romano-British	1
Mundford	Norfolk	Romano-British	2
Runham	Norfolk	Romano-British	1
129 The Mount, York	North Yorkshire	Romano-British	1
1-3 Driffield Terrace, York	North Yorkshire	Romano-British	30
6 Driffield Terrace, York	North Yorkshire	Romano-British	18
Moss Street Depot, York	North Yorkshire	Romano-British	3
The Mount School, York	North Yorkshire	Romano-British	5
Trentholme Drive, York	North Yorkshire	Romano-British	4
Mallows Cotton	Northamptonshire	Romano-British	1
Stanwick	Northamptonshire	Romano-British	6
Water Lane, Towcester	Northamptonshire	Romano-British	2
Great Casterton	Rutland	Romano-British	1
Maiden Castle Long Mound	Dorset	Early medieval	1
Great Chesterford	Essex	Early medieval	1
Bevis's Grave, Southampton	Hampshire	Early medieval	1
Meon Hill	Hampshire	Early medieval	10
Portway West, Andover	Hampshire	Early medieval	1
Winnall	Hampshire	Early medieval	2
Ketton Quarry	Rutland	Early medieval	1
London Road, Staines	Surrey	Early medieval	5
North Elmham	Norfolk	Medieval	1
St Michael, Thetford	Norfolk	Medieval	1
Fishergate, York	North Yorkshire	Medieval	9
George Street, York	North Yorkshire	Medieval	1

Skeletons Analysed by Other Reseaechers

Site	Period	No. individuals	Reference
Sutton Walls, Herefordshire	Iron Age	7	Cornwall 1954
Baldock, Hertfordshire	Iron Age	1	McKinley 2009c
Heslington, York, North Yorkshire	Iron Age	1	Buckberry 2010
South Cadbury, Somerset	Iron Age	5	Jones 2008
Joist Fen, Lakenheath, Suffolk	Iron Age	1	Anderson 2000a
Whitehouse Road, Ipswich, Suffolk	Iron Age	1	Anderson 2000b
Birchfield Road, Great Barford, Bedfordshire	Romano-British	2	Geber and Boston 2007
Kempston, Bedfordshire	Romano-British	12	Boylston and Roberts 2004; Marshall 1999
Babraham Institute, Cambridge, Cambridgeshire	Romano-British	5	Timberlake *et al.* 2007; Dodwell n.d.
Camp Ground, Colne Fen, Cambridgeshire	Romano-British	1	Dodwell 2004
Chesterton Lane Corner, Cambridge, Cambridgeshire	Romano-British	1	Cessford 2007
Fox Cover Farm, Market Deeping, Cambridgeshire	Romano-British	2	Gowland 2000
Foxton, Cambridgeshire	Romano-British	2	Goode and Bardill 1995
Godmanchester, Cambridgeshire	Romano-British	3	Brickley 2003
Jeavons Lane, Cambourne, Cambridgeshire	Romano-British	1	McKinley 2009a
Jesus Lane, Cambridge, Cambridgeshire	Romano-British	3	Alexander *et al.* 2004
Milton Landfill, Cambridgeshire	Romano-British	1	Wallis forthcoming
Orton Longueville, Cambridgeshire	Romano-British	1	Wells and Dallas 1976
Watson's Lane, Little Thetford, Cambridgeshire	Romano-British	1	Dodwell 1996
Poundbury, Dorchester, Dorset	Romano-British	1	Farwell and Molleson 1993
Butt Road, Colchester, Essex	Romano-British	1	Crummy 2000
Chignall St James, Essex	Romano-British	5	Stirland 1998
120-122 London Road, Gloucester, Gloucestershire	Romano-British	1	Simmonds *et al.* 2008
Ashchurch, Gloucestershire	Romano-British	2	Holst 2004a
Bath Gate, Cirencester, Gloucestershire	Romano-British	10	Wells 1982; Bush and Stirland 1991
Cotswold Community, Gloucestershire	Romano-British	1	Dean and Boston 2010
Cowhill, Gloucestershire	Romano-British	1	Holst 2004b

Frocester Court, Gloucestershire	Romano-British	2	Price 2000
Parliament Street, Gloucester, Gloucestershire	Romano-British	1	Gilmore 2008
Roughground Farm, Lechlade, Gloucestershire	Romano-British	2	Allen *et al.* 1993
Syreford Mill, Wycomb, Gloucestershire	Romano-British	1	Firth 1998
Kenchester, Herefordshire	Romano-British	2	Everton 1985
Royston Road, Baldock, Hertfordshire	Romano-British	2	McKinley 1993
Bower Road, Smeeth, Kent	Romano-British	1	Witkin 2006
Worsley Moss, Lancashire	Romano-British	1	Garland, A.N. 1995
Bishop Grosseteste College, Lincoln, Lincolnshire	Romano-British	1	Boylston 1997
Lord Mayor's Walk, York, North Yorkshire	Romano-British	1	Robinson 2005
Parlington Hollins, North Yorkshire	Romano-British	2	Holbrey and Burgess 2001
Slip Gill Windypit, Helmsley, North Yorkshire	Romano-British	1	Leach 2006
Ashton, Northamptonshire	Romano-British	2	Bush and Stirland 1991
Duston, Northamptonshire	Romano-British	2	Harman n.d.(a)
Station Road, Cogenhoe, Northamptonshire	Romano-British	1	Harman n.d.(b)
Vindolanda, Northumberland	Romano-British	1	Loe 2003
Barrow Hills, Radley, Oxfordshire	Romano-British	4	Harman 2007
Claydon Pike, Oxfordshire	Romano-British	2	Witkin 2007
Cold Harbour Farm, Crowmarsh, Oxfordshire	Romano-British	2	Clarke 1996
Horcott Quarry, Oxfordshire	Romano-British	8	Clough n.d.(a)
South Parks Road, Oxford, Oxfordshire	Romano-British	1	Witkin 2005
Stanton Harcourt, Oxfordshire	Romano-British	3	Harman *et al.* 1981
Wroxton St Mary, Oxfordshire	Romano-British	1	Harman 1986
Little Spittle, Ilchester, Somerset	Romano-British	4	Everton and Rogers 1982
Flixton Park Quarry, Suffolk	Romano-British	4	Anderson 2011
Icklingham, Suffolk	Romano-British	6	Wells 1976
Lakenheath, Suffolk	Romano-British	1	Anderson 2005
Rickinghall, Suffolk	Romano-British	1	Anderson 1995
Birch Abbey, Alcester, Warwickshire	Romano-British	1	Denston 1994
Lloyd's Bank, Alcester, Warwickshire	Romano-British	1	Booth and Evans 2001
Stretton-on-Fosse, Warwickshire	Romano-British	1	Ford 2003

Rothwell Haigh, West Yorkshire	Romano-British	1	Manchester 2011
Nettleton, Wiltshire	Romano-British	7	Richardson 1982
Lochend, Dunbar	Roman Iron Age	1	Brothwell and Powers 1966
Sculptor's Cave, Grampion	Roman Iron Age	6	Schulting *et al.* 2010
Kintbury, Berkshire	Early medieval	1	Smith 1998
Chesterton Lane Corner, Cambridge, Cambridgeshire	Early medieval	5	Cessford 2007
Hillside Meadow, Fordham, Cambridgeshire	Early medieval	2	Brickley 2011
Old Dairy Cottage, Winchester, Hampshire	Early medieval	7	Cherryson and Buckberry 2011
Walkington Wold, North Yorkshire	Early medieval	6	Buckberry and Hadley 2007; Buckberry 2008
St John's College, Oxford, Oxfordshire	Early medieval	6	Falys n.d.
Shakenoak, Wilcote, Oxfordshire	Early medieval	1	Brodribb *et al.* 2005
Tubney Woods Quarry, Oxfordshire	Early medieval	1	Clough n.d.(b)
Guildown, Surrey	Early medieval	5	Brants 2005
Roche Court Down, Wiltshire	Early medieval	1	Tildesley 1932
Stonehenge, Wiltshire	Early medieval	1	Pitts *et al.* 2002
St John's, Worcester, Worcestershire	Early medieval	1	Western 2009
Fishergate House, York, North Yorkshire	Medieval	3	Holst 2005
Jewbury, York, North Yorkshire	Medieval	1	Brothwell and Browne 1994
Towton, North Yorkshire	Medieval	4	Novak 2000b; Holst *et al.* 2000; Holst and Coughlan 2000
Hulton Abbey, Staffordshire	Medieval	1	Lewis, M.E. 2008
Woodcock Rise, Brandon, Suffolk	Medieval	1	Tester 2004

Appendix 4

Comparative Sites

Chapter 3: Romano-British

Site name	County	Reference
Rural and small-town cemeteries		
Dunstable	Bedfordshire	Jones and Horne 1981; Matthews 1981
Friary Fields, Dunstable	Bedfordshire	Gardner 2004; Waldron 2004
Great Barford	Bedfordshire	Geber and Boston 2007; Timby *et al.* 2007
Kempston	Bedfordshire	Boylston and Roberts 2004; Dawson 2004
Gayhurst Quarry	Buckinghamshire	Anderson 2007; Chapman 2007
Babraham Institute	Cambridgeshire	Dodwell 2007b, n.d.; Timberlake *et al.* 2007
Camp Ground, Colne Fen	Cambridgeshire	Dodwell 2004
Jeavons Lane, Cambourne	Cambridgeshire	McKinley 2009a; Wright *et al.* 2009
Market Deeping	Cambridgeshire	Gowland 2000; Trimble 2000
Milton Landfill	Cambridgeshire	Gibson *et al.* forthcoming; Wallis forthcoming
Yaxley	Cambridgeshire	Tucker 2008b
Chignall	Essex	Clarke, C.P. 1998; Stirland 1998
Ashchurch	Gloucestershire	Holst 2004a
Cotswold Community	Gloucestershire	Dean and Boston 2010; Powell *et al.* 2010
Frocester	Gloucestershire	Price 2000
Horcott Quarry	Gloucestershire	Clough 2009, n.d.(a); Mullin *et al.* 2009
Roughground Farm, Lechlade	Gloucestershire	Allen *et al.* 1993
Cowdery's Down	Hampshire	Millett and James 1983
Winchester Street, Andover	Hampshire	Jennings 2000
Water Lane, Towcester	Northamptonshire	Walker *et al.* 2008
Cassington	Oxfordshire	Harman *et al.* 1981
Curbridge	Oxfordshire	Harman *et al.* 1981
Radley	Oxfordshire	Harman *et al.* 1981
Radley II	Oxfordshire	Chambers and Boyle 2007; Harman 2007
Stanton Harcourt	Oxfordshire	McGavin 1980; Harman *et al.* 1981
Great Casterton	Rutland	McConnell and Grassam 2005; Phillips and Leach n.d.;
Ilchester	Somerset	Everton and Rogers 1982; Leach 1982
Lakenheath	Suffolk	Anderson 2005; Caruth 2005
Birch Abbey, Alcester	Warwickshire	Denston 1994; Mahany 1994
Urban cemeteries		
Alington Avenue, Dorchester	Dorset	Davies *et al.* 2002; Waldron 2002
Little Keep, Dorchester	Dorset	McKinley and Egging Dinwiddy 2009; McKinley 2009b
Maiden Castle Road, Dorchester	Dorset	Smith *et al.* 1997
Poundbury, Dorchester	Dorset	Farwell and Molleson 1993
122 London Road, Gloucester	Gloucestershire	Simmonds *et al.* 2008

124 London Road, Gloucester	Gloucestershire	Foundations Archaeology 2003
Bath Gate, Cirencester	Gloucestershire	McWhirr *et al.* 1982; Wells 1982
Carfax, Winchester	Hampshire	Ottaway *et al.* 2012
Eagle Hotel, Winchester	Hampshire	Ottaway *et al.* 2012
Hyde Street, Winchester	Hampshire	Ottaway *et al.* 2012
Lankhills I, Winchester	Hampshire	Clarke 1979
Lankhills II, Winchester	Hampshire	Booth *et al.* 2010
St Martin's Close, Winchester	Hampshire	Ottaway *et al.* 2012
Victoria Road, Winchester	Hampshire	Ottaway *et al.* 2012
Eastern London	London	Barber and Bowsher 2000
Trentholme Drive, York	North Yorkshire	Wenham 1968

Chapter 8: Medieval

Site Name	County	Reference
St Nicholas Shambles	London	White 1988
North Elmham	Norfolk	Wells and Cayton 1980
Fishergate, York	North Yorkshire	Stroud 2003a
Helen-on-the-Walls, York	North Yorkshire	Dawes and Magilton 1980
Jewbury, York	North Yorkshire	Brothwell and Browne 1994
SS James and Mary Magdalene, Chichester	West Sussex	Magilton *et al.* 2008

Glossary

Anterior (ventral)	front
Cortical bone	compact, dense bone that forms the outer layer of bones
Diaphysis	shaft of a long bone
Distal	furthest from the centre of the body
Ectocranial	outside of the cranium
Endocranial	inside of the cranium
Epiphysis	end of a long bone
Hypertrophy	increase in size
Hypotrophy	decrease in size
Inferior	bottom
Lateral	furthest from the midline of the body
Medial	nearest to the midline of the body
Metaphysis	portion of a long bone between the diaphysis and epiphysis
Palmar	anterior surface (palm) of the hand
Plantar	distal surface (sole) of the foot
Posterior (dorsal)	back
Proximal	nearest to the centre of the body
Subchondral	bone under a joint surface
Superior	top
Trabecular bone	cancellous, spongy bone that forms the inner structure of bones

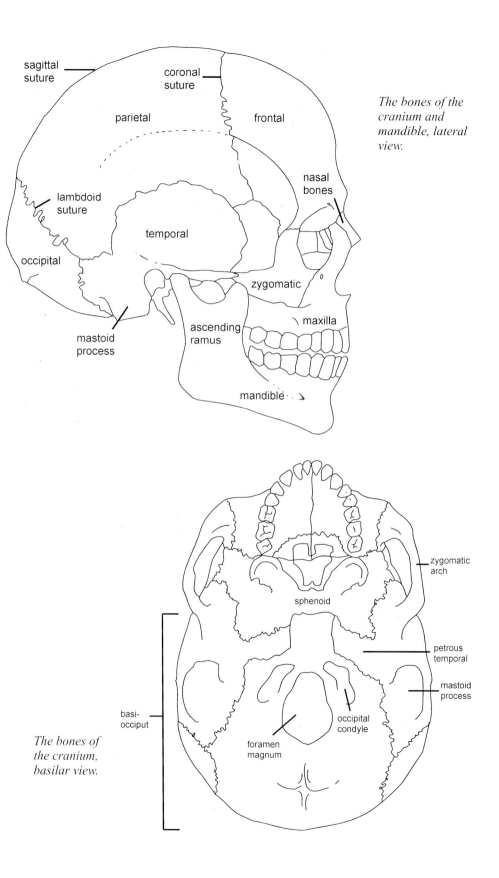

sagittal suture

coronal suture

parietal

frontal

lambdoid suture

nasal bones

occipital

temporal

zygomatic

mastoid process

maxilla

ascending ramus

mandible

The bones of the cranium and mandible, lateral view.

zygomatic arch

sphenoid

petrous temporal

mastoid process

basi-occiput

occipital condyle

foramen magnum

The bones of the cranium, basilar view.

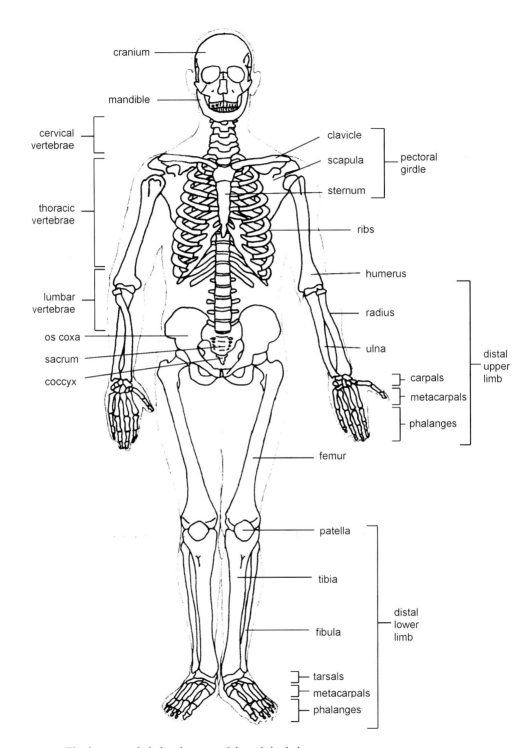

The bones and skeletal areas of the adult skeleton.

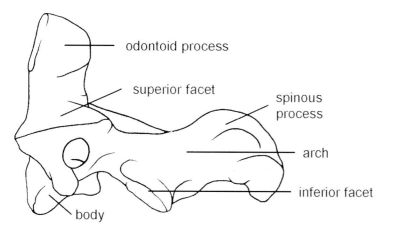

odontoid process

superior facet

spinous process

arch

inferior facet

body

Lateral view of a second cervical vertebra.

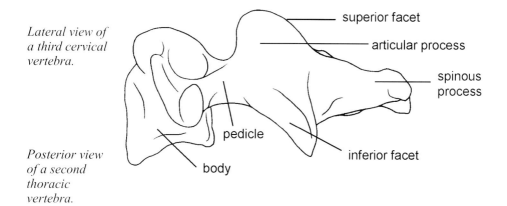

Lateral view of a third cervical vertebra.

superior facet

articular process

spinous process

pedicle

inferior facet

body

Posterior view of a second thoracic vertebra.

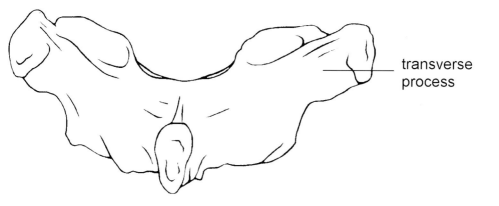

transverse process

203

Acknowledgements

The doctoral research that was the basis of this book was funded by a University of Winchester PhD studentship, and I would like to thank my doctoral supervisors, Prof. Tony King and Dr Nick Thorpe, for all their help and advice during the three years of research. I would also like to thank Prof. Chris Knüsel and Dr Rebecca Redfern for their very useful comments on earlier drafts of the text.

The reconstruction drawings were produced by Alexander 'Alf' Thomas and I would like to thank him for taking on and persevering with a project that was much larger and more complicated than he originally anticipated – *Vielen Dank*, Alf!

The vertebral diagrams were produced especially for the project by Caroline Needham from the Centre for Anatomy and Human Identification, University of Dundee, with additional diagrams being produced by the author. The map of Romano-British decapitation burials was produced by David Ashby, University of Winchester.

Permission to use photographs of burials was very kindly provided by Wessex Archaeology and the York Archaeological Trust.

Access to unpublished data and information was provided by Jim Brown, Jo Buckberry, Anwen Caffell, Cambridge Archaeological Unit, Sharon Clough, Lizzy Craig, English Heritage, Martin Green, David Gurney, Richard Hall, Malin Holst, Sarah Inskip, Sue Jones, Ailsa Mainman, Northamptonshire Archaeology, Liz Pieksma, Rob Poulton, Natasha Powers, Nicky Rogers, Suffolk County Council, Fiona Tucker, Wessex Archaeology, Tony Wilmott, Winchester Research Unit, York Archaeological Trust.

Access to skeletal remains was provided by Leigh Allen (Oxford Archaeology); Martin Biddle; Richard Breward and Jon Murden (Dorset County Museum); Esther Cameron (Oxfordshire Museum Services); Nick Cooper (University of Leicester Archaeological Services); Lorraine Cornwall (Rutland County Museum); Jane Ellis (Salisbury and South Wiltshire Museum); Ceri Falys (Thames Valley Archaeological Services); Martin Green; Laura Hadland (Leicester Arts and Museums Service); Tora Hylton (Northamptonshire Archaeology); Sarah Inskip (formally Southampton University, now Universiteit Leiden); Alan Jacobs (formally

Hampshire Museums Service); Rob Kruszynski (Natural History Museum); Jennifer Macey (Southampton Museums Service); Simon Mays (English Heritage); Christine McDonnell (York Archaeological Trust); Andrew Morrison (York Museums Trust); Sue Nelson (Wessex Archaeology); Helen Rees (Winchester Museums Service); Brett Thorne (Buckinghamshire Museums Service); Gillian Varndell (British Museum); Tim Vickers (Luton Museums Service); and Alan West (Norfolk Museums and Archaeology Service).

From Pen and Sword, I would like to thank Eloise Hansen for seeing the potential in my thesis text and providing encouragement and answers to my numerous queries; and Emma Grundy Haigh for her very useful comments and observations on the first draft of the text.

Finally I would like to thank my parents, Liz and Geoff White, and friends, Si Cleggett, David Ashby, Nathalie Barrett, Briony Lalor, Maria Bergman and Alf Ator, who, over the many years that this project has taken, have provided discussions, encouragement, a sympathetic ear, cups of tea and a place to get away from the research and writing when it all got too much!

Bibliography

Abeghian, M. 1899. *Der Armenische Volksglaube*. Drugulin: Leipzig.

Acsádi, G. and Nemeskéri, J. 1970. *History of Human Life Span and Mortality*. Akadémiai Kiadó: Budapest.

Aich, M., Alam, A.B.M.K., Talukder, D.C., Sarder, M.A.R., Fakir, A.Y. and Hossain, M. 2011. Cut Throat Injury: Review of 67 Cases. *Bangladesh Journal of Otorhinolaryngology* 17: 5-13.

Akerman, J.Y. 1860. Second Report of Researches in a Cemetery of the Anglo-Saxon Period at Brighthampton, Oxon. *Archaeologia* 38: 84-97.

Alberge, D. 2005. Mystery of 49 Headless Romans Who Weren't Meant to Haunt Us. *The Times*, 25 February 2005.

Alexander, M., Dodwell, N. and Evans, C. 2004. A Roman Cemetery at Jesus Lane, Cambridge. *Proceedings of the Cambridge Antiquarian Society* 93: 67-94.

Allen, D. 1958. Belgic Coins as Illustrations of Life in the Late Pre-Roman Iron Age of Britain. *Proceedings of the Prehistoric Society* 24: 43-63.

Allen, T., Darvill, T., Green, S. and Jones, M. 1993. *Excavations at Roughground Farm, Lechlade, Gloucestershire: A Prehistoric and Roman Landscape*. Oxford University Committee for Archaeology: Oxford.

Alunni-Perret, V., Muller-Bolla, M., Laugier, J.P., Lupi-Pegurier, L., Bertrand, M.F., Staccini, P., Bolla, M. and Quatrehomme, G.R. 2005. Scanning Electron Microscopy Analysis of Experimental Bone Hacking Trauma. *Journal of Forensic Sciences* 50: 796-801.

Ambrose, S.H., Buikstra, J. and Krueger, H.W. 2003. Status and Gender Differences in Diet at Mound 72, Cahokia, Revealed by Isotopic Analysis of Bone. *Journal of Anthropological Archaeology* 22: 217-226.

Anderson, S. 1995. A Human Skeleton from Rickinghall (RKN026), Suffolk, in Boulter, S. *A Record of the Archaeological Works Associated with the Rickinghall/Botesdale Bypass*. Suffolk County Council Archaeological Service Report 95/37.

Anderson, S. 1999. Violent Endings: Examples of Unhealed Trauma and Their Interpretations, in Anderson, S. (ed.) *Current and Recent Research in Osteoarchaeology 2: Proceedings of the 4th-6th Meetings of the Osteoarchaeology Research Group*. Oxbow Books: Oxford, pp. 23-30.

Anderson, S. 2000a. A Human Skull from Joist Fen, Lakenheath (LKH 107). Unpublished Suffolk County Council report.

Anderson, S. 2000b. Human Skeletal Remains, in Suffolk County Council Archaeological Service, *Agilent Technologies, Whitehouse Road, Ipswich: Excavation Report*. SCCAS Draft Report 2000/92.

Anderson, S. 2005. Human Skeletal Remains, in Caruth, J. *LKH191: Outdoor Recreation Centre*. Suffolk County Council Archaeological Service Report 2005/54, pp. 62-68.

Anderson, S. 2011. Human Skeletal Remains from Flixton Quarry (FLN 062). Unpublished Suffolk County Council report.

Anderson, T. 2001. Two Decapitations from Roman Towcester. *International Journal of Osteoarchaeology* 11: 400-405.

Anderson, T. 2007. The Late Roman Burials on Barrow 2, in Chapman, A. *A Bronze Age Barrow Cemetery and Later Boundaries, Pit Alignments and Enclosures at Gayhurst Quarry, Newport Pagnell, Buckinghamshire*. Northamptonshire Archaeology Report 06/143, pp. 59-60.

Andrén, A. 2006. A World of Stone: Warrior Culture, Hybridity and Old Norse Cosmology, in Andrén, A., Jennbert, K. and Raudvere, C. (eds) *Old Norse Religion in Long-Term Perspectives: Origins, Changes and Interactions*. Nordic Academic Press: Lund, pp. 33-38.

Andrew, C.K.C. 1939. Headless Burials. *Devon and Cornwall Notes and Queries* 20: 331-332.

Andrew, W.J. 1919. Medieval Relics from a Mysterious Interment at Winchester. *Proceedings of the Hampshire Field Club and Archaeological Society* 8: 323-326.

APC. 2006. *The Roman Way of Death: The Mystery*. Archaeological Planning Consultancy leaflet. Online: http://www.archaeologicalplanningconsultancy.co.uk/mga/projects/89_mount/pdf/mystery.pdf (accessed 7 November 2011).

Arcini, C. 2009. Prone Burials: Buried Face Down. *Current Archaeology* 231: 30-35.

Ardagna, Y., Richier, A., Vernet, G. and Dutour, O. 2005. A Case of Beheading Dating from the Celtic Period (La Tène B, Sarliève-Grande Halle, France). *International Journal of Osteoarchaeology* 15: 73-76.

Armit, I. 2006. Inside Kurtz's Compound: Headhunting and the Human Body in Prehistoric Europe, in Bonogofsky, M. (ed.) *Skull Collection, Modification and Decoration*. BAR International Series 1539. Archaeopress: Oxford, pp. 1-14.

Armit, I. 2007. *Celtic Scotland*. Batsford: London.

Armit, I. 2012. *Headhunting and the Body in Iron Age Europe*. Cambridge University Press: Cambridge.

Armit, I. and Ginn, V. 2007. Beyond the Grave: Human Remains from Domestic Contexts in Iron Age Atlantic Scotland. *Proceedings of the Prehistoric Society* 73: 113-134.

Armit, I., Schulting, R., Knüsel, C.J. and Shepherd, I.A.G. 2011. Death, Decapitation and Display? The Bronze and Iron Age Human Remains from the Sculptor's Cave, Covesea, North-East Scotland. *Proceedings of the Prehistoric Society* 77: 251-278.

Aspöck, E. 2011. Past 'Disturbances' of Graves as a Source: Taphonomy and Interpretation of Reopened Early Medieval Inhumation Graves at Brunn Am Gebirge (Austria) and Winnall II (England). *Oxford Journal of Archaeology* 30: 299-324.

Atkinson, J.C. 1891. *Forty Years in a Moorland Parish*. Macmillan: London.

Aufderheide, A.C. and Rodríguez-Martín, C. 1998. *The Cambridge Encyclopedia of Human Paleopathology*. Cambridge University Press: Cambridge.

Bailey, C.J. 1980. Excavation of Three Round Barrows in the Parish of Kingston Russell. *Proceedings of the Dorset Natural History and Archaeological Society* 102: 19-31.

Balys, J. 1952. Lithuanian Ghost Stories from Pittsburgh, Pennsylvania. *Midwest Folklore* 2 (1): 47-52.

Barber, B. and Bowsher, D. 2000. *The Eastern Cemetery of Roman London: Excavations 1983-1990*. MoLAS Monograph 4. Museum of London: London.

Barber, G., Wiggins, R. and Rogers, J. 1995. The Human Remains, in Coles, J. and Minnitt, S. *'Industrious and Fairly Civilized': The Glastonbury Lake Village*. Somerset Levels Project and Somerset County Council Museums Service, pp. 170-174.

Barrett, J.H, and Richards, M.P.P. 2004. Identity, Gender, Religion and Economy: New Isotope and Radiocarbon Evidence for Marine Resource Intensification in Early Historic Orkney, Scotland, UK. *European Journal of Archaeology* 7: 249-272.

Bass, W.M. 1995. *Human Osteology: A Laboratory and Field Manual*. Missouri Archaeological Society: Columbia.

Bateman, T. 1861. *Ten Year's Diggings in Celtic and Saxon Grave Hills, in the Counties of Derby, Stafford and York from 1848 to 1858*. George Allen and Sons: London.

Bayley, J. 2001. Human Skeletal Material, in Chowne, P., Cleal, R.M.J. and Fitzpatrick, A.P.P. *Excavations at Billingborough, Lincolnshire 1975-1978: A Bronze-Iron Age Settlement and Salt Working Site*. East Anglian Archaeology Monograph 94. Wessex Archaeology: Salisbury, pp. 73-78.

BBC Two. 2006. *Timewatch: Mystery of the Headless Romans*. British Broadcasting Company: London, 21 April 2006.

Becker, M.J. 1995. Children's Cemeteries: Early Christianity, Not Disease. *Paleopathology Newsletter* 80: 10-11.

Becker, T. 2009. Hingerichteter in Römischem Brunnen. *Archäologie im Rheinland 2008*: 86-87.

Bekvalac, J. and Kausmally, T. 2011. The Human Bone, in Grainger, I. and Phillpotts, C. *The Cistercian Abbey of St Mary Graces, East Smithfield, London*. MoLA Monograph 44. Museum of London: London.

Bell, L.S., Skinner, M.F. and Jones, S.J. 1996. The Speed of Post Mortem Change to the Human Skeleton and Its Taphonomic Significance. *Forensic Science International* 82: 129-140.

Bello, S.M., Parfitt, S.A. and Stringer, C.B. 2011. Earliest Directly Dated Human Skull-Cups. *PLoS ONE* 6. Online: http://www.plosone.org/article/info:doi/10.1371/journal.pone.0017026 (accessed 22 November 2011).

Bennike, P.P. 1985. *Palaeopathology of Danish Skeletons: A Comparative Study of Demography, Disease and Injury*. Akademisk Vorlag: Copenhagen.

Berkowitz, B.A. 2002. Decapitation and the Discourse of Antisyncretism in the Babylonian Talmud. *Journal of the American Academy of Religion* 70 (4): 743-769.

Berry, A.C. and Berry, R.J. 1967. Epigenetic Variation in the Human Cranium. *Journal of Anatomy* 101: 361-379.

Bethel, P.H. and Carver, M.O.H. 1987. Detection and Enhancement of Decayed Inhumations at Sutton Hoo, in Boddington, A., Garland, A.N. and Janaway, R.C. (eds) *Death, Decay and Reconstruction*. Manchester University Press: Manchester, pp. 10-21.

Bidder, H. 1906. Excavations in an Anglo-Saxon Burial Ground at Mitcham, Surrey. *Archaeologia* 60: 49-68.

Blair, J. 2005. *The Church in Anglo-Saxon Society*. Oxford University Press: Oxford.

Blair, J. 2009. The Dangerous Dead in Early Medieval England, in Baxter, S., Karkov, C., Nelson, J.L. and Pelleret, D. (eds) *Early Medieval Studies in Memory of Patrick Wormald*. Ashgate: Farnham, pp. 539-559.

Boardman. 2000. The Historical Background to the Battle and the Documentary Evidence, in Fiorato, V., Boylston, A. and Knüsel, C. (eds) *Blood Red Roses: The Archaeology of a Mass Grave from the Battle of Towton AD 1461*. Oxbow: Oxford, pp. 15-28.

Bonogofsky, M. 2005. A Bioarchaeological Study of Plastered Skulls from Anatolia: New Discoveries and Interpretations. *International Journal of Osteoarchaeology* 15: 124-135.

Booth, P. and Evans, J. 2001. *Roman Alcester, Northern Extramural Area: 1969-1988 Excavations*. Council for British Archaeology Research Report 127: York.

Booth, P., Simmonds, A., Boyle, A., Clough, S., Cool, H.E.M. and Poore, D. 2010. *The Late Roman Cemetery at Lankhills, Winchester: Excavations 2000-2005*. Oxford Archaeology Monograph 10: Oxford.

Boulestin, B. 1994. La tête isolée de la Grotte du Queroy: Nouvelles observations, nouvelles considerations. *Bulletin de la société préhistorique française* 91 (6): 440-446.

Boulestin, B. and Gambier, D.H. 2012. *Crânes trophées, crânes d'ancêtres et autres pratiques autour de la tête: Problèmes d'interprétation en archéologie*. BAR International Series 2415. Archaeopress: Oxford.

Boulter, S. 1995. *A Record of the Archaeological Works Associated with the Rickinghall/Botesdale Bypass*. Suffolk County Council Archaeological Service Report 95/37.

Bowman, J.E., MacLaughlin, S.M. and Scheuer, J.L. 1992. The Relationship Between

208

Biological and Chronological Age in the Juveniles from St Bride's Church, Fleet Street. *Annals of Human Biology* 19: 216.

Boyle, A., Boston, C. and Witkin, A. 2005. *The Archaeological Experience at St Luke's Church, Old Street, Islington*. Oxford Archaeology Report.

Boylston, A. 1997. *Report on the Analysis of Two Infant Burials from Bishop Grosseteste College, Lincoln (BGB95)*. Calvin Wells Laboratory Report: Bradford.

Boylston, A. 2000. Evidence for Weapon-Related Trauma in British Archaeological Samples, in Cox, M. and Mays, S. (eds) *Human Osteology in Archaeology and Forensic Science*. Greenwich Medical Media: London, pp. 357-380.

Boylston, A., Holst, M. and Coughlan, J. 2000a. Physical Anthropology, in Fiorato, V., Boylston, A. and Knüsel, C. (eds) *Blood Red Roses: The Archaeology of a Mass Grave from the Battle of Towton AD 1461*. Oxbow Books: Oxford, pp. 45-59.

Boylston, A., Knüsel, C.J., Roberts, C.A. and Dawson, M. 2000b. Investigation of a Romano-British Rural Ritual in Bedford, England. *Journal of Archaeological Science* 27: 241-254.

Boylston, A. and Lee, F. 2008. Joint Disease, in Magilton, J., Lee, F. and Boylston, A. (eds) *'Lepers Outside the Gate': Excavations at the Cemetery of the Hospital of St James and St Mary Magdalene, Chichester 1986-1987 and 1993*. CBA: York, pp. 239-251.

Boylston, A. and Roberts, C. 2004. The Roman Inhumations, Kempston, in Dawson, M. *Archaeology in the Bedford Region*. Bedfordshire Archaeology Monograph 4. BAR British Series 373. Archaeopress: Oxford, pp. 322-350.

Bradbury, J. 2004. *The Routledge Companion to Medieval Warfare*. Routledge: London.

Bradley, I.C. 1995. *The Power of Sacrifice*. Darton, Longman and Todd: London.

Bradley, P., Charles, B., Hardy, A. and Poore, D. 2005. Prehistoric and Roman Activity and a Civil War Ditch: Excavations at the Chemistry Research Laboratory, 2-4 South Parks Road, Oxford. *Oxoniensia* 70: 141-202.

Bradley, R. 1979. The Interpretation of Later Bronze Age Metalwork from British Rivers. *International Journal of Nautical Archaeology* 8: 3-6.

Brants, E.J. 2005. *Reanalysis of the Human Remains from Guildown Pagan Anglo-Saxon Cemetery and Late Anglo-Saxon Execution Cemetery and Comparison with Other Similar Assemblages in Surrey*. MA dissertation, Southampton University.

Brewster, T.C.M. 1984. *The Excavation of Whitegrounds Barrow, Burythorpe*. East Riding Archaeological Research Committee: Malton.

Brickley, M. 2003. Human Remains, in Jones, A. *Settlement, Burial and Industry in Roman Godmanchester: Excavations in the Extramural Area, The Parks 1998, London Road 1997-1998 and Other Investigations*. BAR British Series 346. Archaeopress: Oxford, pp. 69-79.

Brickley, M. 2011. Hillside Meadow, Fordham: Human Bone, in Cuttler, R., Martin-Bacon, H., Nichol, K., Patrick, C., Perrin, R., Ratkai, S., Smith, M. and Williams, J. *Five Sites in Cambridgeshire: Excavations at Woodhurst, Fordham, Soham, Buckden and St Neots, 1998-2002*. BAR British Series 528. Archaeopress: Oxford, pp. 74-79.

Bright, P.P. 1998. Assessment of Human Remains from the Site of the Former Eagle Hotel, Andover Road, Winchester, in Teague, S. *Eagle Hotel, Andover Road, Winchester: Report on Archaeological Excavation 1998*. Winchester Museums Service Report, pp. 49-52.

Bristow, P.H.W. 1998. *Attitudes to Disposal of the Dead in Southern Britain 3500BC-AD43, Volume 2*. BAR British Series 274: Oxford.

Brodribb, A.C.C., Hands, A.R. and Walker, D.R. 2005. *The Roman Villa at Shakenoak Farm, Oxfordshire: Excavations 1960-1976*. BAR 395. Archaeopress: Oxford.

Brooke, J.W. 1892. Discovery of a Roman Skeleton on Manton Downs. *Wiltshire Archaeological Magazine* 26: 412.

Brooke, R. 1857. *Visits to Fields of Battle in England of the Fifteenth Century*. John Russell Smith: London.

Brooks, D.A. 1986. A Review of the Evidence for Continuity in British Towns in the 5th and 6th Centuries. *Oxford Journal of Archaeology* 5: 77-102.

Brooks, S. and Suchey, J.M. 1990. Skeletal Age Determination Based on the Os Pubis: A Comparison of the Acsádi–Nemeskéri and Suchey–Brooks Methods. *Human Evolution* 5: 227-238.

Brothwell, D. 1959. Teeth in Earlier Human Populations. *Proceedings of the Nutrition Society* 18: 59-65.

Brothwell, D. 1971. Forensic Aspects of the So-Called Neolithic Skeleton Q1 from Maiden Castle, Dorset. *World Archaeology* 3: 233-241.

Brothwell, D.R. 1981. *Digging Up Bones* (3rd edition). British Museum: London.

Brothwell, D.R. 1986. *The Bog Man and the Archaeology of People*. British Museum Press: London.

Brothwell, D.R. and Browne, S. 1994. Pathology, in Lilley, J.M., Stroud, G., Brothwell, D.R. and Williamson, M.H. *The Jewish Burial Ground at Jewbury*. CBA: York, pp. 457-494.

Brothwell, D. and Gill-Robinson, H. 2002. Taphonomic and Forensic Aspects of Bog Bodies, in Haglund, W. and Sorg, M. (eds) *Advances in Forensic Taphonomy*. CRC Press: Boca Raton, pp. 119-132.

Brothwell, D. and Powers, R. 1966. Part II: The Iron Age People of Dunbar. *Proceedings of the Society of Antiquaries of Scotland* 98: 184-198.

Brunaux, J.L., Amandry, M., Brouquier-Reddé, V., Delestrée, L.-P., Duday, H., Fercoq du Leslay, G., Lejars, T., Marchand, C., Méniel, P., Petit, B. and Rogéré, B. 1999. Ribemont-sur-Ancre (Somme): Bilan préliminaire et nouvelles hypothèses. *Gallia* 56: 177-283.

Bruzek, J. 2002. A Method for Visual Determination of Sex, Using the Human Hip Bone. *American Journal of Physical Anthropology* 117: 157-168.

Buckberry, J. 2000. Missing, Presumed Buried? Bone Diagenesis and the Under-Representation of Anglo-Saxon Children. *Assemblage* 5. Online: http://ads.ahds.ac.uk/catalogue/adsdata/assemblage/html/5/buckberr.html (accessed 23 November 2011).

Buckberry, J. 2008. Off With Their Heads: The Anglo-Saxon Execution Cemetery at Walkington Wold, East Yorkshire, in Murphy, E.M. (ed.) *Deviant Burial in the Archaeological Record*. Oxbow: Oxford, pp. 148-168.

Buckberry, J. 2010. *Osteological Analysis of the Human Skeletal Remains from Heslington East*. BARC, University of Bradford Report.

Buckberry, J.L. and Chamberlain, A.T. 2002. Age Estimation from the Auricular Surface of the Ilium: A Revised Method. *American Journal of Physical Anthropology* 119: 231-239.

Buckberry, J.L. and Hadley, D.M. 2007. An Anglo-Saxon Execution Cemetery at Walkington Wold, Yorkshire. *Oxford Journal of Archaeology* 26: 309-329.

Bugler, J. and Drew, G. 1974. Roman Dorset. *Proceedings of the Dorset Natural History and Archaeology Society* 95: 57-70.

Buikstra, J.E. and Ubelaker, D.H. 1994. *Standards for Data Collection from Human Skeletal Remains: Proceedings of a Seminar at the Field Museum of Natural History*. Arkansas Archaeological Survey Research Series No. 44. Arkansas Archaeological Survey: Fayetteville.

Bull, S. 2007. *Triumphant Rider: The Lancaster Roman Cavalry Tombstone*. Lancashire Museums: Lancaster.

Burgess, A. 2000. The Excavation and Finds, in Fiorato, V., Boylston, A. and Knüsel, C. (eds) *Blood Red Roses: The Archaeology of a Mass Grave from the Battle of Towton AD1461*. Oxbow: Oxford, pp. 29-36.

Burleigh, G. and Fitzpatrick-Matthews, K. 2007. *Excavations at Baldock 1978-1994: Fieldwork by G.R. Burleigh*. Unpublished report.

Burnham, B.C. 1988. A Survey of Building Types in Romano-British 'Small Towns'. *Journal of the British Archaeological Association* 141: 35-59.

Burnham, B.C. and Wacher, J.S. 1990. *The Small Towns of Roman Britain*. Batsford: London.

Bush, H. and Stirland, A. 1991. Romano-British Decapitation Burials: A Comparison of Osteological Evidence and Burial Ritual from Two Cemeteries. *Anthropologie* 29: 205-210.

Calkin, J.B. 1947. Two Romano-British Burials at Kimmeridge. *Proceedings of the Dorset Natural History and Archaeological Society* 69: 33-41.

Calmet, A. 1850. *The Phantom World: Or, the Philosophy of Spirits, Apparitions, etc., Volume II*. Richard Bentley: London.

Cambridge Archaeological Unit. n.d. *Babraham Park and Ride*. Unpublished report.

Cancelmo, J.J. 1972. Clay Shoveler's Fracture: A Helpful Diagnostic Sign. *American Journal of Roentgenology* 115: 540-543.

Cardew, G. 1865. On the Discovery of Human Skeletons and Ancient Remains at Helmingham, Suffolk. *Journal of the British Archaeological Association* 21: 267-273.

Cardy, A. 1997. The Human Bones, in Hill, P.P. *Whithorn and St Ninian: The Excavation of a Monastic Town 1984-1991*. The Whithorn Trust/Sutton Publishing: Stroud, pp. 519-562.

Carrière, M.G. 1902. Les cimetières de l'époque du Bas Empire de Pouzilhac, Arpaillargues et autres lieux du département du Gard. *Mémoires de l'académie de Nimes* 25: 17-23.

Carter, J.C. 1998. *The Chora of Metaponto: The Necropoleis*. University of Texas Press: Austin.

Caruth, J. 2005. *LKH191: Outdoor Recreation Centre*. Suffolk County Council Archaeological Service Report 2005/54.

Carver, M. 2005. *Sutton Hoo: A Seventh-Century Princely Burial Ground and Its Context*. British Museum Press: London.

Carver, M., Hills, C. and Scheschkewitz, J. 2009. *Wasperton: A Roman, British and Anglo-Saxon Community in Central England*. The Boydell Press: Woodbridge.

Casa-Hatton, R. and Wall, W. 2006. A Late Roman Cemetery at Durobrivae, Chesterton. *Proceedings of the Cambridge Antiquarian Society* 95: 5-24.

Castriota-Scanderbeg, A. and Dallapiccola, B. 2005. *Abnormal Skeletal Phenotypes: From Simple Signs to Complex Diagnoses*. Springer: Berlin.

Cessford, C. 2007. Middle Anglo-Saxon Justice: The Chesterton Lane Corner Execution Cemetery and Related Sequence, Cambridge. *Archaeological Journal* 164: 197-226.

Chacón, S., Peccerelli, F.A., Paiz Diez, L. and Rivera Fernández, C. 2008. Disappearance, Torture and Murder of Nine Individuals in a Community of Nebaj, Guatemala, in Kimmerle, E.H. and Baraybar, J.P.P. *Skeletal Trauma: Identification of Injuries Resulting from Human Rights Abuse and Armed Conflict*. CRC Press: Baco Raton, pp. 300-313.

Chadwick, H. 1976. *Priscillian of Avila: The Occult and the Charismatic in the Early Church*. Clarendon Press: Oxford.

Chamberlain, A.T. 2000. Problems and Prospects in Palaeodemography, in Cox, M. and Mays, S. (eds) *Human Osteology in Archaeology and Forensic Science*. Greenwich Medical Media: London, pp. 101-116.

Chambers, R. and Boyle, A. 2007. The Romano-British Cemetery, in Chambers, R. and McAdam, E. *Excavations at Radley Barrow Hills, Radley, Oxfordshire, Volume 2: The Romano-British Cemetery and Anglo-Saxon Settlement*. Oxford Archaeology: Oxford, pp. 13-84.

Channel 4. 2010. *Gladiators: Back from the Dead*. Channel 4, 14 June 2010.

Chapman, A. 2007. *A Bronze Age Barrow Cemetery and Later Boundaries, Pit Alignments and Enclosures at Gayhurst Quarry, Newport Pagnell, Buckinghamshire*. Northamptonshire Archaeology Report 06/143.

Chapman, M. 1992. *The Celts: Construction of a Myth*. St Martin's Press: New York.

Charmasson, J. 1968. Une nécropole du Bas-Empire: La Brèche, commune de Laudun (Gard). *Cahiers ligures de préhistoire et d'archéologie* 17: 131-150.

Cherryson, A.K. 2005. *In the Shadow of the Church: Burial Practices in the Wessex Heartlands (c.600-1100AD)*. PhD thesis, University of Sheffield.

Cherryson, A.K. 2008. Normal, Deviant and Atypical: Burial Variation in Late Saxon Wessex, c. AD700-1100, in Murphy, E.M. (ed.) *Deviant Burial in the Archaeological Record*. Oxbow: Oxford, pp. 115-130.

Cherryson, A.K and Buckberry, J. 2011. *Old Dairy Cottage (ODC89), Littleton, Winchester: An Analysis of Skeletal Remains and Burial Practices*. Unpublished report.

Chesterman, J.T. 1977. Burial Rites in a Cotswold Long Barrow. *Man* 12: 22-32.

Chilton, C.W. 1955. The Roman Law of Treason under the Early Principate. *Journal of Roman Studies* 45: 73-81.

Cipriani, D. 2009. *Children's Rights and the Minimum Age of Criminal Responsibility: A Global Perspective*. Ashgate: Farnham.

Clark, M.A., Worrell, M.B. and Pless, J.E. 1997. Postmortem Changes in Soft Tissues, in Haglund, W.D and Sorg, M.H. (eds) *Forensic Taphonomy: The Postmortem Fate of Human Remains*. CRC Press: Boca Raton, pp. 151-164.

Clarke, C. 1996. Excavations at Cold Harbour Farm, Crowmarsh. *South Midlands Archaeology* 26: 71-76.

Clarke, C.P. 1998. *Excavations to the South of Chignall Roman Villa, Essex 1977-1981*. East Anglian Archaeology Monograph 83. Essex County Council: Chelmsford.

Clarke, D. 1998. *The Head Cult: Tradition and Folklore Surrounding the Symbol of the Severed Human Head in the British Isles*. PhD thesis, University of Sheffield.

Clarke, G. 1979. *Pre-Roman and Roman Winchester, Part II: The Roman Cemetery at Lankhills*. Winchester Studies 3. Clarendon Press: Oxford.

Clough, S. 2009. Human Remains, in Mullin, D., Laws, G and Smith, A. *Horcott Quarry (Churchberry Manor), Fairford, Gloucestershire: Post-Excavation Assessment and Project Design*. Unpublished Oxford Archaeology report, pp. 42-45.

Clough, S. n.d.(a) *Human Bones from Horcott Quarry*. Unpublished Oxford Archaeology report.

Clough, S. n.d.(b) *The Human Remains from Tubney Wood Quarry*. Unpublished Oxford Archaeology report.

Coale, A.J. and Demeny, P.P. 1983. *Regional Model Life Tables and Stable Populations* (2nd edition). Academic Press: New York.

Cole, G. 2009. *Evidence for Interpersonal Violence at the Anglo-Saxon Cemetery at Bevis's Grave, near Bedhampton*. Unpublished report.

Coleman, K.M. 1990. Fatal Charades: Roman Executions Stages as Mythological Enactments. *Journal of Roman Studies* 80: 44-73.

Collis, J. 2003. *The Celts: Origins, Myths and Inventions*. Tempus: Stroud.

Connolly, R.C. 1986. The Anatomical Description of Lindow Man, in Stead, I.M., Bourke, J.B. and Brothwell, D.R. (eds) *Lindow Man: The Body in the Bog*. Cornell University Press: New York, pp. 54-62.

Cool, H.E.M. and Baxter, M.J. 1999. Peeling the Onion: An Approach to Comparing Vessel Glass Assemblages. *Journal of Roman Archaeology* 12: 72-100.

Cooper, N.J. 2000. Rubbish Counts: Quantifying Portable Material Culture in Roman Britain, in Pearce, S. (ed.) *Researching Material Culture*. Leicester Archaeology Monograph 8. University of Leicester: Leicester, pp. 75-86.

Cornwall, I.W. 1954. The Human Remains, in Kenyon, K.M. Excavations at Sutton Walls, Herefordshire 1948-1951. *Archaeological Journal* 110: 1-87.

Coughlan, J. and Holst, M. 2000. Health Status, in Fiorato, V., Boylston, A. and Knüsel, C. (eds) *Blood Red Roses: The Archaeology of a Medieval Mass Grave from the Battle of Towton 1461*. Oxbow: Oxford, pp. 60-76.

Cox, M. 2000. Ageing Adults from the Skeleton, in Cox, M. and Mays, S. (eds). *Human Osteology in Archaeology and Forensic Science*. Greenwich Medical Media: London, pp. 61-81.

Craig, C.R., Knüsel, C.J. and Carr, G.C. 2005. Fragmentation, Mutilation and Dismemberment: An Interpretation of Human Remains on Iron Age Sites, in Parker-Pearson, M. and Thorpe, I.J.N. (eds) *Warfare, Violence and Slavery in Prehistory*. BAR International Series 1374. Archaeopress: Oxford, pp. 165-180.

Crummy, P.P. 2000. Butt Road Burial. *The Colchester Archaeologist* 13: 19.

Cunha, E. and Pinheiro, J. 2009. Antemortem Trauma, in Blau, S. and Ubelaker, D.H. (eds) *Handbook of Forensic Anthropology and Archaeology*. Left Coast Press: Walnut Creek, pp. 256-262.

Cunliffe, B. 1990. *The Celtic World*. BCA: London.

Cunliffe, B. 2005. *Iron Age Communities in Britain: An Account of England, Scotland and Wales from the Seventh Century BC until the Roman Conquest* (4th edition). Routledge: London.

Cunliffe, B. and Poole, C. 2000. *The Danebury Environs Programme: The Prehistory of a Wessex Landscape, Volume 2, Part 3: Suddern Farm, Middle Wallop, Hampshire 1991 and 1996*. English Heritage and Oxford University Committee for Archaeology Monograph 49. Oxford University Press: Oxford.

Cunnington, M. 1884. Notes on Bowl's Barrow. *Wiltshire Archaeological Magazine* 24: 104-125.

Daniell, C. 1997. *Death and Burial in Medieval England (1066-1550)*. Routledge: London.

Daniell, C. 2002. Conquest, Crime and Theology in the Burial Record 1066-1200, in Lucy, S. and Reynolds, A. (eds) *Burial in Early Medieval England and Wales*. Society for Medieval Archaeology: London, pp. 241-254.

Davies, S.M. 1981. Excavations at Old Down Farm, Andover, Part II: Prehistoric and Roman. *Proceedings of the Hampshire Field Club and Archaeological Society* 37: 81-163.

Davies, S.M., Bellamy, P.S., Heaton, M.J. and Woodward, P.J. 2002. *Excavations at Alington Avenue, Fordington, Dorchester, Dorset 1984-1987*. Dorset Natural History and Archaeology Society Monograph 15: Dorchester.

Davies, S.M. and Thompson, C.N. 1987. Archaeological Evaluation at Southfield House, Dorchester, Dorset. *Proceedings of the Dorset Natural History and Archaeological Society* 109: 126-129.

Dawes, J.D. 1984. Human Bone Report, in Brewster, T.C.M. *The Excavation of Whitegrounds Barrow, Burythorpe*. East Riding Archaeological Research Committee: Malton, pp. 20-27.

Dawes, J.D. and Magilton, J.R. 1980. *The Cemetery of St Helen-on-the-Walls, Aldwark*. CBA: London.

Dawson, M. 2004. *Archaeology in the Bedford Region*. Bedfordshire Archaeology Monograph 4. BAR British Series 373. Archaeopress: Oxford.

Dean, B. and Boston, C. 2010. Human Skeletal Remains, in Smith, A., Powell, K. and Booth, P. (eds) *Evolution of a Farming Community in the Upper Thames Valley: Excavation of a Prehistoric, Roman and Post-Roman Landscape at Cotswold Community, Gloucestershire and Wiltshire, Volume 2: The Finds and Environmental Reports*. Oxford Archaeology: Oxford, pp. 243-268.

Dedouit, F., Tournel, G., Bécart, A., Hédouin, V. and Gosset, D. 2007. Suicidal Hanging

Resulting in Complete Decapitation – Forensic, Radiological and Anthropological Studies: A Case Report. *Journal of Forensic Sciences* 52: 1190-1193.

Denston, C.B. 1994. Human Skeletal Remains, in Mahany, C. *Roman Alcester: Southern Extramural Area 1964-66 Excavations.* CBA Research Report 96. CBA: York, pp. 215-216.

Dias, G. and Tayles, N. 1997. 'Abscess Cavity' – A Misnomer. *International Journal of Osteoarchaeology* 7: 548-554.

Dix, B. 1980. Excavations at Harrold Pit, Odell 1974-8: A Preliminary Report. *Bedfordshire Archaeological Journal* 14: 15-18.

Dobney, K., Jaques, D. and Brothwell, D. 1999. Assessment of the Bone Assemblage from COT93, in Richards, J.D. Cottam: An Anglian and Anglo-Scandinavian Settlement on the Yorkshire Wolds. *Archaeological Journal* 156: 1-110.

Dočkalová, M. 2005. A Mass Grave from the Roman Period in Moravia (Czech Republic). *Anthropologie* 43: 23-43.

Dodwell, N. 1996. Human Remains, in Lucas, G. and Hinman, M. *Archaeological Excavations of an Iron Age Settlement and Romano-British Enclosures at Watson's Lane, Little Thetford, Ely, Cambridgeshire.* Cambridge Archaeological Unit Report 194, pp. 56-63.

Dodwell, N. 2004. Human Bone, in Regan, R., Evans, C. and Webley, L. *The Camp Ground Excavations, Colne Fen, Earith: Assessment Report.* Cambridge Archaeological Unit Report 654, pp. 153-159.

Dodwell, N. 2007a. Human Remains, in Evans, C., Knight, M. and Webley, L. Iron Age Settlement and Romanisation on the Isle of Ely: The Hurst Lane Reservoir Site. *Proceedings of the Cambridge Antiquarian Society* 96: 41-78.

Dodwell, N. 2007b. Human Bone, in Timberlake, S., Dodwell, N., Armour, N. *The Roman Cemetery, The Babraham Institute, Cambridgeshire: An Archaeological Excavation.* Cambridge Archaeological Unit Report 75, pp. 110-116.

Dodwell, N. n.d. *Romano-British Burials at the Babraham Institute: The Skeletal Population.* Cambridge Archaeological Unit unpublished report.

Dogan, K.H., Demirci, S., Deniz, I. and Erkol, Z. 2010. Decapitation and Dismemberment of the Corpse: A Matricide Case. *Journal of Forensic Sciences* 55: 542-545.

Donnelly, S., Donnelly, C., Murphy, E., Donnell, C. 1999. The Forgotten Dead: The Cillíní and Disused Burial Grounds of Ballintoy, County Antrim. *Ulster Journal of Archaeology* 58: 109-113.

Dougherty, S.P. 2004. A Little More Off the Top. *Nekhen News* 16: 11-12.

Dower, J.W. 2008. Devil in the Details. *Throwing Off Asia II.* Visualizing Cultures, Massachusetts Institute of Technology. Online: http://visualizingcultures.mit.edu (accessed 24 November 2011).

Djurić, M., Rakočević, Z. and Djonić, D. 2005. The Reliability of Sex Determination of Skeletons from Forensic Contexts in the Balkans. *Forensic Science International* 147: 159-164.

Duhig, C. n.d. Human Remains, in Cambridge Archaeological Unit. *Babraham Park and Ride.* Unpublished report.

Dunning, G.C. and Wheeler, R.E.M. 1932. A Barrow at Dunstable, Bedfordshire. *Archaeological Journal* 88: 193-217.

Dwight, T. 1890. The Closure of the Sutures as a Sign of Age. *Boston Medical and Surgical Journal* 122: 389-535.

Dymond, C.W. and Tomkins, H.G. 1886. *Worlebury: An Ancient Stronghold in the County of Somerset.* Privately printed.

Edwards, B.J.N. 1970. Lancashire Archaeological Notes: Prehistoric and Roman (Note 8). *Transactions of the Historical Society of Lancashire and Cheshire* 121: 99-106.

214

Egging Dinwiddy, K. 2010. *A Late Roman Cemetery at Little Keep, Dorchester, Dorset*. Wessex Archaeology Report.

Esmonde Cleary, A.S. 1989. *The Ending of Roman Britain*. Routledge: London.

Evans, J. 2001. Material Approaches to the Identification of Different Romano-British Site Types, in James, S. and Millett, M. (eds) *Britons and Romans: Advancing an Archaeological Agenda*. CBA Research Report 125. CBA: York, pp. 26-35.

Everton, R.F. 1985. Human Bone, Kenchester, in Wilmott, T. and Rahtz, S.P.Q. An Iron Age and Roman Settlement Outside Kenchester (Magnis), Herefordshire: Excavations 1977-9. *Transactions of the Woolhope Naturalists Field Club* 45: Microfiche 2.

Everton, R.F. and Rogers, J. 1982. The Human Remains, in Leach, P. *Ilchester, Volume I: Excavations 1974-5*. Western Archaeological Trust: Bristol, pp. 266.

Evison, V.I. 1987. *Dover: The Buckland Anglo-Saxon Cemetery*. Historic Buildings and Monuments Commission: London.

Evison, V.I. 1994. *An Anglo-Saxon Cemetery at Great Chesterford, Essex*. CBA: York.

Faccia, K.J. and Williams, R.C. 2008. Schmorl's Nodes: Clinical Significance and Implications for the Bioarchaeological Record. *International Journal of Osteoarchaeology* 18: 28-44.

Falys, C. n.d. *St John's College, Oxford: The Physical Anthropology and Trauma*. Unpublished report.

Falys, C. 2015. A Late Saxon Mass Grave. The Human Bone, in Wallis, S. (ed.) *The Oxford Henge and Late Saxon Massacre with Medieval and Late Occupation at St John's College, Oxford*. Thames Valley Archaeological Services, Reading, pp.41–130.

Falys, C.G. and Lewis, M.E. 2011. Proposing a Way Forward: A Review of Standardisation in the Use of Age Categories and Ageing Techniques in Osteological Analysis (2004–2009). *International Journal of Osteoarchaeology* 21: 704-716.

Falys, C.G., Schutkowski, H. and Weston, D.A. 2006. Auricular Surface Aging: Worse than Expected? A Test of the Revised Method on a Documented Historic Skeletal Assemblage. *American Journal of Physical Anthropology* 130: 508-513.

Farley, M.E. 1986. Excavations at the Prebendal Court, Aylesbury 1985. *South Midlands Archaeology* 16: 37-38.

Farwell, D.E. and Molleson, T.I. 1993. *Excavations at Poundbury 1966-1980, Volume II: The Cemeteries*. Dorset Natural History and Archaeology Society Monograph 11: Dorchester.

Fields, N. 2005. Headhunters of the Roman Army, in Hopkins, A. and Wyke, M. (eds) *Roman Bodies: Antiquity to the Eighteenth Century*. British School at Rome: London, pp. 55-66.

Finnegan, M. 1978. Non-Metric Variation of the Skeleton. *Journal of Anatomy* 125: 23-37.

Firth, J. 1998. Syreford Mill, in Timby, J. *Excavations at Kingscote and Wycomb, Gloucestershire*. Cotswold Arch Trust: Cirencester, pp. 331-333.

Ford, W.J. 2003. The Romano-British and Anglo-Saxon Settlement and Cemeteries at Stretton-on-Fosse, Warwickshire. *Transactions of the Birmingham and Warwickshire Archaeological Society* 106: 1-116.

Foster, A. 2001. Romano-British Burials in Wiltshire, in Ellis, P. (ed.) *Roman Wiltshire and After: Papers in Honour of Ken Annable*. Wiltshire Archaeology and Natural History Society: Devizes, pp. 165-177.

Foster, W.K. 1883. Account of the Excavation of an Anglo-Saxon Cemetery at Barrington, Cambridgeshire. *Proceedings of the Cambridge Antiquarian Society* 5: 5-32.

Foucault, M. 1977. *Discipline and Punish: The Birth of the Prison*. Penguin: London.

Foundations Archaeology. 2003. *124-130 London Road, Gloucester: Archaeological Excavation Report*. Foundations Archaeology report.

Fox, C. and Lethbridge, T.C. 1926. The La Tene and Romano-British Cemetery at Guilden Morden, Cambridgeshire. *Proceedings of the Cambridge Antiquarian Society* 27: 49-71.

Franklin, D., Oxnard, C.E., O'Higgins, P. and Dadour, I. 2007. Sexual Dimorphism in the Subadult Mandible: Quantification Using Geometric Morphometrics. *Journal of Forensic Sciences* 52: 6-10.

Frayer, D.W. 1997. Ofnet: Evidence for a Mesolithic Massacre, in Martin, D.L. and Frayer, D.W. (eds) *Troubled Times: Violence and Warfare in the Past*. OPA: Amsterdam, pp. 181-216.

Frend, W.H.C. 1955. Religion in Roman Britain in the Fourth Century AD. *Journal of the British Archaeological Association* 18: 1-18.

Frere, S.S. 1983. *Verulamium Excavations II*. Society of Antiquaries of London Research Report 41. Society of Antiquaries: London.

Galer, D. 2007. The Human Remains, in Benson, D. and Whittle, A. (eds) *Building Memories: The Neolithic Cotswold Long Barrow at Ascott-under-Wychwood, Oxfordshire*. Oxbow Books: Oxford, pp. 189-220.

Gallien, V., Langlois, J.-Y., Cousyn, P. and Gerber, F. 2009. Les décapités d'Évreux (Eure, Haute-Normandie): Témoignage d'une catastrophe de la fin de l'Antiquité?, in Buchet, L., Séguy, I., Rigeade, C. and Signoli, M. (eds) *Vers une anthropologie des catastrophes*. Antibes/INED: Paris.

Gardner, R. 2004. Investigations at 24 Friary Fields, Dunstable, Bedfordshire. *Bedfordshire Archaeological Journal* 25: 159-189.

Garland, A.N. 1995. Worsley Man, England, in Turner, R.C. and Scaife, R.G. (eds) *Bog Bodies: New Discoveries and New Perspectives*. British Museum Press: London, pp. 104-107.

Garland, R. 1995. *The Eye of the Beholder: Deformity and Disability in the Graeco-Roman World*. Duckworth: London.

Gatty, R.A. 1905. Lord Strafford's Burial-Place. *Cornhill Magazine* 19: 104-109.

Geber, J. 2012. Comparative Study of Perimortem Weapon Trauma in Two Early Medieval Skeletal Populations (AD 400–1200) from Ireland. *International Journal of Osteoarchaeology*, Early View November 2012. Online: http://onlinelibrary.wiley.com/doi/10.1002/oa.2281/abstract (accessed 27 March 2014).

Geber, J. and Boston, C. 2007. Human Remains, in Timby, J., Brown, R., Hardy, A., Leech, S., Poole, C. and Webley, L. *Settlement on the Bedfordshire Claylands: Archaeology along the A421 Great Barford Bypass*. Oxford Archaeological Unit/Bedfordshire Archaeological Council: Oxford, pp. 303-327.

Gerard, E. 1888. *The Land Beyond the Forest: Facts, Figures and Fancies from Transylvania*. Harper and Brothers: New York.

Gibson, M., Marquez-Grant, N. and Webb, H. Forthcoming. The Human Skeletal Assemblage, in Wallis, H. *Romano-British Cambridgeshire: Recent Excavations*. East Anglian Archaeology: Cambridge.

Gilbert, B.M. and McKern, T.W. 1973. A Method for Ageing the Female Os Pubis. *American Journal of Physical Anthropology* 38: 31-38.

Gilmore, T. 2008. The Human Remains, in Holbrook, N. and Bateman, C. The South Gate Cemetery of Roman Gloucester: Excavations at Parliament Street 2001. *Transactions of the Bristol and Gloucestershire Archaeological Society* 126: 100-103.

Girling, R. 2006. A Cemetery of Secrets. *Sunday Times Magazine*, 26 March 2006.

Glass, G.B. 1991. Continuous Eruption and Periodontal Status in Pre-industrial Dentitions. *International Journal of Osteoarchaeology* 1: 265-271.

Glendor, U., Marcenes, W. and Andreason, J.O. 2007. Classification, Epidemiology and Etiology, in Andreason, J.O., Andreason, F.M. and Andersson, L. (eds) *Textbook and Color Atlas of Traumatic Injuries to the Teeth*. Blackwell Munksgaard: Oxford, pp. 217-254.

Glob, P.V. 1969. *The Bog People: Iron Age Man Preserved*. Faber and Faber: London.

Goode, J.L. and Bardill, M. 1995. St Neots to Duxford Pipeline 1994: Human Remains, in John Price Engineering Archaeological Services. *St Neots to Duxford 900mm Gas Pipeline 1994: Archaeological Report, Volume 3*. John Price Engineering Archaeological Services Report, pp. 857-890.

Gordon, C.C. and Buikstra, J.E. 1981. Soil pH, Bone Preservation and Sampling Bias at Mortuary Sites. *American Antiquity* 46: 566-571.

Gosden, C. 2006. Race and Racism in Archaeology: Introduction. *World Archaeology* 38: 1-7.

Gowland, R. 2000. Report on the Human Bone from Site 4 (DBF97) on the Market Deeping Bypass, in Trimble, D. (ed.) *Archaeological Excavations Undertaken along the Route of the Market Deeping Bypass, Volume 3: Appendices 7-13*. Archaeological Project Services Report 2000/93.

Grant, A. 2004. Domestic Animals and Their Uses, in Todd, M. (ed.) *A Companion to Roman Britain*. Blackwell: Oxford, pp. 371-392.

Gravett, C. 2003. *Towton 1461: England's Bloodiest Battle*. Osprey: Oxford.

Green, H.J.M. 1986. Religious Cults at Roman Godmanchester, in Henig, M. and King, A. (eds) *Pagan Gods and Shrines of the Roman Empire*. Oxford University Committee for Archaeology Monograph 8. Oxford University: Oxford, pp. 29-55.

Green, M. 1976. *A Corpus of Religious Material from the Civilian Areas of Roman Britain*. BAR British Series 24. British Archaeological Reports: Oxford.

Green, M. 1998. Humans as Ritual Victims in the Later Prehistory of Western Europe, *Oxford Journal of Archaeology* 17: 169-189.

Green, M.A. 2002. *Dying for the Gods: Human Sacrifice in Iron Age and Roman Europe*. Tempus: Stroud.

Green, M.A. 2004. Chaining and Shaming: Images of Defeat from Llyn Cerrig Bach to Sarmitzegetusa. *Oxford Journal of Archaeology* 23: 319-340.

Green, M.A. 2010. *Caesar's Druids: Story of an Ancient Priesthood*. Yale University Press: New Haven.

Greenwell, W. 1877. *British Barrows: A Record of the Examination of Sepulchral Mounds in Various Parts of England*. Clarendon Press: Oxford.

Grinsell, L.V. 1936. *The Ancient Burial Mounds of England*. Methuen: London.

Grinsell, L.V. 1959. *Dorset Barrows*. Dorset Natural History and Archaeology Society/Council for British Archaeology: Dorchester.

Grossschmidt, K. and Kanz, F. 2002. Leben, Lied und Tod der Gladiatoren: Texte und Bilder der Austellung, in *Ephesos: Tod am Nachmittag; Eine Austellung in Ephesos Museum Selçuk Seit 20 April 2002*, pp. 60-71.

Grundy, G.B. 1919. The Saxon Land Charters of Wiltshire. *Archaeological Journal* 76: 143-301.

Hadman, J. 1978. Aisled Buildings in Roman Britain, in Todd, M. (ed.) *Studies in the Romano-British Villa*. Leicester University Press: Leicester, pp. 187-195.

Hanna, J., Bouwman, A.S., Brown, K.A., Parker Pearson, M. and Brown, T.A. 2012. Ancient DNA Typing Shows that a Bronze Age Mummy Is a Composite of Different Skeletons. *Journal of Archaeological Science* 39: 2774-2779.

Harman, M. 1986. The Human Remains, in Chambers, R.A. Romano-British Burials from Wroxton, Oxon 1980. *Oxoniensia* 51: 43-44.

Harman, M. 2007. Human Bone, in Chambers, R. and McAdam, E. *Excavations at Radley Barrow Hills, Radley, Oxfordshire, Volume 2: The Romano-British Cemetery and Anglo-Saxon Settlement*. Oxford Archaeology: Oxford, pp. 38-43.

Harman, M. n.d.(a). *The Human Remains from Duston*. Unpublished report.

Harman, M. n.d.(b). *Cogenhoe: The Human Skeleton*. Unpublished report.

Harman, M., Molleson, T.I. and Price, J.L. 1981. Burials, Bodies and Beheadings in Romano-British and Anglo-Saxon Cemeteries. *Bulletin of the British Museum of Natural History (Geology)* 35 (3): 145-188.

Hartnett, K.M. 2010. Analysis of Age-at-Death Estimation Using Data from a New, Modern Autopsy Sample – Part 1: Pubic Bone. *Journal of Forensic Sciences* 55: 1145-1151.

Hawkey, D.E. and Merbs, C.F. 1995. Activity-Induced Musculoskeletal Stress Markers (MSM) and Subsistence Strategy Changes among Ancient Hudson Bay Eskimos. *International Journal of Osteoarchaeology* 5: 324-338.

Hayman, G. and Reynolds, A. 2005. A Saxon and Saxo-Norman Execution Cemetery at 42-54 London Road, Staines. *Archaeological Journal* 162: 215-255.

Hencken, T.C. 1939. The Excavation of the Iron Age Camp on Bredon Hill, Gloucestershire 1935-7. *Archaeological Journal* 95 (1): 1-111.

Henderson, J. 1987. Factors Determining the State of Preservation of Human Remains, in Boddington, A., Garland, A.N. and Janaway, R.C. (eds) *Death, Decay and Reconstruction*. Manchester University Press: Manchester, pp. 43-54.

Henig, M. 1984. *Religion in Roman Britain*. BT Batsford: London.

Henig, M. and Booth, P. 2000. *Roman Oxfordshire*. Sutton Publishing: Stroud.

Herdman, R.C., Langer, L.O. and Good, R.A. 1966. Dyschondrosteosis: The Most Common Cause of Madelung's Deformity. *The Journal of Pediatrics* 68: 432-441.

Heron, J. 1889. Report on the Stapenhill Explorations. *Transactions of the Burton-on-Trent Natural History and Archaeological Society* 1: 156-193.

Hershkovitz, I., Bedford, L., Jellema, L.M. and Latimer, B. 1996. Injuries to the Skeleton Due to Prolonged Activity in Hand-to-Hand Combat. *International Journal of Osteoarchaeology* 6: 167-178.

Hershkovitz, I., Latimer, B., Dutour, O., Jellema, L.M., Wish-Baratz, S., Rothschild, C. and Rothschild, B.M. 1997. Why Do We Fail in Ageing the Skull from the Sagittal Suture? *American Journal of Physical Anthropology* 103: 393-400.

Hight, G.A. 1914. *The Saga of Grettir the Strong: A Story of the Eleventh Century*. Dent: London.

Hill, N.G. 1937. Excavations on Stockbridge Down 1935-1936. *Proceedings of the Hampshire Field Club and Archaeological Society* 13: 247-259.

Hillson, S. 2005. *Teeth*. Cambridge Manuals in Archaeology. Cambridge University Press: Cambridge.

Hingley, R. 1989. *Rural Settlement in Roman Britain*. Seabey: London.

Hirsch, C.S. and Kaufman, B. 1975. Contrecoup Skull Fractures. *Journal of Neurosurgery* 42: 530-534.

Hirst, S.M. 1985. *An Anglo-Saxon Inhumation Cemetery at Sewerby, East Yorkshire*. CBA: York.

Ho, V.K. 2000. Butchering Fish and Executing Criminals: Public Executions and the Meanings of Violence in Late Imperial and Modern China, in Aijmer, G. and Abbink, J. (eds) *Meanings of Violence: A Cross Cultural Perspective*. Berg: Oxford, pp. 141-160.

Hogg, A.H.A. 1977. Two Cairns at Aber Camddwr, near Ponterwyd, Cardiganshire. *Archaeologica Cambrensis* 126: 24-37.

Holbrey, R. and Burgess, A. 2001. Parlington Hollins, in Roberts, I., Burgess, A. and Berg, D. (eds) *A New Link to the Past: The Archaeological Landscape of the M1-A1 Link Road*. Yorkshire Archaeology Monograph 7. West Yorkshire Archaeology Service: Leeds, pp. 83-105.

Hollingworth, E.J. and O'Reilly, M.M. 1925. *The Anglo-Saxon Cemetery at Girton College, Cambridge: A Report Based on the MS Notes of the Excavations Made by the Late FJH Jenkinson, MA*. Cambridge University Press: Cambridge.

Homes Hogue, S. 2006. Determination of Warfare and Interpersonal Conflict in the

Protohistoric Period: A Case Study from Mississippi. *International Journal of Osteoarchaeology* 16: 236-248.

Holst, M. 2004a. *Osteological Analysis, Ashchurch Railway Bridge, Ashchurch, Gloucestershire*. York Osteoarchaeology Report 1304.

Holst, M. 2004b. *Osteological Analysis, Wessex Water, Cowhill, Oldbury-on-Severn, Gloucestershire*. York Osteoarchaeology Report 1504.

Holst, M. 2005. Blue Bridge Lane and Fishergate House: The Human Remains, in Spall, C.A. and Toop, N.J. (eds) *Blue Bridge Lane and Fishergate House, York: Report on Excavations July 2000-July 2002*. Archaeological Planning Consultancy: York. Online: http://www.archaeologicalplanningconsultancy.co.uk/mono/001/rep_bone_hum3f.html (accessed 2 April 2009).

Holst, M. and Coughlan, J. 2000. Dental Health and Disease, in Fiorato, V., Boylston, A. and Knüsel, C. (eds) *Blood Red Roses: The Archaeology of a Mass Grave from the Battle of Towton AD1461*. Oxbow: Oxford, pp. 77-89.

Holst, M., Coughlan, J. and Boylston, A. 2000. Catalogue of the Palaeopathology, in Fiorato, V., Boylston, A. and Knüsel, C. (eds) *Blood Red Roses: The Archaeology of a Mass Grave from the Battle of Towton AD1461*. Oxbow: Oxford, pp. 201-210.

Hooper, B. 1991. The Anatomical Considerations, in Cunliffe, B. and Poole, C. *Danebury: An Iron Age Hillfort in Hampshire, Volume 5: The Excavations 1979-1988: The Finds*. Council for British Archaeology Research Report 73: London, pp. 425-431.

Hope, V.M. 2000. Contempt and Respect: The Treatment of the Corpse in Ancient Rome, in Hope, V.M. and Marshall, E. (eds) *Death and Disease in the Ancient City*. Routledge: London, pp. 104-127.

Hope, V. 2007. *Death in Ancient Rome: A Source Book*. Routledge: London.

Hoppenfeld, S. and Vasantha, L.M. 2000. *Treatment and Rehabilitation of Fractures*. Lippincott Williams and Wilkins: Philadelphia.

Houck, M. 1998. Skeletal Trauma and the Individualization of Knife Marks in Bones, in Reichs, K. (ed.) *Forensic Osteology: Advances in the Identification of Human Remains* (2nd edition). Charles C. Thomas: Springfield, pp. 410-424.

Housley, R.A., Walker, A.J., Otlet, R.L. and Hedges, R.E.M. 1995. Radiocarbon Dating of the Lindow III Bog Body, in Turner, R.C. and Scaife, R.G. (eds) *Bog Bodies: New Discoveries and New Perspectives*. British Museum Press: London, pp. 39-46.

Howells, W.W. 1973. *Cranial Variation in Man*. Peabody Museum of Archaeology and Ethnology Papers: Cambridge.

Howells, W.W. 1995. Who's Who in Skulls: Ethnic Identification of Crania from Measurements. *Papers of the Peabody Museum of Archaeology and Ethnology* 82: 1-108.

Hrdlicka, A. 1939. *Practical Anthropometry*. Wistar Institute: Philadelphia.

Humphrey, J.H. and Hutchinson, D.L. 2001. Macroscopic Characteristics of Hacking Trauma. *Journal of Forensic Sciences* 46: 228-233.

Humphreys, J., Ryland, J.W., Welstood, F.C., Barnard, E.A.B. and Barnett, T.G. 1925. An Anglo-Saxon Cemetery at Bidford-on-Avon, Warwickshire: Second Report on the Excavations. *Archaeologia* 74: 271-288.

Hunt, D.R. and Bullen, L. 2007. The Frequency of *os acromiale* in the Robert J. Terry Collection. *International Journal of Osteoarchaeology* 17: 309-317.

Hunter-Mann, K. 2006. *Romans Lose Their Heads: An Unusual Cemetery at The Mount, York*. Archaeology of York Web Series no. 6. York Archaeological Trust. Online: http://www.iadb.co.uk/driffield6/driffield6.php (accessed 3 November 2011).

Hutton, R. 1991. *The Pagan Religions of the Ancient British Isles*. Blackwell: Oxford.

Igarashi, Y., Uesu, K., Wakebe, T. and Kanazawa, E. 2005. New Method for Estimation of Adult Skeletal Age at Death from the Morphology of the Auricular Surface of the Ilium. *American Journal of Physical Anthropology* 128: 324-339.

Ingraham Kip, W. 1854. *The Catacombs of Rome as Illustrating the Church of the First Three Centuries*. Redfield: New York.

Işcan, M.Y., Loth, S.R. and Wright, R.K. 1984. Metamorphosis at the Sternal Rib End: A New Method to Estimate Age at Death in White Males. *American Journal of Physical Anthropology* 65: 147-156.

Işcan, M.Y., Loth, S.R. and Wright, R.K. 1985. Age Estimation from the Rib by Phase Analysis: White Females. *Journal of Forensic Sciences* 30: 853-863.

Isserlin, R.M.J. 1997. Thinking the Unthinkable: Human Sacrifice in Roman Britain, in Meadows, K., Lemke, C. and Heron, J. (eds) *TRAC 96: Proceedings of the 6th Annual Theoretical Roman Archaeology Conference Sheffield 1996*. Oxbow: Oxford, pp. 91-100.

Janes, R. 1991. Beheadings. *Representations* 35: 21-51.

Janes, R. 2005. *Losing Our Heads: Beheadings in Literature and Culture*. New York University Press: London.

Jennings, K. 2000. The Excavation of Nine Romano-British Burials at Andover, Hampshire in 1984 and 1987. *Proceedings of the Hampshire Field Club and Archaeological Society* 55: 114-132.

Jimenez, S.B. 1994. Occupational Hazards in 19th-Century Upper Canada, in Herring, A. and Chan, L. (eds) *Strength in Diversity*. Canadian Scholars: Toronto, pp. 345-364.

Jones, A. 2003. *Settlement, Burial and Industry in Roman Godmanchester: Excavations in the Extramural Area, The Parks 1998, London Road 1997-8 and Other Investigations*. BAR British Series 346. Archaeopress: Oxford.

Jones, C. 2011. *Finding Fulford: The Search for the First Battle of 1066*. WPS: London.

Jones, E.V. and Horne, B. 1981. The Skeletons, in Matthews, C.L. A Romano-British Inhumation Cemetery at Dunstable. *Bedfordshire Archaeological Journal* 15: 37-44.

Jones, P. n.d. *Archaeological Fieldwork at Abbey Meads, Chertsey*. Unpublished report.

Jones, R.F.J. 1987. A False Start? The Roman Urbanization of Western Europe. *World Archaeology* 19: 47-57.

Jones, S. 2008. *'Slain at the Gate': A Reassessment of the Massacre Deposits from Cadbury Castle, Somerset*. MSc dissertation, Bournemouth University .

Jovanović, A. 2006. Prologue to the Research of Inhumation in Moesia Superior in the First to Third Centuries AD. *Journal of the Serbian Archaeological Society* 22: 23-44.

Jurmain, R. 1999. *Stories from the Skeleton: Behavioral Reconstruction in Human Osteology*. Routledge: London.

Jurmain, R. and Kilgore, L. 1995. Skeletal Evidence of Osteoarthritis: A Palaeopathological Perspective. *Annals of the Rheumatic Diseases* 54: 443-450.

Kanjou, Y. 2009. Study of Neolithic Human Graves from Tell Qaramel in North Syria. *International Journal of Modern Anthropology* 1: 25-37.

Kanz, F. and Grossschmidt, K. 2006. Head Injuries of Roman Gladiators. *Forensic Science International* 160: 207-216.

Kanz, F. and Grossschmidt, K. 2009. Dying in the Arena: The Osseous Evidence from Ephesian Gladiators, in Wilmott, T. (ed.) *Roman Amphitheatres and Spectacula: A 21st-Century Perspective*. BAR International Series 1946. Archaeopress: Oxford.

Karlsson, E., Arcini, C. and Sandén, A. 2012. The Punishment of Death: Concerning an Archaeological Excavation of an Execution Site in Vadstena (Sweden), in Auler, J. (ed.) *Richtstättenarchäologie* 3. Archaeotopos: Dormagen, pp. 140-159.

Keller, E. 1979. *Das Spätrömische Gräberfeld von Neuburg an der Donau*. Kallmünz: Lassleben.

Kenyon, K.M. 1954. Excavations at Sutton Walls, Herefordshire 1948-51. *Archaeological Journal* 110: 1-87.

Keys, D. 2010. Day the Vikings Got Their Comeuppance. The Independent 12 March

220

2010. Online: http://independent.co.uk/news/uk/this-britain-day-the-vikings-got-their-comeuppence-1920111.html (accessed 08.11.11)

Kilfeather, S. 2002. Oliver Plunkett's Head. *Textual Practice* 16: 229-248.

Killgrove, K. 2011. Mutiny in Modena? Decapitated Slaves in Roman Modena. *Powered by Osteons*. Online: http://www.poweredbyosteons.org/2011/10/mutiny-in-mutina-decapitated-slaves-in.html (accessed 25 November 2011).

Kimmerle, E.H. and Baraybar, J.P. 2008. *Skeletal Trauma: Identification of Injuries Resulting from Human Rights Abuse and Armed Conflict*. CRC Press: Boca Raton.

King, A.C. 1984. Animal Bones and the Dietary Identity of Military and Civilian Groups in Roman Britain, Germany and Gaul, in Blagg, T.F.C. and King, A.C. (eds) *Military and Civilian in Roman Britain*. BAR British Series 136. BAR: Oxford, pp. 187-217.

King, A.C. 1999. Animals and the Roman Army: The Evidence of Animal Bones. *Journal of Roman Archaeology* Suppl. 34: 139-150.

Kitson, P.R. 1995. The Nature of Old English Dialect Distributions, Mainly as Exhibited in Charter Boundaries, in Fisiak, J. (ed.) *Medieval Dialectology*. Trends in Linguistics Studies and Monographs 79. Mouton de Gruyter: Berlin, pp. 43-136.

Klaus, H.D., Centurión, J. and Curo, M. 2010. Bioarchaeology of Human Sacrifice: Violence, Identity and the Evolution of Ritual Killing at Cerro Cerrilos, Peru. *Antiquity* 84: 1102-1122.

Knight, B. 1991. *Forensic Pathology*. Edward Arnold: London.

Knüsel, C. 2000a. Bone Adaptation and Its Relationship to Physical Activity in the Past, in Cox, M. and Mays, S. (eds) *Human Osteology in Archaeology and Forensic Science*. Greenwich Medical Media: London, pp. 381-401.

Knüsel, C. 2000b. Activity-Related Skeletal Change, in Fiorato, V., Boylston, A. and Knüsel, C. (eds) *Blood Red Roses: The Archaeology of a Mass Grave from the Battle of Towton AD1461*. Oxbow: Oxford, pp. 103-118.

Knüsel, C. 2005. The Physical Evidence of Warfare: Subtle Stigmata?, in Parker Pearson, M. and Thorpe, I.J.N. (eds) *Warfare, Violence and Slavery in Prehistory*. BAR International Series 1374. Archaeopress: Oxford, pp. 49-65.

Knüsel, C.J., Janaway, R.C. and King, S.E. 1996. Death, Decay and Ritual Reconstruction: Archaeological Evidence of Cadaveric Spasm. *Oxford Journal of Archaeology* 15: 121-128.

Knüsel, C.J. and Ripley, K.M. 2000. The Man-Woman or 'Berdache' in Anglo-Saxon England and Post-Roman Europe, in Frazer, W. and Tyrrell, A. (eds) *Social Identity in Early Medieval Britain*. Continuum Press: London, pp. 157-191.

Kramis, S. 2009. Unusual Treatment of the Dead outside Cemeteries in Roman Times, in Brambilla, E., Deschler-Erb, S., Lamboley, J.-L., Klemeshov, A. and Moretto, G. (eds) Routines of Existence: Time, Life and After Life in Society and Religion. Edizioni Plus: Pisa, pp. 86-105.

Kunos, C.A., Simpson, S.W., Russell, K.F. and Hershkovitz, I. 1999. First Rib Metamorphosis: Its Possible Utility for Human Age-at-Death Estimation. *American Journal of Physical Anthropology* 110: 303-323.

Lai, P. and Lovell, N. 1992. Skeletal Markers of Occupational Stress in the Fur Trade: A Case Study from a Hudson's Bay Company Fur Trade Post. *International Journal of Osteoarchaeology* 2: 221-234.

Lanciani, R. 1892. *Pagan and Christian Rome*. Riverside Press: Cambridge.

Larsen, C.S. 1997. *Bioarchaeology: Interpreting Behaviour from the Human Skeleton*. Cambridge University Press: Cambridge.

Lavigne, S.E. and Molto, J.E. 1995. System of Measurement of the Severity of Periodontal Disease in Past Populations. *International Journal of Osteoarchaeology* 5: 265-273.

Leach, P. 1982. *Ilchester, Volume I: Excavations 1974-1975*. Western Archaeological Trust: Bristol.

Leach, S. 2006. *Going Underground: An Anthropological and Taphonomic Study of Human Skeletal Remains from Caves and Rock Shelters in Yorkshire*. PhD thesis, University of Winchester.

Leahy, K. 2007. *'Interrupting the Pots': The Excavation of Cleatham Anglo-Saxon Cemetery, North Lincolnshire*. Council for British Archaeology: York.

Leech, R. 1980. Religion and Burials in South Somerset and North Dorset, in Rodwell, W. (ed.) *Temples, Churches and Religion: Recent Research in Roman Britain*. BAR British Series 77: Oxford, pp. 329-366.

Lethbridge, T.C. 1929. The Anglo-Saxon Cemetery at Burwell, Cambridgeshire, Part IV. *Proceedings of the Cambridge Antiquarian Society* 30: 97-109.

Lethbridge, T.C. 1936. Further Excavations in the Early Iron Age and Romano-British Cemetery at Guilden Morden. *Proceedings of the Cambridge Antiquarian Society* 36: 109-120.

Lethbridge, T.C. and Palmer, W.M. 1929. Excavations in the Cambridgeshire Dykes VI: Bran's Ditch Second Report. *Proceedings of the Cambridge Antiquarian Society* 30: 78-96.

Lewis, J.E. 2008. Identifying Sword Marks on Bone: Criteria for Distinguishing between Cut Marks Made by Different Classes of Bladed Weapons. *Journal of Archaeological Science* 35: 2001-2008.

Lewis, M.E. 2000. Non-Adult Palaeopathology: Current Status and Future Potential, in Cox, M. and Mays, S. (eds) *Human Osteology in Archaeology and Forensic Science*. Greenwich Medical Media: London, pp. 39-58.

Lewis, M.E. 2007. *The Bioarchaeology of Children: Perspectives from Biological and Forensic Anthropology*. Cambridge University Press: Cambridge.

Lewis, M.E. 2008. A Traitor's Death? The Identity of a Drawn, Hanged and Quartered Man from Hulton Abbey, Staffordshire. *Antiquity* 82: 113-124.

Lewis, M.E. and Roberts, C. 1997. Growing Pains: The Interpretation of Stress Markers. *International Journal of Osteoarchaeology* 7: 581-586.

Liddell, D.M. 1934. Excavations at Meon Hill. *Proceedings of the Hampshire Field Club and Archaeological Society* 12: 127-162.

Lieverse, A.R. 1999. Diet and the Aetiology of Dental Calculus. *International Journal of Osteoarchaeology* 9: 219-232.

Lilley, J.M., Stroud, G., Brothwell, D.R. and Williamson, M.H. 1994. *The Jewish Burial Ground at Jewbury*. CBA: York.

'L.M.M.R.,' 1852. Discovery of the Body of a Beheaded Man. *Notes and Queries* 6: 386-387.

Loe, L. 2003. Specialist Report on the Human Skull (8658) from Vindolanda, Northumberland, in Birley, A. *Vindolanda Report 2003, Volume 1: The Excavations of 2001-2002: Civilian Settlement, Severan and Second Century Forts and the Pre-Hadrianic Occupation, with a Report on the Trial Excavations at Carvoran*. Vindolanda Trust: Hexham, pp. 213-249.

Loe, L. 2009. Peri-mortem Trauma, in Blau, S. and Ubelaker, D.H. (eds) *Handbook of Forensic Anthropology and Archaeology*. Left Coast Press: Walnut Creek, pp. 263-283.

Loe, L., Boyle, A., Webb, H. and Score, D. 2014. *'Given to the Ground': A Viking Mass Grave on Ridgeway Hill, Weymouth*. Dorset Natural History and Archaeological Society: Dorchester.

Looper, M. 2002. Women-Men (and Men-Women): Classic Maya Rulers and the Third Gender, in Ardren, T. (ed.) *Ancient Maya Women*. AltaMira Press: Walnut Creek, pp. 171-202.

Lovejoy, C.O. 1985. Dental Wear in the Libben Population: Its Functional Pattern and Role in the Determination of Adult Skeletal Age at Death. *American Journal of Physical Anthropology* 68: 47-56.

Lovejoy, C.O., Meindl, R.S., Mensforth, R.P. and Barton, T.J. 1985a. Multifactorial Determination of Skeletal Age at Death: A Method and Blind Tests of Its Accuracy. *American Journal of Physical Anthropology* 68: 1-14.

Lovejoy, C.O., Meindl, R.S., Pryzbeck, T.R. and Mensforth, R.P. 1985b. Chronological Metamorphosis of the Auricular Surface of the Ilium: A New Method for the Determination of Adult Skeletal Age at Death. *American Journal of Physical Anthropology* 68: 15-28.

Lovell, N.C. 1989. Test of Phenice's Technique for Determining Sex from the Os Pubis. *American Journal of Physical Anthropology* 79: 117-120.

Lovell, N.C. 1997. Fracture Analysis in Paleopathology. *Yearbook of Physical Anthropology* 40: 139-170.

Lowther, A.W.G. 1931. The Saxon Cemetery at Guildown, Guildford, Surrey. *Surrey Archaeological Collections* 39: 1-50.

Lucy, S. 1994. Children in Early Medieval Cemeteries. *Archaeological Review from Cambridge* 13: 21-34.

Lucy, S. 2000. *The Anglo-Saxon Way of Death: Burial Rites in Early England*. Sutton Publishing: Stroud.

Lucy, S. and Reynolds, A. 2002. Burial in Early Medieval England and Wales: Past, Present and Future, in Lucy, S. and Reynolds, A. (eds) *Burial in Early Medieval England and Wales*. Society for Medieval Archaeology: London, pp. 1-23.

Luff, R. 1984. The Human Remains from the Legionary Ditch, in Crummy, P. *Excavations at Lion Walk, Balkerne Lane and Middleborough, Colchester, Essex*. Colchester Archaeological Report 3. Colchester Archaeological Trust: Colchester, pp. 97.

Lyon, R.M. 2011. The Influence of Roman Military Camps on Town Planning. *Presidential Scholars Projects, Stanford University*. Online: http://dspace.sunyconnect.suny.edu/handle/1951/50737 (accessed 24 November 2011).

Maat, G.J.R. 2005. Two Millennia of Male Stature Development and Population Health and Wealth in the Low Countries. *International Journal of Osteoarchaeology* 15: 276-290.

Maat, G.J.R., Mastwijk, R.W. and Van der Welde, E.A. 1997. On the Reliability of Non-metrical Morphological Sex Determination of the Skull Compared with That of the Pelvis in the Low Countries. *International Journal of Osteoarchaeology* 7: 575-580.

MacLaughlin, S.M. and Bruce, M.F. 1990. The Accuracy of Sex Identification in European Skeletal Remains Using Phenice Characters. *Journal of Forensic Sciences* 35: 1384–1392.

Magilton, J., Lee, F. and Boylston, A. 2008. *'Lepers Outside the Gate': Excavations at the Cemetery of the Hospital of St James and St Mary Magdalene, Chichester, 1986-1987 and 1993*. CBA: York.

Mahany, C. 1994. *Roman Alcester: Southern Extramural Area 1964-1966 Excavations*. CBA Research Report 96. CBA: York.

Maish, A. 2003. Not Just Another Cut Throat. *Nekhen News* 15: 26.

Maltby, M. 1989. Urban Rural Variations in the Butchering of Cattle in Romano-British Hampshire, in Serjeantson, D. and Waldron, T. (eds) *Diet and Craft in Towns: The Evidence of Animal Remains from the Roman to the Post-Medieval Periods*. BAR British Series 199: Oxford, pp. 75-106.

Maltby, M. 1994. The Meat Supply in Roman Dorchester and Winchester, in Hall, A.R. and Kenward, H.K. (eds) *Urban-Rural Connexions: Perspectives from Environmental Archaeology*. Oxbow: Oxford, pp. 85-102.

Maltby, M. 2007. Chop and Change: Specialist Cattle Carcass Processing in Roman Britain, in Croxford, B., Ray, N. and Roth, R. (eds) *TRAC 2006: Proceedings of the 16th Annual Theoretical Roman Archaeology Conference*. Oxbow: Oxford, pp. 59-76.

223

Maltby, M. 2010. *Feeding a Roman Town: Environmental Evidence from Excavations in Winchester, 1972-1985*. Winchester Museums: Winchester.

Manchester, K. 1978. Executions in West Yorkshire. *Sciant Presentes* 5: 4.

Manchester, K. 1990. Resurrecting the Dead: The Potential of Palaeopathology, in Southworth, E. (ed.) *Anglo-Saxon Cemeteries: A Reappraisal*. Alan Sutton: Stroud, pp. 87-96.

Manchester, K. 2011. Human Bone, in Richardson, J. *Rothwell Haigh, Rothwell, Leeds, West Yorkshire: Excavation Report*. West Yorkshire Archaeological Service Report 2170, pp. 54-55.

Mansell-Pleydell, J. 1893. Anniversary Address of the President. *Proceedings of the Dorset Natural History and Antiquarian Field Club* 14: 1-28.

Maples, R. 1986. Trauma Analysis by the Forensic Anthropologist, in Reichs, K. (ed.) *Forensic Osteology: Advances in the Identification of Human Remains*. Charles C Thomas: Springfield, pp. 218-228.

Marcsik, A. and Oláh, S. 1991. Case Report of Osteomyelitis. *International Journal of Osteoarchaeology* 1: 147-150.

Maresh, M.M. 1970. Measurements from Roentgenograms, in McCammon, R.W. (ed.) *Human Growth and Development*. C.C. Thomas: Springfield, pp. 157-200.

Marshall, C.E. 1999. *'And the Head Shall Remain Uncorrupted': A Taphonomic Analysis of Romano-British Decapitation Burials*. MSc dissertation, University of Bradford.

Martín, L.A. 2008. Evidencias de ejecución y tortura pública de los soldados sertorianos en el pórtico del foro de *Valentia*, in Roca de Togores, C. and Rodes, F. (eds) *Antropología física y forense en contextos arqueològicos*. Instituto de Cultura Juan Gil Albert: Alicante, pp. 50-58.

Masur, L.J. 2009. Stature Trends in Ancient Maya Populations: Re-examining Studies from Tikal and Altar de Sacrificios. *Totem: The University of Western Ontario Journal of Anthropology* 17: 12-22.

Matos, V. and Santos, A.L. 2006. On the Trail of Pulmonary Tuberculosis Based on Rib Lesions: Results from the Human Identified Skeletal Collection from the Museu Bocage (Lisbon, Portugal). *American Journal of Physical Anthropology* 130: 190-200.

Matthews, C.L. 1976. *Occupation Sites on a Chiltern Ridge: Excavations at Puddlehill and Sites near Dunstable, Bedfordshire, Part 1: Neolithic, Bronze Age and Early Iron Age*. BAR 29: Oxford.

Matthews, C.L. 1979. The Excavation of a Roman Inhumation Cemetery at Dunstable, Bedfordshire. *The Manshead Magazine* 25: 3-41.

Matthews, C.L. 1981. A Romano-British Inhumation Cemetery at Dunstable. *Bedfordshire Archaeological Journal* 15: 1-73.

Matthews, C.L. 1989. *Ancient Dunstable* (revised and enlarged by J.P. Schneider). Manshead Archaeology Society: Dunstable.

Mattingly, D. 2006. *An Imperial Possession: Britain in the Roman Empire 54BC-AD409*. Allen Lane: London.

Mays, S. 2002. The Relationship between Molar Wear and Age in an Early 19th Century AD Archaeological Human Skeletal Series of Documented Age at Death. *Journal of Archaeological Science* 29: 861-871.

Mays, S. and Cox, M. 2000. Sex Determination in Skeletal Remains, in Cox, M. and Mays, S. (eds) *Human Osteology in Archaeology and Forensic Science*. Greenwich Medical Media: London, pp. 117-130.

Mays, S. and Steele, J. 1996. A Mutilated Human Skull from Roman St Albans, Hertfordshire, England. *Antiquity* 70: 155-161.

McConnell, D. and Grassam, A. 2005. *Land Adjacent to Great Casterton Primary. School, Pickworth Road, Great Casterton, Rutland: Archaeological Excavation Interim*

Report. Archaeological Solutions Report 1903.

McCulloch, P.M. 1991. Littleton, Old Dairy Cottage. *Archaeology in Hampshire Annual Report for 1990*: 38-39.

McDonald, J.L. 1979. Religion, in Clarke, G. *Pre-Roman and Roman Winchester, Part II: The Roman Cemetery at Lankhills*. Winchester Studies 3. Clarendon Press: Oxford, pp. 404-433.

McGavin, N. 1980. A Roman Cemetery and Trackway at Stanton Harcourt. *Oxoniensia* 45: 112-123.

McKern, T.W. and Stewart, T.D. 1957. *Skeletal Age Changes in Young American Males, Analysed from the Standpoint of Age Estimation*. Headquarters Quartermaster Research and Development Command Technical Report EP-45.

McKinley, J. 1987. Burial 33, in Rogerson, A., Ashley, S.J., Williams, P. and Harris, A. *Three Norman Churches in Norfolk*. Norfolk Museums Service/Norfolk Archaeological Unit: Dereham, pp. 74.

McKinley, J. 1993. *Human Skeletal Report from Baldock, Hertfordshire*. Unpublished report.

McKinley, J. 1997. *Sovell Down, Gussage-All-Saints, Dorset: Human Bone Archive Report*. Unpublished report.

McKinley, J.I. 2000. The Analysis of Cremated Bone, in Cox, M. and Mays, S. (eds) *Human Osteology in Archaeology and Forensic Science*. Greenwich Medical Media: London, pp. 403-422.

McKinley, J.I. 2004. The Human Remains and Aspects of Pyre Technology and Cremation Rituals, in Cool, H.E.M. *The Roman Cemetery at Brougham, Cumbria: Excavations 1966-1967*. Britannia Monograph Series 21. Society for Promotion of Roman Studies: London, pp. 283-309.

McKinley, J.I. 2008. The Human Remains, in Mercer, R. and Healy, F. *Hambledon Hill, Dorset, England: Excavation and Survey of a Neolithic Monument Complex and Its Surrounding Landscape*. English Heritage: Swindon, pp. 477-521.

McKinley, J.I. 2009a. Human Bone, in Wright, J., Leivers, M., Seagar Smith, R. and Stevens, C.J. *Cambourne New Settlement: Iron Age and Romano-British Settlement on the Clay Uplands of West Cambridgeshire*. Wessex Archaeology Report 23. Wessex Archaeology: Salisbury, pp. 71-81.

McKinley, J.I. 2009b. Human Bone, in Egging Dinwiddy, K. *A Late Roman Cemetery at Little Keep, Dorchester, Dorset*. Wessex Archaeology Report, pp. 11-35.

McKinley, J.I. 2009c. Human Remains, in Phillips, M. *Four Millennia of Human Activity along the A505 Baldock Bypass, Hertfordshire*. EAA Report 128. Albion Archaeology: Bedford, pp. 80-83.

McKinley, J.I. and Egging Dinwiddy, K. 2009. 'Deviant' Burials from a Late Romano-British Cemetery at Little Keep, Dorchester. *Proceedings of the Dorset Natural History and Archaeological Society* 130: 43-61.

McWhirr, A., Viner, L. and Wells, C. 1982. *Romano-British Cemeteries at Cirencester*. Cirencester Excavation Committee: Cirencester.

Meaney, A.L. 1964. *A Gazetteer of Early Anglo-Saxon Burial Sites*. George Allen and Unwin: London.

Meaney, A.L. 1995. Pagan English Sanctuaries, Place-Names and Hundred Meeting-Places. *Anglo-Saxon Studies in Archaeology and History* 8: 29-42.

Meaney, A.L. and Hawkes, S.C. 1970. *Two Anglo-Saxon Cemeteries at Winnall*. Society for Medieval Archaeology Monograph 4: London.

Mein, A.G. 1997. Trostrey Castle, Trostrey. *Archaeology in Wales* 37: 59-60.

Meindl, R.S., Lovejoy, C.O., Mensforth, R.P. and Don Carlos, L. 1985. Accuracy and Direction of Error in the Sexing of the Skeleton: Implications for Paleodemography. *American Journal of Physical Anthropology* 68: 79-85.

225

Mercer, R. and Healy, F. 2008. *Hambledon Hill, Dorset, England: Excavation and Survey of a Neolithic Monument Complex and Its Surrounding Landscape*. English Heritage: Swindon.

Merrifield, R. 1987. *The Archaeology of Ritual and Magic*. Batsford: London.

Miles, A.E.W. 1963. The Dentition in the Assessment of Individual Age in Skeletal Material, in Brothwell, D.R. (ed.) *Dental Anthropology*. Pergamon: Oxford, pp. 191-209.

Millett, M. 1990. *The Romanization of Britain: An Essay in Archaeological Interpretation*. Cambridge University Press: Cambridge.

Millett, M. and James, S. 1983. Excavations at Cowdery's Down, Basingstoke, Hampshire 1978-81. *Archaeological Journal* 140: 151-279.

Mitchell, P.D., Boston, C., Chamberlain, A.T., Chaplin, S., Chauhan, V., Evans, J., Fowler, L., Powers, N., Walker, D., Webb, H. and Witkin, A. 2011. The Study of Anatomy in England from 1700 to the Early 20th Century. *Journal of Anatomy* 219: 91-99.

Moir, J.R. and Maynard, G. 1931. The Roman Villa at Castle Hill, Whitton, Ipswich. *Proceedings of the Suffolk Institute of Archaeology* 21: 240-260.

Molleson, T. and Cox, M. 1993. *The Spitalfields Project, Volume 2. The Anthropology: The Middling Sort*. CBA Research Report 86. Council for British Archaeology: York.

Molleson, T., Cruse, K. and Mays, S. 1998. Some Sexually Dimorphic Features of the Human Juvenile Skull and Their Value in Sex Determination in Immature Juvenile Remains. *Journal of Archaeological Science* 25: 719-728.

Montgomery, J., Knüsel, C. and Tucker, K. 2011. Identifying the Origins of Decapitated Male Skeletons from 3 Driffield Terrace, York, through Isotope Analysis: Reflections on the Cosmopolitan Nature of Roman York in the Time of Caracalla, in Bonogofsky, M. (ed.) *The Bioarchaeology of the Human Head: Decapitation, Deformation, and Decoration*. University Press of Florida: Gainesville, pp. 141-178.

Moore, M. 2010. 'Gladiator Burial Ground' Discovered in York. *The Telegraph*, 7 June 2010.

Moorrees, C.F.A., Fanning, E.A. and Hunt, E.E. 1963. Age Variation of Formation Stages for Ten Permanent Teeth. *Journal of Dental Research* 42: 1490-1502.

Morant, G.M. and Goodman, C.N. 1943. Human Bones, in Wheeler, R.E.M. *Maiden Castle, Dorset*. Society of Antiquaries: Oxford, pp. 337-360.

Morland, J. 1894. On Some Roman Remains at Long Sutton, Somerset. *Proceedings of the Somerset Archaeological and Natural History Society* 40: 272-274.

Mortimer, J.R. 1905. *Forty Years Researches in British and Saxon Burial Mounds of East Yorkshire*. A. Brown and Sons: London.

Mousourakis, G. 2003. *The Historical and Institutional Context of Roman Law*. Ashgate: Aldershot.

Müldner, G., Chenery, C. and Eckardt, H. 2011. The 'Headless Romans': Multi-isotope Investigations of an Unusual Burial Ground from Roman Britain. *Journal of Archaeological Science* 38: 280-290.

Mulhern, D.M. and Jones, E.B. 2005. Test of Revised Method of Age Estimation from the Auricular Surface of the Ilium. *American Journal of Physical Anthropology* 126: 61-65.

Mullin, D., Laws, G. and Smith, A. 2009. *Horcott Quarry (Churchberry Manor), Fairford, Gloucestershire: Post-Excavation Assessment and Project Design*. Unpublished Oxford Archaeology report.

Murphy, E., Gokhman, I., Chistov, Y. and Barkova, L. 2002. Prehistoric Old World Scalping: New Cases from the Cemetery of Aymyrlyg, South Siberia. *American Journal of Archaeology* 106: 1-10.

Murray, K.A. and Murray, T. 1991. A Test of the Auricular Surface Ageing Techniques. *Journal of Forensic Sciences* 36: 1162-1169.

Museum Syndicate. 2010. Execution by Decapitation in Japan. *Museum Syndicate*. Online: http://www.museumsyndicate.com/item.php?item=43122 (accessed 24 November 2011).

Myres, J.N.L. and Green, B. 1973. *The Anglo-Saxon Cemeteries of Caistor-by-Norwich and Markshall, Norfolk*. Reports of the Research Committee of the Society of Antiquaries of London 30. Society of Antiquaries: London.

Nenquin, J. 1953. *La nécropole de Furfooz*. De Tempel: Bruges.

Neville, R.C. 1854. Anglo-Saxon Cemetery on Linton Heath, Cambridgeshire. *Archaeological Journal* 11: 95-115.

Nickens, P.R. 1976. Stature Reduction as an Adaptive Response to Food Production in Mesoamerica. *Journal of Archaeological Science* 3: 31-41.

Niinimäki, S. 2009. What Do Muscle Marker Ruggedness Scores Actually Tell Us? *International Journal of Osteoarchaeology* 21: 292-299.

Ning, Z. 2008. The Political Origins of Death Penalty Exceptionalism: Mao Zedong and the Practice of Capital Punishment in Contemporary China. *Punishment and Society* 10: 117-136.

Novak, S.A. 2000a. Battle-Related Trauma, in Fiorato, V., Boylston, A. and Knüsel, C. (eds) *Blood Red Roses: The Archaeology of a Mass Grave from the Battle of Towton AD1461*. Oxbow: Oxford, pp. 90-102.

Novak, S.A. 2000b. Case Studies, in Fiorato, V., Boylston, A. and Knüsel, C. (eds) *Blood Red Roses: The Archaeology of a Mass Grave from the Battle of Towton AD1461*. Oxbow: Oxford, pp. 240-268.

O'Brien, E. 1999. *Post-Roman Britain to Anglo-Saxon England: Burial Practices Reviewed*. BAR British Series 289: Oxford.

O'Connor, S., Ali, E., Al-Sabah, S., Anwar, D., Bergström, E., Brown, K.A., Buckberry, J., Buckley, S., Collins, M., Denton, J., Dorling, K.M., Dowle, A., Duffey, P., Edwards, H.G.M., Faria, E.C., Gardner, P., Gledhill, A., Heaton, K., Heron, C., Janaway, R., Keely, B.J., King, D., Masinton, A., Penkman, K., Petzold, A., Pickering, M.D., Rumsby, M., Schutkowski, H., Shackleton, K.A., Thomas, J., Thomas-Oates, J., Usai, M.-R., Wilson, A.S. and O'Connor, T. 2011. Exceptional Preservation of a Prehistoric Human Brain from Heslington, Yorkshire, UK. *Journal of Archaeological Science* 38: 1641-1654.

Ogilvie, M.D. and Hilton, C.E. 2000. Ritualized Violence in the Prehistoric American Southwest. *International Journal of Osteoarchaeology* 10: 27-48.

Ordnance Survey. 2011. *Roman Britain* (6th edition). Ordnance Survey Historical Maps. Ordnance Survey: Southampton.

Ortner, D.J. 2003. *Identification of Pathological Conditions in Human Skeletal Remains*. Academic Press: London.

Osborne, D.L., Simmons, T.L. and Nawrocki, S.P. 2004. Reconsidering the Auricular Surface as an Indicator of Age at Death. *Journal of Forensic Sciences* 49: 905-911.

Osgood, R. 2005. *The Unknown Warrior: An Archaeology of the Common Soldier*. Sutton: Stroud.

Ottaway, P. 2004. *Roman York*. The History Press: Stroud.

Ottaway, P. 2005. *1-3 Driffield Terrace, York: Assessment Report on an Archaeological Excavation*. York Archaeological Trust Report 2005/27.

Ottaway, P. 2011. *Archaeology in the Environs of Roman York: Excavations 1976-2005*. York Archaeological Trust: York.

Ottaway, P.J., Qualmann, K.E., Rees, H. and Scobie, G.D. 2012. *The Roman Cemeteries and Suburbs of Winchester: Excavations 1971-1986*. Winchester Museums Service: Winchester.

Otten, T. 2003. *Die Ausgrabungen unter St Viktor zu Xanten: Dom und Immunität*. Verlag Philipp von Zabern: Mainz am Rhein.

Ousley, S.D. and Jantz, R.L. 2005. *FORDISC 3.0: Personal Computer Forensic Discriminant Functions*. University of Tennessee: Knoxville.

227

Palmer, S. 1871. Archaeological Notes. *Transactions of the Newbury and District Field Club* 1: 205-209.

Parker-Pearson, M., Chamberlain, A., Craig, O., Marshall, P., Mulville, J., Smith, H., Chenery, C., Collins, M., Cook, G., Craig, G., Evans, J., Hiller, J., Montgomery, J., Schwenninger, J.-L., Taylor, G. and Wess, T. 2005. Evidence for Mummification in Bronze Age Britain. *Antiquity* 79: 529-546.

Parker-Pearson, M., Chamberlain, A., Collins, M., Cox, C., Craig, G., Craig, O., Hiller, J., Marshall, P., Mulville, J. and Smith, H. 2007. Further Evidence for Mummification in Bronze Age Britain. *Antiquity* 81: Project Gallery. Online: http://antiquity.ac.uk/projgall/parker/index.html (accessed 28 October 2011).

Parry, T.W. 1928. Holes in the Skulls of Prehistoric Man and Their Significance. *Archaeological Journal* 85: 91-102.

Passmore, A.D. 1942. Chute Barrow I. *Wiltshire Archaeological and Natural History Magazine* 50: 100-101.

Patrick, C. and Ratkai, S. 2011. Hillside Meadow, Fordham, in Cuttler, R., Martin-Bacon, H., Nichol, K., Patrick, C., Perrin, R., Ratkai, S., Smith, M. and Williams, J. *Five Sites in Cambridgeshire: Excavations at Woodhurst, Fordham, Soham, Buckden and St Neots, 1998-2002*. BAR British Series 528. Archaeopress: Oxford, pp. 41-54.

Pearson, K. and Morant, G.M. 1934. The Wilkinson Head of Oliver Cromwell and Its Relationship to Busts, Masks and Portraiture. *Biometrika* 26: 1-116.

Penn, W.S. 1961. Springhead: Temples III and IV. *Archaeologia Cantiana* 74: 113-140.

Perry, M.A. 2005. Redefining Childhood through Bioarchaeology: Toward an Archaeological and Biological Understanding of Children in Antiquity. *Archeological Papers of the American Anthropological Association* 15: 89-111.

Peter, T.C. 1905. St Pirans Old Church. *Journal of the Royal Institution of Cornwall* 16: 133-143.

Peterson, F., Shepherd, I.A.G. and Tuckwell, A.N. 1975. A Short Cist at Horsbrugh Castle Farm, Peeblesshire. *Proceedings of the Society of Antiquaries of Scotland* 105: 43-62.

Pettigrew, T.J. 1858. On the Antiquities of Cuma. *Journal of the British Archaeological Association* 14: 294-305.

Petts, D. 2003. *Christianity in Roman Britain*. Tempus: Stroud.

Phenice, T.W. 1969. A Newly Developed Method of Sexing the Os Pubis. *American Journal of Physical Anthropology* 30: 297-302.

Phillips, C. and Leach, S. n.d. *The Human Bone: P1649 Great Casterton, Rutland (HAT 619)*. Unpublished report.

Philpott, R. 1991. *Burial Practices in Roman Britain: A Survey of Grave Treatment and Furnishing AD43-410*. BAR British Series 219. Tempus Reparatum: Oxford.

Pinhasi, R. and Mays, S. 2008. *Advances in Human Palaeopathology*. John Wiley: Chichester.

Pitt-Rivers, A.H.L.F. 1887. *Excavations in Cranbourne Chase near Rushmore, Volume I: Excavations in a Romano-British Village on Woodcutts Common and Romano-British Antiquities in Rushmore Park*. Privately printed.

Pitt-Rivers, A.H.L.F. 1892. *Excavations in Bokerly and Wansdyke, Dorset and Wiltshire 1888-1891*. Privately printed.

Pitt-Rivers, A.H.L.F. 1898. *Excavations in Cranbourne Chase, Volume IV*. Privately printed.

Pitts, M., Bayliss, A., McKinley, J., Boylston, A., Budd, P., Evans, J., Chenery, C., Reynolds, A. and Semple, S. 2002. An Anglo-Saxon Decapitation and Burial at Stonehenge. *Wiltshire Archaeological and Natural History Magazine* 95: 131-146.

Pollard, A.M., Ditchfield, P., Piva, E., Wallis, S., Falys, C. and Ford, S. 2012. 'Sprouting Like Cockle amongst the Wheat': The St Brice's Day Massacre and the Isotopic Analysis of Human Bones from St John's College, Oxford. *Oxford Journal Of Archaeology* 31: 83-102.

Poplin, F. 1985. Les Gaulois dépecés de Gournay-sur-Aronde. *Revue archéologique de Picardie* 4: 147-164.

Portable Antiquities Scheme. 2007. Knife (LIN-536F87). *Portable Antiquities Scheme.* Online: http://finds.org.uk/database/artefacts/record/id/163020 (accessed 25 November 2011).

Poulton, R. 1989. Rescue Excavations on an Early Saxon Cemetery Site and a Later (Probably Late Saxon) Execution Site at the Former Goblin Works, Ashtead, near Leatherhead. *Surrey Archaeological Collections* 79: 67-97.

Powell, K., Smith, A. and Laws, G. 2010. *Evolution of a Farming Community in the Upper Thames Valley: Excavation of a Prehistoric, Roman and Post-Roman Landscape at Cotswold Community, Gloucestershire and Wiltshire, Volume 1: Site Narrative and Overview.* Oxford Archaeology: Oxford.

Powell, T.G.E. 1958. *The Celts.* Thames and Hudson: London.

Price, E. 2000. *Frocester: A Romano-British Settlement, Its Antecedents and Successors.* Gloucester and District Arch Res Group: Stonehouse.

Rak, Y., Avensburg, B. and Nathan, H. 1976. Evidence of Violence on Human Bones in Israel, First and Third Centuries CE. *Palestine Exploration Quarterly* 108: 55-58.

R.C.H.M. 1962. *An Inventory of the Historical Monuments in the City of York, Volume I: Ebvracvm: Roman York.* HMSO: London.

Reaney, P. 1960. *The Origin of English Place-Names.* Routledge: London.

Redfern, R.C. 2005. *A Gendered Analysis of Health from the Iron Age to the End of the Romano-British Period in Dorset, England.* PhD thesis, University of Birmingham.

Redfern, R.C. 2008. A Bioarchaeological Analysis of Violence in Iron Age Females: A Perspective from Dorset, England (Fourth Century BC to First Century AD), in Davis, O., Sharples, N. and Waddington, K. (eds) *Changing Perspectives on the First Millennium BC.* Oxbow: Oxford, pp. 139-160.

Redfern, R.C. 2009. Does Cranial Trauma Provide Evidence for Projectile Weaponry in Late Iron Age Dorset. *Oxford Journal of Archaeology* 28: 399-424.

Redfern, R. 2011. A Re-appraisal of the Evidence for Violence in the Late Iron Age Human Remains from Maiden Castle Hillfort, Dorset, England. *Proceedings of the Prehistoric Society* 77: 111-138.

Redfern, R. and Bonney, H. 2014. Headhunting and Amphitheatre Combat in Roman London, England: New Evidence from the Walbrook Valley. *Journal of Archaeological Science* 43: 214-226.

Reece, R. 1980a. Religion, Coins and Temples, in Rodwell, W. (ed.) *Temples, Churches and Religion: Recent Research in Roman Britain.* BAR British Series 77. BAR: Oxford.

Reece, R. 1980b. Town and Country: The End of Roman Britain. *World Archaeology* 12: 77-92.

Reece, R. 1988. *My Roman Britain.* Cotswold Studies, Volume 3. Oxbow: Oxford.

Reece, R. 1991. *Roman Coins from 140 Sites in Britain.* Cotswold Studies, Volume 4: Cirencester.

Reece, R. 1995. Site-Finds in Roman Britain. *Britannia* 26: 179-206.

Reynolds, A. 1997. The Definition and Ideology of Anglo-Saxon Execution Sites and Cemeteries, in De Boe, G. and Verhaeghe, F. (eds) *Death and Burial in Medieval Europe: Papers of the 'Medieval Europe Brugge 1997' Conference.* Instituut voor het Archeologisch Patrimonium: Zellik, pp. 33-41.

Reynolds, A. 2009. *Anglo-Saxon Deviant Burial Customs.* Oxford University Press: Oxford.

Ribot, I. and Roberts, C. 1996. A Study of Non-specific Stress Indicators and Skeletal Growth in Two Mediaeval Subadult Populations. *Journal of Archaeological Science* 23: 67-79.

Richards, G.D. 1985. Analysis of a Microcephalic Child from the Late Period (c. AD 1100-1700) of Central California. *American Journal of Physical Anthropology* 68: 343-357.

Richards, L.C. and Miller, S.L. 1991. Relationships between Age and Dental Attrition in Australian Aboriginals. *American Journal of Physical Anthropology* 84: 159-164.

Richardson, E.W. 1982. The Cut Human Bones from the Shrine, in Wedlake, W.J. 1982. *The Excavation of the Shrine of Apollo at Nettleton, Wiltshire, 1956-1971.* Society of Antiquaries of London: London, pp. 179-180.

Ripper, S., Beamish, M., Bayliss, A., Bronk Ramsey, C., Brown, A., Collins, M., Cooper, N.J., Cook, G., Cook, J., Gouldwell, A., Greig, J., Hatton, J., Marshall, P.D., Meadows, J., Monckton, A., Van Der Plicht, H., Smith, D. and Tetlow, E. 2012. Bogs, Bodies and Burnt Mounds: Visits to the Soar Wetlands in the Neolithic and Bronze Age. *Proceedings of the Prehistoric Society* 78: 173-206.

Rissech, C., Garcia, M. and Malgosa, A. 2003. Sex and Age Diagnosis by Ischium Morphometric Analysis. *Forensic Science International* 135: 188-196.

Roberts, C. 2000a. Trauma in Biocultural Perspective: Past, Present and Future, in Cox, M. and Mays, S. (eds) *Human Osteology in Archaeology and Forensic Science.* Greenwich Medical Media: London, pp. 337-356.

Roberts, C. 2000b. Infectious Disease in Biocultural Perspective: Past, Present and Future Work in Britain, in Cox, M. and Mays, S. (eds) *Human Osteology in Archaeology and Forensic Science.* Greenwich Medical Media: London, pp. 145-162.

Roberts, C. 2007. A Bioarchaeological Study of Maxillary Sinusitis. *American Journal of Physical Anthropology* 133: 792-807.

Roberts, C. and Cox, M. 2003. *Health and Disease in Britain from Prehistory to the Present Day.* Sutton: Stroud.

Robertson-Mackay, R. 1987. The Neolithic Causewayed Enclosure at Staines, Surrey: Excavations 1961-1963. *Proceedings of the Prehistoric Society* 53: 23-128.

Robinson, O.F. 1995. *The Criminal Law of Ancient Rome.* Johns Hopkins University Press: Baltimore.

Robinson, T. 2005. *Lord Mayor's Walk, York: Report on an Archaeological Watching Brief.* On-Site Archaeology report.

Rolleston, G. 1869. On the Various Forms of the So-Called 'Celtic' Cranium. *Journal of Anatomy and Physiology* 3: 252-255.

Rolleston, G. 1876. On the People of the Long Barrow Period. *Journal of the Royal Anthropological Institute* 5: 120-173.

Ross, A. 1967. *Pagan Celtic Britain.* Cardinal: London.

Ross, A. 1986. *The Pagan Celts.* Batsford: London.

Ross, A. and Feachem, R. 1984. Heads Baleful and Benign, in Miket, R. and Burgess, C. (eds) *Between and Beyond the Walls: Essays on the Prehistory and History of North Britain in Honour of George Jobey.* John Donald: Edinburgh, pp. 338-352.

Ross, T. 1909. Purchases for the Museum and Library. *Proceedings of the Society of Antiquaries of Scotland* 43: 8-21.

Roth, J.P. 1998. *The Logistics of the Roman Army at War (264BC-AD235).* Brill: Leiden.

Royce, D. 1882. 'Finds' on, or near to, the Excursion of the Society at Stow-on-the-Wold. *Transactions of the Bristol and Gloucestershire Archaeological Society* 7: 69-80.

Rudsdale, E.J. 1931. Inhumation Burials of the Roman Period Discovered at Colchester. *Transactions of the Essex Archaeological Society* 20: 289-291.

St Hoyme, L.E. and İşcan, M.Y. 1989. Determination of Sex and Race: Accuracy and Assumptions, in İşcan, M.Y. and Kennedy, K.A.R. (eds) *Reconstruction of Life from the Skeleton.* Alan R. Liss: New York, pp. 53-93.

Salisbury, J.E. 2004. *The Blood of Martyrs: Unintended Consequences of Ancient Violence.* Routledge: London.

Sanidopolous, J. 2011. Third-Century Skulls of Christian Martyrs Discovered in Lagonisi. *Mystagogy*. Online: http://www.johnsanidopoulos.com/2011/03/third-century-skulls-of-christian.html (accessed 26 February 2014).

Santos, A.L. and Roberts, C.A. 2001. A Picture of Tuberculosis in Young Portuguese People in the Early 20th Century: A Multidisciplinary Study of the Skeletal and Historical Evidence. *American Journal of Physical Anthropology* 115: 38-49.

Saponetti, S.S., Scattarella, V., Di Nunno, C., Emanuel, P. and Di Nunno, N. 2008. A Case of Decapitation in Canosa, South Italy (5th-6th Century AD). *Forensic Science International* 176: e11-e16.

Sauer, E.W. 2005. *Linear Earthwork, Tribal Boundary and Ritual Beheading: Aves Ditch from the Iron Age to the Early Middle Ages*. BAR 402. Archaeopress: Oxford.

Sauer, N.J. 1998. The Timing of Injuries and Manner of Death: Distinguishing Among Antemortem, Perimortem and Postmortem Trauma, in Reichs, K. (ed.) *Forensic Osteology: Advances in the Identification of Human Remains* (2nd edition). Charles C. Thomas: Springfield, pp. 321-332.

Saunders, S.R. 2000. Juvenile Skeletons and Growth-Related Studies, in Katzenberg, M.A. and Saunders, S.R. (eds) *Biological Anthropology of the Human Skeleton*. John Wiley and Sons: Hoboken, pp. 117-148.

Saunders, S.R., Fitzgerald, C., Rogers, T., Dudar, C. and McKillop, H. 1992. A Test of Several Methods of Skeletal Age Estimation Using a Documented Archaeological Sample. *Canadian Society of Forensic Science Journal* 25: 97-118.

Scheuer, L. and Black, S. 2000a. *Developmental Juvenile Osteology*. Academic Press: London.

Scheuer, L. and Black, S. 2000b. Development and Ageing of the Juvenile Skeleton, in Cox, M. and Mays, S. (eds) *Human Osteology in Archaeology and Forensic Science*. Greenwich Medical Media: London, pp. 9-21.

Scheuer, J.L., Musgrave, J.H. and Evans, S.P. 1980. The Estimation of Late Fetal and Perinatal Age from Limb Bone Length by Linear and Logarithmic Regression. *Annals of Human Biology* 7: 257-265.

Schofield, J. and Maloney, C. 1998. *Archaeology in the City of London 1907-1991: A Guide to Records of Excavations by the Museum of London and Its Predecessors*. Museum of London: London.

Schulting, R. 2006. Skeletal Evidence and Contexts of Violence in the European Mesolithic and Neolithic, in Gowland, R. and Knüsel, C. (eds) *Social Archaeology of Funerary Remains*. Oxbow: Oxford, pp. 224-237.

Schulting, R.J., Armit, I. and Knüsel, C.J. 2010. Bronze Age Deposition and Iron Age Decapitation at the Sculptor's Cave, Covesea, in Trythall, J. and Dalgarno, B. (eds) *Beakers, Bones and Birnie*. The Moray Society: Elgin, pp. 69-81.

Schulting, R.J. and Wysocki, M. 2005. 'In This Chambered Tumulus Were Found Cleft Skulls…': An Assessment of the Evidence for Cranial Trauma in the British Neolithic. *Proceedings of the Prehistoric Society* 71: 107-138.

Schutkowski, H. 1993. Sex Determination of Infant and Juvenile Skeletons: 1. Morphognostic Features. *American Journal of Physical Anthropology* 90: 199-205.

Seetah, K. 2006. Multidisciplinary Approach to Romano-British Cattle Butchery, in Maltby, M. (ed.) *Integrating Zooarchaeology: Proceedings of the 9th Conference of the International Council of Archaeozoology, Durham, August 2002*. Oxbow: Oxford, pp. 109-116.

Shapland, F. and Armit, I. 2012. The Useful Dead: Bodies as Objects in Iron Age and Norse Atlantic Scotland. *European Journal of Archaeology* 15: 116-198.

Simmonds, A., Anderson-Whymark, H. and Norton, A. 2011. Excavations at Tubney Woods Quarry, Oxfordshire, 2001-2009. *Oxoniensia* 76: 105-172.

231

Simmonds, A., Marquez-Grant, N. and Loe, L. 2008. *Life and Death in a Roman City: Excavation of a Roman Cemetery with a Mass Grave at 120-122 London Road, Gloucester*. Oxford Archaeology: Oxford.

Simpson, L. 1982. Other Doings of St Alban and Amphibalus and Their Companions. Written in English in the Year 590. Translated by William the Monk of St Albans. *Hertfordshire Archaeology* 8: 67-77.

Singer, R. 1953. Estimation of Age from Cranial Suture Closure: A Report on Its Unreliability. *Journal of Forensic Medicine* 1: 52-59.

Skeat, W.W. 1881. *Aelfric's Lives of the Saints*. Early English Text Society: London.

Smith, A. 1998. Trauma Most Foul: The Human Remains from Kintbury, Berkshire, in Anderson, S. (ed.) *Current and Recent Research in Osteoarchaeology: Proceedings of the Third Meeting of the Osteoarchaeological Research Group*. Oxbow: Oxford, pp. 27-30.

Smith, B.H. 1991. Standards of Human Tooth Formation and Dental Age Assessment, in Kelley, M.A. and Larsen, C.S. (eds) *Advances in Dental Anthropology*. Wiley-Liss: New York, pp. 143-168.

Smith, K. 1977. The Excavation of Winklebury Camp, Basingstoke, Hampshire. *Proceedings of the Prehistoric Society* 43: 31-129.

Smith, P. 1977. The Human Skeletal Remains from the Abba Cave. *Israel Exploration Journal* 27: 121-124.

Smith, M.J. and Brickley, M.B. 2004. Analysis and Interpretation of Flint Toolmarks Found on Bones from West Tump Long Barrow, Gloucestershire. *International Journal of Osteoarchaeology* 14: 18-33.

Smith, M. and Brickley, M. 2009. *People of the Long Barrows: Life, Death and Burial in the Earlier Neolithic*. History Press: Stroud.

Smith, R.J.C., Healy, F., Allen, M.J., Morris, E.L., Barnes, I. and Woodward, P.J. 1997. *Excavations along the Route of the Dorchester By-pass, Dorset 1986-8*. Wessex Archaeology Report 2. Wessex Archaeology: Salisbury.

Sparey Green, C. 1982. The Cemetery of a Romano-British Christian Community at Poundbury, Dorchester, Dorset, in Pearce, S.M. (ed.) *The Early Church in West Britain and Ireland*. BAR British Series 102. British Archaeological Reports: Oxford, pp. 61-76.

Spars, S.A. 2005. *Interpreting Conflict Mortuary Behaviour: Applying Non-linear and Traditional Quantitative Methods to Conflict Burials*. PhD thesis, University of Glasgow.

Spierenburg, P.C. 1984. *The Spectacle of Suffering: Executions and the Evolution of Repression from a Preindustrial Metropolis to the European Experience*. Cambridge University Press: Cambridge.

Startin, D.W.A. 1981. Excavations at the Old Vicarage, Fordington, Dorchester, Dorset 1971. *Proceedings of the Dorset Natural History and Archaeology Society* 103: 43-66.

Stary, J. 2005. Slave and Master, Archaeology and Literature: Inhumation Grave F II at Stengade II in Denmark (translated by A. Millar). *Archeologické Rozhledy* 57: 750-786.

Stead, I.M. 1971. Yorkshire before the Romans: Some Recent Discoveries, in Butler, R.M. (ed.) *Soldier and Civilian in Roman Yorkshire*. Leicester University Press: Leicester, pp. 21-43.

Steele, J. 2000. Skeletal Indicators of Handedness, in Cox, M. and Mays, S. (eds) *Human Osteology in Archaeology and Forensic Science*. Greenwich Medical Media: London, pp. 307-323.

Steele, D.G. and Bramblett, C.A. 1988. *The Anatomy and Biology of the Human Skeleton*. Texas A&M University Press: College Station.

Stirland, A. 1992. *Asymmetry and Activity-Related Change in Selected Bones of the Human Male Skeleton*. PhD thesis, University College, London.

Stirland, A.J. 1993. Asymmetry and Activity-Related Change in the Male Humerus. *International Journal of Osteoarchaeology* 3: 105-113.

Stirland, A. 1998. The Human Skeletal Material, in Clarke, C.P. *Excavations to the South of Chignall Roman Villa, Essex 1977-1981*. East Anglian Archaeology 83. Essex County Council: Chelmsford, pp. 119-122.

Stojanowski, C.M. and Schillaci, M.A. 2006. Phenotypic Approaches for Understanding Intracemetery Biological Variation. *American Journal of Physical Anthropology* 131: 49-88.

Stone, J.F.S. 1932. Saxon Interments on Roche Court Down, Winterslow. *Wiltshire Archaeological and Natural History Magazine* 45: 568-582.

Stone, J.F.S. 1934. A Case of Bronze Age Cephalotaphy on Easton Down in Wiltshire. *Man* 34: 38-42.

Stone, J.F.S. 1939. An Early Bronze Age Grave in Fargo Plantation near Stonehenge. *Wiltshire Archaeological and Natural History Magazine* 48: 357-370.

Stoodley, N. 2006. Changing Burial Practice in Seventh Century Hampshire: The Anglo-Saxon Cemetery at Portway West, Andover. *Proceedings of the Hampshire Field Club and Archaeological Society* 61: 63-80.

Storm, R. 2008. Cranial Asymmetry and Developmental Abnormalities, in Magilton, J., Lee, F. and Boylston, A. (eds) *'Lepers Outside the Gate': Excavations at the Cemetery of the Hospital of St James and St Mary Magdalene, Chichester 1986-1987 and 1993*. CBA: York, pp. 164-173.

Stroud, G. 1993a. The Human Bones, in Stroud, G. and Kemp, R.L. *Cemeteries of St Andrew, Fishergate: The Archaeology of York, Volume 12: The Medieval Cemeteries*. CBA: York, pp. 160-241.

Stroud, G. 1993b. Human Skeletal Material, in Dallas, C. *Excavations in Thetford by B.K. Davison between 1964 and 1970*. Norfolk Museums Service: Dereham, pp. 168-176.

Stroud, G. and Kemp, R.L. 1993. *Cemeteries of St Andrew, Fishergate: The Archaeology of York, Volume 12: The Medieval Cemeteries*. CBA: York.

Stuckert, C.M. in press. *The People of Early Winchester*. Winchester Studies vol. 9i. Clarendon Press: Oxford.

Sutherland, L.D. and Suchey, J.M. 1991. Use of the Ventral Arc in Pubic Sex Determination. *Journal of Forensic Sciences* 36: 501-511.

Sutton, M.Q., Malik, M. and Ogram, A. 1996. Experiments on the Determination of Gender from Coprolites by DNA Analysis. *Journal of Archaeological Science* 23: 263-268.

SWAT Archaeology. 2009. Interim Archaeological Excavation Report for 28 Church Street, Hoo St Werburgh, Rochester, Kent. SWAT Archaeology report.

Syrmos, N.C. 2011. Microcephaly in Ancient Greece: The Minoan Microcephalus of Zakros. *Child's Nervous System* 27: 685-686.

Ta'ala, S.C., Berg, G.E. and Haden, K. 2006. Blunt Force Cranial Trauma in the Cambodian Killing Fields. *Journal of Forensic Sciences* 51: 996-1001.

Tague, R.G. 1989. Variation in Pelvic Size between Males and Females. *American Journal of Physical Anthropology* 80: 59-71.

Tague, R.G. 1992. Sexual Dimorphism in the Human Bony Pelvis, with a Consideration of the Neandertal Pelvis from Kebara Cave, Israel. *American Journal of Physical Anthropology* 88: 1-21.

Tarlow, S. 2011. *Ritual, Belief and the Dead in Early Modern Britain and Ireland*. Cambridge University Press: Cambridge.

Taylor, A. 2003. Burial with the Romans. *British Archaeology* 69. Online: http://www.britarch.ac.uk/ba/ba69/feat2.shtml (accessed 1 November 2010).

Taylor, A. 2008. Aspects of Deviant Burial in Roman Britain, in Murphy, E.M. (ed.) *Deviant Burial in the Archaeological Record*. Oxbow: Oxford, pp. 91-114.

Tester, A. 2004. *46-48 Woodcock Rise, Brandon (BRD165): A Report on the Archaeological Excavation 2003*. Suffolk County Council Archaeology Service Report 2004/25.

Tester, P.J. 1963. A Decapitated Burial at Cuxton. *Archaeologia Cantiana* 78: 181-182.

Thacker, A. 1995. Membra Disjecta: The Division of the Body and the Diffusion of the Cult, in Stancliffe, C. and Cambridge, E. (eds) *Oswald: Northumbrian King to European Saint*. Paul Watkins: Stamford, pp. 97-127.

Thomas, C., Sloane, B. and Phillpotts, C. 1997. *Excavations at the Priory and Hospital of St Mary Spital, London*. MoLAS Monograph 1. Museum of London: London.

Thomas, G.W. 1887. On Excavations in an Anglo-Saxon Cemetery at Sleaford, in Lincolnshire. *Archaeologia* 50: 383-406.

Tiesler, V. 2007. Funerary or Nonfunerary? New References in Identifying Ancient Maya Sacrificial and Postsacrificial Behaviors from Human Assemblages, in Tiesler, V. and Cucina, A. (eds) *New Perspectives on Human Sacrifice and Ritual Body Treatments in Ancient Maya Society*. Springer: New York, pp. 14-44.

Tildesley, M.L. 1932. The Human Remains from Roche Court Down. *Wiltshire Archaeological and Natural History Magazine* 45: 583-599.

Tildesley, M.L. 1934. Report on Human Remains from Meon Hill, in Liddell, D.M. Excavations at Meon Hill. *Proceedings of the Hampshire Field Club and Archaeological Society* 12: 127-162.

Tildesley, M.L. 1934b. Report on the Human Remains, in Stone, J.F.S. A Case of Bronze Age Cephalotaphy on Easton Down in Wiltshire. *Man* 34: 41-42.

Timberlake, S., Dodwell, N. and Armour, N. 2007. *The Roman Cemetery, The Babraham Institute, Cambridgeshire: An Archaeological Excavation*. Cambridge Archaeological Unit Report 75.

Timby, J., Brown, R., Hardy, A., Leech, S., Poole, C. and Webley, L. 2007. *Settlement on the Bedfordshire Claylands: Archaeology along the A421 Great Barford Bypass*. Oxford Archaeological Unit/Bedfordshire Archaeological Council: Oxford.

Todd, M. 1969. The Roman Settlement at Margidunum: The Excavations of 1966-8. *Transactions of the Thoroton Society of Nottinghamshire* 73: 7-104.

Todd, T.W. 1920. Age Changes in the Pubic Bone: I. The Male White Pubis. *American Journal of Physical Anthropology* 3: 285-334.

Todd, T.W. 1921a. Age Changes in the Pubic Bone: II. The Pubis of the Male Negro-White Hybrid; III: The Pubis of the White Female; IV: The Pubis of the Female Negro-White Hybrid. *American Journal of Physical Anthropology* 4: 1-70.

Todd, T.W. 1921b. Age Changes in the Pubic Bone: VI. The Interpretation of Variations in the Symphyseal Area. *American Journal of Physical Anthropology* 4: 407-424.

Todd, T.W. 1923. Age Changes in the Pubic Symphysis: VII. The Anthropoid Strain in Human Pubic Symphyses of the Third Decade. *Journal of Anatomy* 57: 274-294.

Todd, T.W. and Lyon, D.W. 1924. Endocranial Suture Closure, Its Progress and Age Relationship, Part I: Adult Males of White Stock. *American Journal of Physical Anthropology* 7: 325-384.

Todd, T.W. and Lyon, D.W. 1925a. Cranial Suture Closure, Its Progress and Age Relationship Part II: Ectocranial Closure in Adult Males of White Stock. *American Journal of Physical Anthropology* 8: 23-45.

Todd, T.W. and Lyon, D.W. 1925b. Cranial Suture Closure, Its Progress and Age Relationship Part III: Endocranial Closure in Adult Males of Negro Stock. *American Journal of Physical Anthropology* 8: 47-71.

Todd, T.W. and Lyon, D.W. 1925c. Suture Closure, Its Progress and Age Relationship Part

IV: Ectocranial Closure in Adult Males of Negro Stock. *American Journal of Physical Anthropology* 8: 149-168.

Toop, N. 2008. Excavations at Moss Street Depot, Moss Street, York. *Yorkshire Archaeology Journal* 80: 21-42.

Töppen, M. 1867. *Aberglauben aus Masuren*. Bertling: Danzig.

Trimble, D. 2000. *Archaeological Excavations Undertaken along the Route of the Market Deeping Bypass, Volume 1: Descriptions of the Excavations*. Archaeological Project Services Report 2000/93.

Trinkaus, E. 1975. Squatting among the Neandertals: A Problem in the Behavioral Interpretation of Skeletal Morphology. *Journal of Archaeological Science* 2: 327-351.

Trotter, M. 1970. Estimation of Stature from Intact Long Bones, in Stewart, T.D. (ed.) *Personal Identification in Mass Disasters*. Smithsonian Institute Press: Washington, DC, pp. 71-83.

Tucker, K. 2007. *Analysis of the Inhumations and Disarticulated Human Bone from the Cemetery of the Lost Church of St Stephen, George Street, York*. Unpublished YAT report.

Tucker, K. 2008a. The Human Bone, in Toop, N. Excavations at Moss Street Depot, Moss Street, York. *Yorkshire Archaeological Journal* 80: 21-42.

Tucker, K. 2008b. Appendix 3: Catalogue of Burials, in Brown, J. *Late Iron Age Occupation and the Emergence of a Roman Farming Settlement at Broadway Fields, Yaxley, Huntingdonshire July-October 2005*. Northamptonshire Archaeology Report 08/135, pp. 18-33.

Tucker, K. 2012. A Note on the Decapitation Burials, in Ottawa, P.J., Qualmann, K.E., Rees, H. and Scobie, G.D. *The Roman Cemeteries and Suburbs of Winchester: Excavations 1976–86*. Winchester Museums Service: Winchester, pp. 240-242.

Tucker, K. in press a. LH 427: Amputation of Digits of the Left Hand, in Stuckert, C.M. (ed.) *The People of Early Winchester*. Winchester Studies vol. 9.i. Clarendon Press: Oxford.

Tucker, K. in press b. The Physical Evidence for Decapitation at Lankhills, in Stuckert, C.M. (ed.) *The People of Early Winchester*. Winchester Studies vol. 9.i. Clarendon Press: Oxford.

Turner, C.H. 2006. Bone Strength: Current Concepts. *Annals of the New York Academy of Sciences* 1068: 429-446.

Tyrrell, A. 2000. Skeletal Non-metric Traits and the Assessment of Inter- and Intra-population Diversity: Past Problems and Future Potential, in Cox, M. and Mays, S. (eds) *Human Osteology in Archaeology and Forensic Science*. Greenwich Medical Media: London, pp. 289-306.

Ubelaker, D.H. 1978. *Human Skeletal Remains: Excavation, Analysis and Interpretation*. Smithsonian Institute Press: Washington, DC.

van der Sanden, W.A.B. 1996. *Through Nature to Eternity: The Bog Bodies of Northwest Europe*. Batavian Lion International: Amsterdam.

van Doorselaer, A. 1967. *Les nécropoles d'époque Romaine en Gaule septentrionale*. De Tempel: Brugge.

Varner, E.R. 2001. Punishment after Death: Mutilation of Images and Corpse Abuse in Ancient Rome. *Mortality* 6: 45-64.

Varner, E.R. 2005. Execution in Effigy: Severed Heads and Decapitated Statues in Imperial Rome, in Hopkins, A. and Wyke, M. (eds) *Roman Bodies: Antiquity to the Eighteenth Century*. The British School at Rome: London, pp. 67-82.

Venables, E. 1860. *A Guide to the Isle of Wight*. Edward Stanford: London.

Verano, J.W. 2000. Paleopathological Analysis of Sacrificial Victims at the Pyramid of the Moon, Moche River Valley, Northern Peru. *Chungara* 32: 61-70.

Verano, J. 2001. The Physical Evidence of Human Sacrifice in Ancient Peru, in Benson,

E. and Cook, A. (eds) *Ritual Sacrifice in Ancient Peru*. National Gallery of Art: Washington, pp. 111-125.

Verano, J. 2008. Trophy Head-Taking and Human Sacrifice in Andean South America, in Silverman, H. and Isbell, W.H. (eds) *Handbook of South American Archaeology*. Springer: New York, pp. 1047-1060.

Viciano, J., López-Lázaro, S., Cesana, D.T., D'Anastasio, R. and Capasso, L. 2012. Multiple Traumatic Dental Injuries: A Case Report in a Young Individual from the Samnitic Necropolis of Opi Val Fondillo (VI–V century BC; Central Italy). *Journal of Archaeological Science* 39: 566-572.

Villa, P. and Mathieu, E. 1991. Breakage Patterns of Human Long Bones. *Journal of Human Evolution* 21: 27-48.

Villotte, S., Castex, D., Couallier, V., Dutour, O., Knüsel, C. and Henry-Gambier, D. 2010. Enthesopathies as Occupational Stress Markers: Evidence from the Upper Limb. *American Journal of Physical Anthropology* 142: 224-234.

Voisin, J.L. 1984. Les Romains, chasseurs de têtes, in *Du châtiment dans la cité: Supplices corporels et peine de mort dans le monde antique: Table ronde (Rome 9-11 novembre 1982)*. École Française de Rome: Rome, pp. 241-293.

von Tettau, W.J.A. and Temme, J.D.H. 1837. *Die Volssagen Ostpreussens, Litthauens und Westpreussens*. Nicolaischen Buchhandlung: Berlin.

Wacher, J. 1975. *The Towns of Roman Britain*. Batsford: London.

Wainwright, J. 2010. *Archaeological Investigations in St John's, Worcester*. Historic Environment and Archaeology Service, Worcestershire Report 1751.

Wainwright, M. 2010. Scars from Lion Bite Suggest Headless Romans Found in York Were Gladiators. *The Guardian*, 7th June 2010.

Wait, G.A. 1985. *Ritual and Religion in Iron Age Britain*. BAR British Series 149: Oxford.

Wait, G.A. 1995. Burial and the Otherworld, in Green, M.J. (ed.) *The Celtic World*. Routledge: London, pp. 489-509.

Wakely, J. 1997. Identification and Analysis of Violent and Non-violent Head Injuries in Osteo-archaeological Material, in Carman, J. (ed.) *Material Harm: Archaeological Studies of War and Violence*. Cruithne Press: Glasgow, pp. 24-46.

Waldron, T. 1987. The Relative Survival of the Human Skeleton: Implications for Palaeopathology, in Boddington, A., Garland, A.N. and Janaway, R.C. (eds) *Death, Decay and Reconstruction*. Manchester University Press: Manchester, pp. 55-64.

Waldron, T. 2002. The Human Remains, in Davies, S.M., Bellamy, P.S., Heaton, M.J. and Woodward, P.J. *Excavations at Alington Avenue, Fordington, Dorchester, Dorset 1984-1987*. Dorset Natural History and Archaeological Society Monograph 15: Dorchester, pp. 147-154.

Waldron, T. 2004. Human Remains in Gardner, R. Investigations at 24 Friary Fields, Dunstable, Bedfordshire. *Bedfordshire Archaeological Journal* 25: 178-180.

Waldron, T. and Waldron, G. 1988. Two Felons from Surrey. *London Archaeologist* 5: 443-445.

Walker, C., Thorne, A. and Holmes, M. 2008. *Water Lane, Towcester: Archaeological Excavations on the Site of the Safeway Supermarket 1997-1998*. Northamptonshire Archaeology Report 08/59.

Walker, L. 1984. The Deposition of the Human Remains, in Cunliffe, B. *Danebury: An Iron Age Hillfort in Hampshire, Volume 2: The Excavations 1969-1978: The Finds*. Council for British Archaeology Research Report 52: London, pp. 442-463.

Walker, P.L. 2001. A Bioarchaeological Perspective on the History of Violence. *Annual Review of Anthropology* 30: 573-596.

Walker, P.L. 2005. Greater Sciatic Notch Morphology: Sex, Age and Population Differences. *American Journal of Physical Anthropology* 127: 385-39.

Walker, P.L., Bathurst, R.R., Richman, R., Gjerdrum, T. and Andrushko, V.A. 2009. The Causes of Porotic Hyperostosis and Cribra Orbitalia: A Reappraisal of the Iron-Deficiency-Anemia Hypothesis. *American Journal of Physical Anthropology* 139: 109-125.

Walker, P.L., Johnson, J.R. and Lambert, P.M. 1988. Age and Sex Biases in the Preservation of Human Skeletal Remains. *American Journal of Physical Anthropology* 76: 183-188.

Wallis, H. Forthcoming. *Romano-British Cambridgeshire: Recent Excavations*. East Anglian Archaeology: Cambridge.

Watkins, T. 1982. The Excavation of an Early Bronze Age Cemetery at Barns Farm, Dalgety, Fife. *Proceedings of the Society of Antiquaries of Scotland* 112: 48-141.

Watts, D. 1991. *Christians and Pagans in Roman Britain*. Routledge: London.

Watts, D. 1998. *Religion in Late Roman Britain: Forces of Change*. Routledge: London.

Weaver, D.S. 1980. Sex Differences in the Ilia of a Known Sex and Age Sample of Fetal and Infant Skeletons. *American Journal of Physical Anthropology* 52: 191-195.

Wedlake, W.J. 1982. *The Excavation of the Shrine of Apollo at Nettleton, Wiltshire, 1956-1971*. Society of Antiquaries of London: London.

Weinberg, J. 2008. Sword of Justice? Beheadings Rise in Saudi Arabia. *Arabia Today*. Online: http://arabia2day.com/reports/sword-of-justice-beheadings-rise-in-saudi-arabia (accessed 24th November 2011).

Weiss, E. 2003. Understanding Muscle Markers: Aggregation and Construct Validity. *American Journal of Physical Anthropology* 121: 230-240.

Weiss, E. 2004. Understanding Muscle Markers: Lower Limbs. *American Journal of Physical Anthropology* 125: 232-238.

Weiss, E., Corona, L. and Schultz, B. 2012. Sex Differences in Musculoskeletal Stress Markers: Problems with Activity Pattern Reconstructions. *International Journal of Osteoarchaeology* 22: 70-80.

Wells, C. 1964a. An Early Case of Birth Injury: Multiple Abnormalities in a Romano-British Skeleton. *Developmental Medicine and Child Neurology* 6: 397-402.

Wells, C. 1964b. The Human Skeleton, in Smedley, N. and Owles, E.J. Some Suffolk Kilns IV: Saxon Kilns in Cox Lane, Ipswich, 1961. *Proceedings of the Suffolk Institute of Archaeology* 29: 304-335.

Wells, C. 1967a. Report on the Human Skeletons from Red Castle, Thetford. *Norfolk Archaeology* 34: 155-186.

Wells, C. 1967b. A Leper Cemetery at South Acre, Norfolk. *Medieval Archaeology* 11: 242-248.

Wells, C. 1975. Prehistoric and Historical Changes in Nutritional Diseases and Associated Conditions. *Progress in Food and Nutrition Science* 1: 729-779.

Wells, C. 1976. Icklingham: The Human Burials, in West, S.E. (ed.) *East Anglian Archaeology Report, no. 3: Suffolk*. Suffolk County Planning Department: Ipswich, pp. 103-119.

Wells, C. 1981. Report on Three Series of Romano-British Cremations and Four Inhumations from Skeleton Green, in Partridge, C. *Skeleton Green: A Late Iron Age and Romano-British Site*. Britannia Monograph 2. Society for the Promotion of Roman Studies: London, pp. 277-304.

Wells, C. 1982. The Human Burials, in McWhirr, A., Viner, L. and Wells, C. Romano-British Cemeteries at Cirencester. Cirencester Excavation Committee: Cirencester, pp. 135-202.

Wells, C. and Cayton, H. 1980. The Human Bones, in Wade-Martins, P. *Excavations in North Elmham, Volume II*. Norfolk Archaeology Unit and Norfolk Museums Service: Dereham, pp. 247-374.

Wells, C. and Dallas, C. 1976. Romano-British Pathology. *Antiquity* 50: 53-55.

Wenham, L.P. 1968. *The Romano-British Cemetery at Trentholme Drive, York*. HMSO: London.

Wenham, S.J. 1989. Anatomical Interpretations of Anglo-Saxon Weapon Injuries, in Hawkes, S.C. (ed.) *Weapons and Warfare in Anglo-Saxon England*. Oxford University Press, Oxford, pp. 123-139.

Western, G. 2009. *Osteological Analysis of Human Remains from Sainsbury's Site, St Johns, Worcester*. Ossafreelance report.

Weston, D.A. 2008. Investigating the Specificity of Periosteal Reactions in Pathology Museum Specimens. *American Journal of Physical Anthropology* 137: 48-59.

Wheeler, R.E.M. 1943. *Maiden Castle, Dorset*. Society of Antiquaries: Oxford.

Wheeler, R.E.M. 1954. *The Stanwick Fortifications, North Riding of Yorkshire*. Society of Antiquaries: Oxford.

Whimster, R. 1981. *Burial Practices in Iron Age Britain: A Discussion and Gazetteer of the Evidence c. 700BC-AD43*. BAR 90: Oxford.

White, B. 1988. *Skeletal Remains from the Cemetery of St Nicholas Shambles, City of London*. London and Middlesex Archaeological Society: London.

White, B. 2000. The Cemetery Population, in Mackinder, A. *A Romano-British Cemetery on Watling Street: Excavations at 165 Great Dover Street, Southwark, London*. MoLAS: London, pp. 26-27.

White, K. 2003. *The Archaeology of Intersex and Gender*. MSc dissertation, University of Bradford.

Whittaker, D.K., Griffiths, S., Robson, A., Roger Davies, P. and Thomas, G. 1990. Continuing Tooth Eruption and Alveolar Crest Height in an Eighteenth-Century Population from Spitalfields, East London. *Archives of Oral Biology* 35: 81-85.

Wiedemann, T. 1992. *Emperors and Gladiators*. Routledge: London.

Wilkinson, J.L. and Barker, P.A. 1997. Human Skull Fragments, in Barker, P., White, R., Pretty, K., Bird, H. and Corbishley, M. *The Baths Basilica Wroxeter: Excavations 1966-90*. English Heritage: London, pp. 368-370.

Williams, H.M.R. 1999. Identities and Cemeteries in Roman and Early Medieval Britain, in Baker, P. (ed.) *TRAC 98: Proceedings of the 8th Annual Theoretical Roman Archaeology Conference Leicester 1998*. Oxbow: Oxford, pp. 96-107.

Willey, P. and Emerson, T.E. 1993. The Osteology and Archaeology of the Crow Creek Massacre. *The Plains Anthropologist* 38: 227-269.

Wilmott, T. and Rahtz, S.P.Q. 1985. An Iron Age and Roman Settlement outside Kenchester (Magnis), Herefordshire: Excavations 1977-9. *Transactions of the Woolhope Naturalists Field Club* 45: 36-185.

Wilson, C.E. 1981. Burials within Settlements in Southern Britain during the Pre-Roman Iron Age. *Institute of Archaeology Bulletin* 18: 127-169.

Wilson, D. 1992. *Anglo-Saxon Paganism*. Routledge: London.

Wilson, D.M. and Hurst, J.G. 1960. Medieval Britain in 1959. *Medieval Archaeology* 4: 134-165.

Wilson, D.M. and Wright, R.P. 1965. Roman Britain in 1964. *Journal of Roman Studies* 55: 199-228.

Wiltschke-Schrotta, K. and Stadler, P. 2005. Beheading in Avar Times (630-800 AD). *Acta Medica Lituanica* 12: 58-64.

Witkin, A. 2005. Human Bones, in Bradley, P., Charles, B., Hardy, A. and Poore, D. Prehistoric and Roman Activity and a Civil War Ditch: Excavations at the Chemistry Research Laboratory, 2-4 South Parks Road, Oxford. *Oxoniensia* 70: 141-202.

Witkin, A. 2006. *Human Remains from a Roman Settlement at Bower Road, Smeeth, Kent*. CTRL Specialist Report Series.

Witkin, A. 2007. Human Remains, in Miles, D., Palmer, S., Smith, A. and Perpetua Jones, G. *Iron Age and Roman Settlement in the Upper Thames Valley: Excavations at Claydon Pike and Other Sites within the Cotswold Water Park*. Oxford Archaeology: Oxford, pp. 201-203.

Wood, J.W., Milner, G.R., Harpending, H.C. and Weiss, K.M. 1992. The Osteological Paradox: Problems of Inferring Prehistoric Health from Skeletal Samples. *Current Anthropology* 33: 343-370.

Wood-Jones, F. 1908. The Examination of the Bodies of 100 Men Executed in Nubia in Roman Times. *British Medical Journal* 1: 736-737.

Woods, P.J. 1969. *Excavations at Hardingstone, Northamptonshire, 1967-8*. Northamptonshire County Council: Northampton.

Woodward, A. 1992. *Shrines and Sacrifice*. BT Batsford: London.

Wright, J., Leivers, M., Seagar Smith, R. and Stevens, C.J. 2009. *Cambourne New Settlement: Iron Age and Romano-British Settlement on the Clay Uplands of West Cambridgeshire*. Wessex Archaeology Report 23. Wessex Archaeology: Salisbury.

Wright, L.R. and Yoder, C.J. 2003. Recent Progress in Bioarchaeology: Approaches to the Osteological Paradox. *Journal of Archaeological Research* 11: 43-70.

Wymer, J.J. 1996. *Barrow Excavations in Norfolk 1984-88*. Norfolk Museums Service: Dereham.

YAT. 2004. *33rd Annual Report: 2004-2005*. York Archaeological Trust: York.

Yates, D. and Bradley, R. 2010. Still Water, Hidden Depths: The Deposition of Bronze Age Metalwork in the English Fenland. *Antiquity* 84: 405-415.

York, J. 2002. The Life Cycle of Bronze Age Metalwork from the Thames. *Oxford Journal of Archaeology* 21: 77-92.

Young, C.J. 1972. Excavations at the Churchill Hospital 1971: Interim Report. *Oxoniensia* 37: 10-31.

Zanier, W. 1992. *Das Römische Kastell Ellingen*. Römisch-Germanische Kommission des Deutschen Archäologischen Instituts: Frankfurt am Main.

Zanoni, V. 2013. Beneath the Surface of Water: Hydraulic Structures and Human Skeletal Remains in Ancient Italy. *Traces in Time* 3. Online: http://www.archaeologicaltraces.org /OJS/index.php/traces_in_time/article/view/27/91 (accessed 20 February 2014).

Zias, J. 1983. Anthropological Evidence of Interpersonal Violence in First-Century AD Jerusalem. *Current Anthropology* 24: 233-234.

Zissu, B. and Ganor, A. 2009. Horvat 'Ethri: A Jewish Village from the Second Temple Period and the Bar Kokhba Revolt in the Judean Foothills. *Journal of Jewish Studies* 60: 90-136.

Notes

1 Pitt-Rivers described Wor Barrow as a Roman tumulus with burials, but it is more likely to be a prehistoric or Roman barrow with intrusive Saxon burials. See Pitt-Rivers 1887: 18, 36; 1892: 211; 1898.
2 Pitt-Rivers 1887: 18, 36.
3 Mansell-Pleydell 1893: 24.
4 The vertebrae are hereafter referred to by their letter and number, i.e. C1-C7 (cervical), T1-T12 (thoracic), L1-L5 (lumbar).
5 See Brooke 1892; Palmer 1871; Royce 1882; Cardew 1865.
6 Heron 1889; Neville 1854; Foster 1883; Akerman 1860.
7 Thomas 1887; Wilson 1992: 94; Reynolds 2009: 77.
8 Cunnington 1884: 107; Smith and Brickley 2009: 144.
9 Rolleston 1876; Smith and Brickley 2009: 51.
10 Bateman 1861; Greenwell 1877; Mortimer 1905.
11 Dymond and Tomkins 1886.
12 Hencken 1939; Wheeler 1943, 1954; Kenyon 1954.
13 Fox and Lethbridge 1926; Moir and Maynard 1931; Rudsdale 1931; Lethbridge 1936; Calkin 1947.
14 Lethbridge and Palmer 1929; Lowther 1931; Dunning and Wheeler 1932; Stone 1932; Liddell 1934; Hill 1937.
15 Cornwall 1954; Tildesley 1934a; Morant and Goodman 1943.
16 Wells 1964a, 1964b, 1967a, 1967b, 1976, 1982; Manchester 1978; Brothwell 1971.
17 Clarke 1979: 372-375.
18 Clarke 1979: 372-374.
19 Harman *et al.* 1981.
20 Philpott 1991: 305-309.
21 Philpott 1991: 80.
22 Wells 1981: 279; McKinley 2004: 301; Sue Jones *pers. comm.* 2009.
23 Philpott 1991: 79, table 14.
24 O'Brien 1999.
25 Roberts and Cox 2003: 153, 158, 168-169.
26 Roberts and Cox 2003: 153.
27 Roberts and Cox 2003: 168.
28 Reynolds 2009.
29 Reynolds 2009: 44.
30 Ibid.
31 Reynolds 2009: 166.
32 Reynolds 2009: 38.
33 Reece 1988: 98.
34 Ibid.; Stirland 1998: 121; Boylston *et al.* 2000b: 250; Jones 2003: 35; Taylor 2003; Witkin 2005: 184; Harman 2007: 43.
35 Bradley 1995: 9-10; Green 1998: 173, 2002: 40; Armit 2006: 3.
36 Cessford 2007: 212.
37 Hayman and Reynolds 2005; Buckberry and Hadley 2007; Cessford 2007; Buckberry 2008; Cherryson 2008: 122.
38 Whimster 1981; Bristow 1998; Schulting and Wysocki 2005; Schulting 2006; Armit and Ginn 2007; Smith and Brickley 2009; Armit 2012.
39 Bateman 1861; Greenwell 1877; Mortimer 1905.

40 Barber *et al.* 1995.
41 Robertson-Mackay 1987.
42 Grinsell 1959: 25, 87.
43 Bateman 1861: 186.
44 Mortimer 1905: 105.
45 Taylor 2008: 101-102
46 Armit and Ginn 2007: 128.
47 Smith and Brickley 2009: 51.
48 Schulting and Wysocki 2005; Schulting 2006.
49 Grinsell 1936: 37.
50 Powell 1958: 108; Ross 1967: 127, 1986: 121; Walker 1984: 453; Wait 1985: 120; Cunliffe 1990: 83, 87; Watts 1998: 81-82; Green 2002: 96.
51 Ross and Feachem 1984: 340.
52 Ross 1986: 121.
53 Hutton 1991: 195; Chapman 1992.
54 Whimster 1981: 184; Wilson 1981: 162; Collis 2003: 215-216; Cunliffe 2005: 573; Armit 2006: 1.
55 Andrén 2006: 35-36.
56 Henig 1984: 24; Watts 1998: 82.
57 Wells 1976; Mays and Steele 1996; Wilkinson and Barker 1997; Mattingly 2006: 477.
58 Leech 1980: 342; Wilmott and Rahtz 1985: 173; Watts 1991: 197, 1998; Holst 2004a: 11; Witkin 2005: 184; Mattingly 2006: 478-479; Timby *et al.* 2007: 156.
59 Bugler and Drew 1974: 65.
60 Frend 1955: 12.
61 Green 1976: 63; Watts 1991: 66, 1998; Foster 2001: 170; Petts 2003: 149; Sauer 2005: 52; Timby *et al.* 2007: 156.
62 Esmonde Cleary 1989: 134; Williams 1999: 102.
63 Watts 1991.
64 Hollingworth and O'Reilly 1925: 17; Todd 1969: 76.
65 Reynolds 1997: 38.
66 McDonald 1979, and see Merrifield 1987: 72-74.
67 Green 2002: 33.
68 Henig 1984: 23; Green 1998: 172; Watts 1998: 2.
69 Philpott 1991: 85.
70 Williams 1999: 102.
71 Isserlin 1997; Green 1998: 174.
72 Garland 1995; Housley *et al.* 1995.
73 Merrifield 1987: 74-75; Philpott 1991: 86.
74 Philpott 1991: 86; Esmonde Cleary 2000: 135; Anderson 2001: 404; Jones 2003: 35; Witkin 2005: 184-185; Timberlake *et al.* 2007: 57.
75 Penn 1961: 122; McDonald 1979: 416; Harman *et al.* 1981: 167; Taylor 2008: 94.
76 Merrifield 1987: 75-76; Philpott 1991: 86; Boylston *et al.* 2000b: 252; Henig and Booth 2000: 133; Casa-Hutton and Wall 2006: 19.
77 Lucretius, *De Rerum Natura* III. 902-906.
78 Wait 1995: 507-509; Watts 1998: 82; Green 2004: 330.
79 Lethbridge 1936: 117; Wait 1985: 203; Merrifield 1987: 71; Philpott 1991: 84; Jones 2003: 35; Taylor 2008: 111; McKinley and Egging-Dinwiddy 2009: 58.
80 Reynolds 2009: 93.
81 Barber and Bowsher 2000: 320.
82 Lethbridge 1936: 117; Calkin 1947: 33-34; Green 1976; Green 1986: 131; Philpott 1991: 84.

83 Harman *et al.* 1981: 168; Watts 1991: 197; Woodward 1992: 94; Wait 1995: 509; Jones 2003: 35; Taylor 2008: 96.

84 Varner 2001, 2005.

85 Hope 2000.

86 Varner 2001: 57; Janes 2005: 35.

87 Brooke 1892: 412; Pitt-Rivers 1898: 79; Calkin 1947: 37; Wells 1976: 119; Matthews 1981; Wells 1982: 194.

88 Morland 1894: 273; Peter 1905: 138; Sparey-Green 1982: 74.

89 Moir and Maynard 1931: 257.

90 See, for example, Janes 1991; Ho 2000; Kilfeather 2002.

91 Philpott 1991: 77; Jones 2003: 35; Janes 2005: 22, 34.

92 Watts 1998: 74.

93 Philpott 1991: 84; Harman *et al.* 1981: 168.

94 Richardson 1982; Wedlake 1982: 85; Boylston *et al.* 2000b: 249; Anderson 2001: 405.

95 Bidder 1906; Meaney 1964: 18.

96 Wells 1967a: 170-171.

97 O'Brien 1999: 7.

98 Lethbridge and Palmer 1929; Lowther 1931; Dunning and Wheeler 1932; Stone 1932; Liddell 1934; Hill 1937; Poulton 1989; McCulloch 1991; Wymer 1996; Reynolds 1997: 37, 2009; Lucy 2000: 75; Lucy and Reynolds 2002: 21; Carver 2005; Hayman and Reynolds 2005; Buckberry and Hadley 2007; Cessford 2007; Buckberry 2008; Cherryson 2008: 122.

99 Reynolds 1997: 38.

100 Lowther 1931; Waldron and Waldron 1988.

101 See, for example, Bennike 1985; Stary 2005; Wiltschke-Schrotta and Stadler 2005; Pinhasi and Mays 2008: 320.

102 Lethbridge 1929: 103; Lowther 1931: 30; Manchester 1990: 90.

103 Carver 2005: 348; Leahy 2007: 56-57.

104 Leahy 2007: 56-57.

105 Meaney 1964: 18; Meaney and Hawkes 1970: 31; Wilson 1992: 92.

106 Watts 1998: 88.

107 Wilson and Hurst 1960: 140; Stroud 1993a; Novak 2000; Holst 2005; Osgood 2005: 95.

108 Daniell 2002: 254; Lewis, M.E. 2008.

109 Greenwell 1877: 500-501, 507; Cunnington 1884.

110 Cunnington 1884: 107.

111 Passmore 1942: 100.

112 Mercer and Healy 2008; McKinley 2008: 513.

113 Robertson-Mackay 1987.

114 Schulting and Wysocki 2005.

115 Bateman 1861: 227-228.

116 Mein 1997.

117 McKinley 2000: 410.

118 Brewster 1984.

119 Dawes 1984.

120 Chesterman 1977.

121 Galer 2007: 207-208.

122 Greenwell 1877: 500-501.

123 Smith and Brickley 2004, 2009: 51.

124 Kanjou 2009; Bonogofsky 2005; Maish 2003; Dougherty 2004.

125 Greenwell 1877: 206; Edwards 1970.

126 Watkins 1982: 81-82.
127 Jones n.d.; Rob Poulton *pers. comm.* 2011.
128 Stone 1934; Tildesley 1934b.
129 Ripper *et al.* 2012.
130 Ibid.
131 Grinsell 1959: 25, 87; Stone 1939; Mortimer 1905: 105.
132 Bailey 1980: 23-24; Hogg 1977.
133 Peterson *et al.* 1975.
134 Cambridge Archaeological Unit n.d.; Duhig n.d.
135 Parker-Pearson *et al.* 2005, 2007.
136 Hanna *et al.* 2012.
137 Dix 1980: 16; Liz Pieksma *pers. comm.* 2010.
138 Burleigh and Fitzpatrick-Matthews 2007: 66.
139 Roberts and Cox 2003: 103; Redfern 2005: 87; unless otherwise noted, the
   comparative data for the following section is taken from Roberts and Cox 2003: 89-
   106 and Redfern 2005.
140 Walker *et al.* 2009.
141 Lewis and Roberts 1997.
142 Wells 1975; Brothwell 1959.
143 Lieverse 1999; Hillson 2005: 291; Roberts and Cox 2003: 131.
144 Lavigne and Molto 1995.
145 Glass 1991; Whittaker *et al.* 1990.
146 Dias and Tayles 1997.
147 Jurmain and Kilgore 1995.
148 Faccia and Williams 2008.
149 Lovell 1997: 164, 166.
150 Hershkovitz *et al.* 1996.
151 Hooper 1991: 429.
152 Craig *et al.* 2005.
153 Ibid.
154 Cunliffe and Poole 2000: 155,167.
155 Walker 1984: 450-451.
156 Smith, K. 1977: 75.
157 Farley 1986.
158 Anderson 2000a.
159 Wheeler 1954.
160 Hirsch and Kaufman 1975.
161 O'Connor *et al.* 2011.
162 Buckberry 2010.
163 Jones 2008.
164 Kenyon 1954.
165 Cornwall 1954.
166 Matthews 1976, 1989.
167 Schulting *et al.* 2010; Armit *et al.* 2011.
168 Davies 1981: 122, 132-133.
169 Knüsel 2000a.
170 Kimmerle and Baraybar 2008: 170-171; Cunha and Pinheiro 2009: 259.
171 Novak 2000b: 257.
172 McKinley 1997: 1.
173 Kenyon 1954: 4, 31.
174 Redfern 2011.

175 Spars 2005: 1.
176 O'Connor *et al.* 2010.
177 Wheeler 1954.
178 Woods 1969: 40.
179 Parry 1928.
180 Ross 1909: 18.
181 Shapland and Armit 2012.
182 Dodwell 2007a: 66.
183 For a review of the evidence for scalping in Old World prehistory, see Murphy *et al.* 2002.
184 For skull-cups in the Upper Palaeolithic, see Bello *et al.* 2011.
185 Bayley 2001.
186 A settlement of a large or small size but which does not appear to show much evidence of planning, amenities or building associated with local government. See Burnham and Wacher 1990 and Millett 1990: 143-147.
187 These include coins (Reece 1991, 1995), glass vessels (Cool and Baxter 1999), ceramics (Cooper 2000; Evans 2001) and animal bone (King 1984, 1999; Maltby 1994, 2007; Grant 2004: 376-381).
188 Hingley 1989: 25-29; Burnham and Wacher 1990: 1.
189 Reece 1980a: 120.
190 Clarke 1979; Harman *et al.* 1981; Philpott 1991.
191 Chapman 2007.
192 Tester 1963.
193 Anderson 1995.
194 Richard Hall *pers. comm.* 2009.
195 Clarke 1979: 374; Philpott 1991: 79, 81.
196 Wainwright, J. 2010.
197 Carver *et al.* 2009.
198 Bethel and Carver 1987.
199 Philpott 1991: 78.
200 This comparison was made in late 2011 and more sites have potentially been added since.
201 Clarke 1979: 374-375; Harman *et al.* 1981: 166.
202 Garland 1995.
203 Manchester 2011.
204 Redfern and Bonney 2014.
205 Young 1972: 16.
206 Luff 1984.
207 Mays and Steele 1996.
208 Wilkinson and Barker 1997.
209 Harman *et al.* 1981: 166; Philpott 1991: 74, 76.
210 Harman *et al.* 1981: 165; Philpott 1991: 80.
211 Harman *et al.* 1981: 164; Green 1976: 48.
212 Such as those produced by the Office of Population Research at Princeton University; see Coale and Demeny 1983.
213 Chamberlain 2000: 104.
214 For examples of this practice in other periods, see Lucy 1994; Becker 1995; and Donnelly *et al.* 1999.
215 Evison 1987; Waldron 1987; Lewis 2000: 40; Buckberry 2000.
216 Gordon and Buikstra 1981; Henderson 1987; Walker *et al.* 1988.
217 See, for example, Saunders 2000: 121; Lewis 2007: 20; Perry 2005: 91.

218 Bell *et al.* 1996.
219 Matthews 1981.
220 Hunt and Bullen 2007.
221 Marcsik and Oláh 1991.
222 See, for example, Ribot and Roberts 1996; Larsen 1997: 82-92; and Roberts 2000b, although it has recently been argued that new bone could have multiple aetiologies, including trauma, localised ulceration or hypertrophic osteoarthropathy, none of which are infectious diseases; see Weston 2008.
223 Roberts 2007.
224 Santos and Roberts 2001; Matos and Santos 2006.
225 Wells 1982.
226 Tucker in press a.
227 Booth *et al.* 2010; Clough n.d.(a); Boylston and Roberts 2004.
228 An abnormal lateral positioning of the neck with a degree of head rotation and tilt that can have either a muscular or non-muscular involvement and is usually the result of an underlying congenital or pathological disorder, or a response to trauma; see Storm 2008: 169.
229 Timberlake *et al.* 2007.
230 Arthritis secondary to an infection of a joint as a result of organisms circulating in the bloodstream or through bacteria gaining direct access to the joint following trauma; see Boylston and Lee 2008: 251.
231 Alexander *et al.* 2004.
232 Clarke 1979.
233 Tucker in press b.
234 Ibid.
235 Tucker in press b.
236 Wells 1964a.
237 For similar examples of cut marks on Peruvian skeletal remains, see Klaus *et al.* 2010.
238 For a dramatic demonstration of this in a modern forensic case, see Dedouit *et al.* 2007.
239 Bradley *et al.* 2005.
240 Witkin 2005.
241 Pitt-Rivers 1892.
242 Chambers and Boyle 2007.
243 Harman 2007.
244 Access to unpublished site archive for 1-3 Driffield Terrace provided by York Archaeological Trust.
245 Boulter 1995.
246 Anderson 1995.
247 Millett and James 1983.
248 Clarke 1979.
249 Tucker in press b.
250 Ottaway *et al.* 2012.
251 Tucker 2012.
252 Jennings 2000.
253 Kimmerle and Baraybar 2008: figure 6.4, 6.5.
254 Verano 2000, 2008; Klaus *et al.* 2010.
255 Glob 1969: 48; Brothwell and Gill-Robinson 2002: 127.
256 Verano 2000, 2008.
257 See, for example, Dogan *et al.* 2010; Aich *et al.* 2011; Kimmerle and Baraybar 2008: figure 6.4, 6.5; Ning 2008: 129.
258 Reynolds 2009: 77-78.

259 Pearson and Morant 1934: 10.
260 Glendor *et al.* 2007.
261 Kimmerle and Baraybar 2008: 213-215.
262 Ogilvie and Hilton 2000; Tiesler 2007: 26.
263 Holst and Coughlan 2000: 87-88.
264 Viciano *et al.* 2012.
265 Connolly 1986: 60.
266 Schulting *et al.* 2010.
267 Tucker in press b.
268 Clarke 1979.
269 Access to unpublished site archive for Stanwick provided by English Heritage.
270 Davies and Thompson 1987.
271 Walker *et al.* 2008.
272 Wells 1964a.
273 Matthews 1981.
274 Startin 1981.
275 See, for example, Dower 2008; Weinberg 2008; Museum Syndicate 2010.
276 Daniell 1997: 81.
277 Matthews 1981.
278 Access to unpublished site archive provided by the Winchester Research Unit; see Stuckert in press.
279 Tucker in press b.
280 Hunter-Mann 2006.
281 McKinley and Egging Dinwiddy 2009.
282 Hunter-Mann 2006.
283 Ibid.
284 Tucker 2012.
285 A fracture that can occur when a blow to the superior of the cranial vault causes the cervical column to be pushed against the basi-occiput, fracturing the area around the foramen magnum, although it can also be produced by falling from height and landing on the sacrum; see Ta'ala *et al.* 2006: 1000.
286 Hunter-Mann 2006.
287 Matthews 1981.
288 Although an earlier analysis reported that there were cuts present on C6 and C7; see Matthews 1979.
289 Simmonds *et al.* 2011: 121.
290 Clough n.d.(b).
291 Peterborough City Council HER 10090.
292 Goode and Bardill 1995.
293 Ordnance Survey 2011.
294 Waldron 2002.
295 Maltby 1989, 2007, 2010: 283-287.
296 Maltby 1989; Seetah 2006.
297 Seetah 2006: 112-113.
298 Maltby 2007: figure 1; Seetah 2006.
299 R.C.H.M. 1962; Ottaway 2004.
300 R.C.H.M. 1962.
301 Wenham 1968.
302 Ottaway 2011.
303 For an earlier discussion of the remains, see Montgomery *et al.* 2011.
304 Ailsa Mainman *pers. comm.* 2009.

305 Ottaway 2005; Hunter-Mann 2006.
306 Wenham 1968.
307 Wells 1982.
308 Barber and Bowsher 2000.
309 Clarke 1979: 123.
310 Millett 1990: 87; Lyon 2011: 5-7.
311 Wenham 1968: 153.
312 For summaries of the excavations of all these sites, see Ottaway 2011.
313 Toop 2008; Tucker 2008a.
314 APC 2006; Robinson 2005.
315 Montgomery *et al.* 2011; Müldner *et al.* 2011.
316 Müldner *et al.* 2011.
317 YAT 2004: 6; Nicky Rogers *pers. comm.* 2005.
318 Knüsel *et al.* 1996.
319 Clark *et al.* 1997: 152.
320 Knight 1991: 57, figure 2.6; Knüsel *et al.* 1996.
321 Castriota-Scanderbeg and Dallapiccola 2005: 5-11. For other archaeological cases of the condition, see Richards 1985 and Syrmos 2011.
322 BBC Two 2006; Girling 2006.
323 Channel 4 2010; Moore 2010; Wainwright, M. 2010.
324 Wainwright, M. 2010.
325 Hunter-Mann 2006.
326 A very similar case in a North American individual is illustrated in Buikstra and Ubelaker 1994: figure 69b. The trauma to the scapula of this individual was not noted during the present research, undertaken before the 'lion bite' theory was publicised.
327 Hope 2007: 109.
328 Grossschmidt and Kanz 2002; Kanz and Grossschmidt 2006, 2009.
329 Grossschmidt and Kanz 2002: 70-71.
330 Roth 1998: 10.
331 Vegetius, *Epitoma Rei Militaris* 1.5.
332 Vegetius, *Epitoma Rei Militaris* 1.4, 1.19, 1.21.
333 Vegetius, *Epitoma Rei Militaris* 1.4.
334 Knüsel 2000b: 114.
335 Stirland 1992: 173.
336 Coughlan and Holst 2000: 68-69.
337 Knüsel 2000b: 114.
338 Robinson 2005.
339 Montgomery *et al.* 2011: 145.
340 For execution as spectacle in the early modern period, see Foucault 1977 and Spierenburg 1984.
341 Alberge 2005.
342 Polybius, *The Histories*, III.67.1-3.
343 Diodorus Siculus, *Bibliotheca Historica*, V.29.4-5; Strabo, *Geographica* IV.4.5.
344 Livy, *Ab Urbe Condita Libri*, XXIII.24.
345 Diodorus Siculus, *Bibliotheca Historica*, XIV.115.5.
346 Polybius, *The Histories*, III.67.1-3.
347 Caesar, *De Bello Hispaniensi*, 32.
348 Livy, *Ab Urbe Condita Libri*, XXIII.15.2-7.
349 Suetonius, *De Vita Caesarum Galba*, XX.5-7; Herodian, *History of the Roman Empire*, III.7.7, V.8.9; Cassius Dio, *Historia Romana*, LXXV.8.3; Scriptores Historiae Augustae, *Diadumenus*, 9.4.

350 Lucan, *Pharsalia (Bellum Civile)*, VIII.668-674.
351 Lucan, *Pharsalia (Bellum Civile)*, VIII.678-681.
352 Scriptores, Historiae Augustae, *Severus*, 11.6-9.
353 Lucan, *Pharsalia (Bellum Civile)*, V.360-363.
354 Eusebius, *Historia Ecclesiastica*, V.1.47, V.21.4; *Digesta*, XLVIII.19; *Acta Pauli et Theclae*, X.
355 Robinson 1995: 11.
356 Wiedemann 1992: 69.
357 Ammianus Marcellinus, *Res Gestae*, XIV.11.23.
358 *Digesta*, XLVIII.19.8; Berkowitz 2002: 746.
359 Eusebius, *Historia Ecclesiastica*, VII.12.1.
360 *Digesta*, XLVIII.24.1, 3.
361 For a complete translation into English of the Latin text, see Simpson 1982.
362 Scenes XXIV and LXXII; scenes XXIV and CXIII; scene LVI; Voisin 1984: 285-289.
363 Slab VI and VII; scene LXVI; Fields 2005.
364 Scene LXI; metope VII/51; Fields 2005: 62, 66.
365 Varner 2005: 71.
366 Voisin 1984: 253.
367 Lanciani 1892: 339.
368 Ingraham Kip 1854: 95.
369 Varner 2005: 71-72, 75.
370 Green 2004: 328-329.
371 Bull 2007.
372 Fields 2005: 63.
373 Portable Antiquities Scheme 2007.
374 Merrifield 1987: 104-105.
375 Armit 2007: 95.
376 Stead 1971: 32.
377 Stead 1971: 34; Mortimer 1905: plate LXIV; Wheeler 1943: 181-183.
378 Allen 1958: 61.
379 Collis 2003: 216.
380 Green 2010: 50.
381 Armit 2012.
382 Blair 2009: 539-540.
383 Walter Map, *De Nugis Curialium*, book II, 22.
384 *Saga of Grettir the Strong*, chapters 18 and 32-35; Hight 1914.
385 Saxo Grammaticus, *Gesta Danorum*, book I.
386 Balys 1952.
387 Gerard 1888: 185.
388 Abeghian 1899: 11.
389 von Tettau and Temme 1837: 276.
390 Töppen 1867: 114.
391 Calmet 1850: 32, 34, 52, 58, 63.
392 Atkinson 1891: 127.
393 For evidence from earlier periods, particularly the Iron Age, see, for example, Poplin 1985; Boulestin 1994; Brunaux *et al.* 1999; Ardagna *et al.* 2005; Boulestin and Gambier 2012. For evidence from later periods, see, for example, Bennike 1985: 106-108; Wiltschke-Schrotta and Stadler 2005; Geber 2012; Karlsson *et al.* 2012, amongst many others.
394 Lanciani 1892: 273.
395 Pettigrew 1858: 298-299.

396 Carter 1998.
397 Nenquin 1953.
398 Charmasson 1968: 142.
399 Carrière 1902: 20.
400 Sanidopolous 2011.
401 van Doorselaer 1967.
402 Otten 2003: 415.
403 Jovanović 2006: 28.
404 Salisbury 2004: 72.
405 Chadwick 1976: 233.
406 Killgrove 2011; Zanoni 2013.
407 Keller 1979.
408 Kramis 2009: 95.
409 Becker 2009.
410 Zanier 1992.
411 Gallien *et al.* 2009.
412 Dočkalová 2005: 32.
413 Martín 2008.
414 Saponetti *et al.* 2008.
415 Wood-Jones 1908.
416 Zissu and Ganor 2009: 100.
417 Zias 1983.
418 Smith, P 1977.
419 Rak *et al.* 1976.
420 Cherryson 2005: figure 4.5, 4.6.
421 Cherryson 2005: figure 4.6.
422 Cherryson 2005: 112, 121, table 4.3.
423 Meaney and Hawkes 1970.
424 Reynolds 2009: figure 9.
425 Aspöck 2011: 317.
426 Stoodley 2006: 67.
427 Wells 1967a.
428 Myres and Green 1973.
429 Buckberry and Hadley 2007.
430 Liddell 1934.
431 Hill 1937: 254.
432 Cherryson and Buckberry 2011.
433 Wilson and Wright 1965: 210; Watts 1998: 86-87, and see chapter 1.
434 Pitts *et al.* 2002.
435 Patrick and Ratkai 2011.
436 Dobney *et al.* 1999.
437 Schofield and Maloney 1998: 284.
438 Reynolds 2009: 45.
439 Loe *et al.* 2014.
440 Pollard *et al.* 2012.
441 Keys 2010.
442 Pollard *et al* 2012.
443 Falys n.d. The results from the skeletal analysis have now been published, see
    Falys 2015.
444 As given in Cherryson 2005: figure 8.4.
445 Calculated from 966 individuals and given in Roberts and Cox 2003: 195.

446 Roberts and Cox 2003: 28, 164-220.
447 For examples of fracture patterns that may be specific to different activities, see Cancelmo 1972; Jimenez 1994.
448 Liddell 1934.
449 Pitts *et al*. 2002.
450 Cole 2009.
451 Liddell 1934.
452 Cessford 2007.
453 Brickley 2011; Patrick and Ratkai 2011.
454 Liddell 1934.
455 Buckberry and Hadley 2007; Buckberry 2008.
456 Hayman and Reynolds 2005.
457 Ibid.
458 Liddell 1934.
459 Evison 1994.
460 Falys n.d.
461 Wheeler 1943.
462 Brothwell 1971.
463 Lewis 2008.
464 Pollard *et al*. 2012.
465 Reynolds 2009: 44.
466 Reynolds 2009: figure 7, and also see figure 5.
467 Reynolds 2009: 91.
468 Dobney *et al*. 1999.
469 Monument no. 211443, *Pastscape*. Online: http://www.pastscape.org.uk/hob.aspx?hob_id=211443 (accessed 22 May 2011).
470 Humphreys *et al*. 1925: 273.
471 Buckberry and Hadley 2007; Buckberry 2008.
472 Grundy 1919: 178.
473 Kitson 1995: 96.
474 Skeat 1881: 492; Reaney 1960: 158; Meaney 1995: 30; Reynolds 2009: 31.
475 *Laws of Aethelstan* II, As. 1.
476 *Laws of Aethelstan* II, As. 1; *Laws of King Alfred*, Alf. 7; *Laws of King Edmund* II, Edm. 6.
477 For the beheading of 4,500 Saxon nobles at Verden, Germany in AD 785, see Bradbury 2004: 125.
478 Blair 2009: 551.
479 Clarke 1998: 114.
480 Blair 2005: 62.
481 Thacker 1995: 101-102.
482 Brooke 1857: 50.
483 Venables 1860: 313
484 Gatty 1905: 89
485 Andrew 1919.
486 'L.M.M.R' 1852.
487 Andrew 1939.
488 SWAT Archaeology 2009.
489 Cardy 1997: 551.
490 Thomas *et al*. 1997: 122.
491 McKinley 1987.
492 Mitchell *et al*. 2011.

493 Tarlow 2011: 76-77.
494 Bekvalac and Kausmally 2011: figure 115.
495 Anderson 1999: 28.
496 See appendix 4 for a list of these sites.
497 Roberts and Cox 2003: 248.
498 Roberts and Cox 2003: 221-286.
499 Novak 2000b.
500 Access to the unpublished site archive provided by the York Archaeological Trust.
501 Stroud 1993b.
502 Access to the unpublished site archive provided by the York Archaeological Trust.
503 Lilley *et al.* 1994.
504 Brothwell and Browne 1994.
505 Lewis, M.E. 2008; and see chapter 7 for an early medieval individual from Maiden Castle, Dorset, who seems to have undergone the same type of treatment.
506 From the location and type of the grave, an iron fragment that compares well in shape with a fifteenth-century armour attachment, and a radiocarbon date of cal AD 1440-1640 (Burgess 2000), as well as the demographic profile of the individuals and the evidence of extensive peri-mortem trauma (Boardman 2000: 25).
507 Stroud and Kemp 1993: 232-241.
508 Boylston 2000: 371; Jones 2011: 236.
509 Stroud and Kemp 1993: 241.
510 There was also a young adult female from the George Street cemetery (SK86) with multiple peri-mortem cranial injuries as well as defensive injuries to the proximal humerus; see Tucker 2007.
511 Lewis, M.E. 2008.
512 See chapter 1 and Reynolds 2009: 68-76.
513 Wilson 1992: 82.
514 Rolleston 1869: 477; Egging Dinwiddy 2010: 44.
515 Although there is evidence that the cranium may have been displayed on top of the coffin or grave fill in two individuals: a mature adult male (AR) from Dunstable, Bedfordshire (see Matthews 1981), and an older adult female (5336) from Baldock, Hertfordshire (see McKinley 1993).
516 This is known as the osteological paradox; see Wood *et al.* 1992; Wright and Yoder 2003.
517 'Beauty and wholeness' being regarded as a mark of divine favour, with 'ugliness and deformity' interpreted as representing the opposite; see Garland, R. 1995: 2.
518 Hirst 1985: 37.
519 Although the meanings of prone burial are as much up for debate as decapitation; see Harman *et al.* 1981: 167-168; Philpott 1991: 71-75; Arcini 2009.
520 Matthews 1981: 37.
521 Waldron 2002.
522 Peterborough City Council HER 10090.
523 Brothwell 1986: 28; Green 1998: 179.
524 Bradley 1979; York 2002; Yates and Bradley 2010.
525 Garland, R. 1995: 64.
526 A form of mesomelic dysplasia with deformity of the distal upper limb; see Herdman *et al.* 1966; van der Sanden 1996.
527 Green 1998, 2002.
528 See Reece 1980b and Jones 1987 for the decline of urbanism in these centuries; for contrary evidence, see Brooks 1986; Frere 1983: 21; and Wacher 1975: 305.
529 See chapter 4.

530 Mousourakis 2003: 320; Cipriani 2009: 73.

531 Chilton 1955: 78; Coleman 1990: 66.

532 Chilton 1955: 78.

533 Walker 2001.

534 Redfern 2008, 2009.

535 Willey and Emerson 1993; Frayer 1997.

536 As was seen at Towton, North Yorkshire, described as the 'largest and bloodiest battle' ever to take place on British soil; see Gravett 2003: 7.

537 See, for example, Bright 1998: 51; White 2000: 26; Mattingly 2006: 468.

538 Paulus, *Sententiae ad Filium*, V.23.14-19.

539 Pliny, *Naturalis Historia*, 30.4; Tacitus, *Annales* 14.30.

540 Lactantius, *Divinae Institutiones*, 1.21.

541 Isserlin 1997: 92.

542 See, for example, Harman *et al.* 1981: 168; Philpott 1991: 80-81; Watts 1998: 74.

543 Millett 1990: 157-164.

544 See Hadman 1978 and Burnham 1988: 44-45 for the distinctively Romano-British aisled buildings.

545 Reynolds 2009: 245.

546 Reynolds 2009: 245-246.

547 The most commonly used and best known of these collections are from Christ Church, Spitalfields, St Bride's Church, Fleet Street, and St Luke's Church, Islington; see Molleson and Cox 1993; Bowman *et al.* 1992; Boyle *et al.* 2005.

548 Ubelaker 1978.

549 Moorrees *et al.* 1963; Smith 1991.

550 Scheuer and Black 2000a: 158.

551 Scheuer and Black 2000b: 11, 13.

552 Scheuer and Black 2000a; Maresh 1970; Scheuer *et al.* 1980.

553 For details of all these times of fusion, see Scheuer and Black 2000a.

554 Scheuer and Black 2000b: 12.

555 Todd 1920, 1921a, 1921b, 1923.

556 McKern and Stewart 1957; Gilbert and McKern 1973; Acsádi and Nemeskéri 1970; Brooks and Suchey 1990; Hartnett 2010.

557 Cox 2000: 69.

558 Lovejoy *et al.* 1985b.

559 Murray and Murray 1991; Saunders *et al.* 1992; Osborne *et al.* 2004.

560 Buckberry and Chamberlain 2002; Igarashi *et al.* 2005; Mulhern and Jones 2005; Falys *et al.* 2006.

561 Işcan *et al.* 1984, 1985.

562 Kunos *et al.* 1999.

563 Dwight 1890; Todd and Lyon 1924, 1925a, 1925b, 1925c.

564 Hrdlicka 1939; Singer 1953; Saunders *et al.* 1992; Hershkovitz *et al.* 1997.

565 Miles 1963; Brothwell 1981.

566 Lovejoy 1985; Lovejoy *et al.* 1985a; Richards and Miller 1991; Mays 2002.

567 Falys and Lewis 2011.

568 Mays and Cox 2000: 117.

569 See, for example, Steele and Bramblett 1988: 53-56; Sutton *et al.* 1996; Ambrose *et al.* 2003; Barrett and Richards 2004.

570 See, for example, Knüsel and Ripley 2000; Looper 2002; White 2003.

571 Mays and Cox 2000: 118.

572 See, for example, Weaver 1980; Schutkowski 1993; Molleson *et al.* 1998; Rissech *et al.* 2003; Franklin *et al.* 2007.

573 Tague 1989, 1992.
574 Phenice 1969; Buikstra and Ubelaker 1994: 18.
575 Sutherland and Suchey 1991; Lovell 1989; MacLaughlin and Bruce 1990; Bruzek 2002.
576 Walker 2005; Bruzek 2002.
577 Meindl *et al.* 1985; Bruzek 2002.
578 Mays and Cox 2000: 119.
579 Buikstra and Ubelaker 1994: 20.
580 Djurić *et al.* 2005; St Hoyme and İşcan 1989; Maat *et al.* 1997.
581 Meindl *et al.* 1985; Mays and Cox 2000: 120.
582 Meindl *et al.* 1985; Boylston et al. 2000a: 47.
583 Trotter 1970.
584 Larsen 1997: 349.
585 See, for example, Nickens 1976; Maat 2005; Masur 2009.
586 Gosden 2006.
587 Bass 1995: 88-92.
588 Ousley and Jantz 2005; Howells 1973, 1995.
589 Knüsel 2000a; Steele 2000.
590 Tyrrell 2000: 290.
591 Berry and Berry 1967; Trinkaus 1975; Finnegan 1978; Jurmain 1999: 179-182; Stojanowski and Schillaci 2006.
592 Knüsel 2000a: 397.
593 Lai and Lovell 1992; Stirland 1993; Hawkey and Merbs 1995.
594 Weiss 2003, 2004; Niinimäki 2009; Weiss *et al.* 2010.
595 Villotte *et al.* 2010.
596 Aufderheide and Rodríguez-Martín 1998; Ortner 2003.
597 Maples 1986.
598 Lovell 1997: 145; Knüsel 2005: 52-53.
599 Lovell 1997: 145.
600 Lovell 1997: 145; Sauer 1998: 325; Knüsel 2005: 52.
601 Cited in Sauer 1998.
602 Sauer 1998: 322; Cunha and Pinheiro 2009: 251.
603 Hoppenfeld and Vasantha 2000.
604 Lovell 1997.
605 Lovell 1997: 150-151; Roberts 2000a: 346-350.
606 Villa and Mathieu 1991; Knüsel 2005: 53.
607 Sauer 1998: 325.
608 Knüsel 2005: 53; Turner 2006: 434.
609 Kimmerle and Baraybar 2008: 159.
610 Loe 2009: 267.
611 Boylston 2000: 361.
612 Loe 2009: 272; Kimmerle and Baraybar 2008: 267; Wakely 1997: 32.
613 Smith and Brickley 2004: 20, 22.
614 Homes Hogue 2006.
615 Novak 2000a: 91.
616 Boylston 2000: 361; Knüsel 2005: 55.
617 See, for example, Wenham 1989; Houck 1998; Humphrey and Hutchinson 2001.
618 Alunni-Perret *et al.* 2005.
619 Lewis, J.E. 2008.
620 Lovell 1997: 166; Chacón *et al.* 2008: figure 6.53, 313.
621 Available at http://www.graphpad.com/quickcalcs/index.cfm (accessed 26 July 2014).

Index

256